THE GLOBAL NEGOTIATOR

ALSO BY JESWALD W. SALACUSE

*The Wise Advisor: What Every Professional
Should Know About Consulting and Counseling*

Making Global Deals: Negotiating in the International Marketplace

The Art of Advice: How to Give It and How to Take It

International Business Planning: Law and Taxation
(with W. P. Streng, six volumes)

Social Legislation in the Contemporary Middle East
(co-editor with L. Michalak)

*An Introduction to Law in French-Speaking Africa:
North Africa*

*An Introduction to Law in French-Speaking Africa:
Africa South of the Sahara*

Nigerian Family Law (with A. B. Kasunmu)

THE GLOBAL NEGOTIATOR

Making, Managing, and Mending Deals Around the World in the Twenty-First Century

JESWALD W. SALACUSE

First published 2003 by
PALGRAVE MACMILLAN™
175 Fifth Avenue, New York, N.Y. 10010 and
Houndmills, Basingstoke, Hampshire, England RG21 6XS.
Companies and representatives throughout the world.

PALGRAVE MACMILLAN is the global academic imprint of the Palgrave Macmillan division of St. Martin's Press, LLC and of Palgrave Macmillan Ltd. Macmillan® is a registered trademark in the United States, United Kingdom and other countries. Palgrave is a registered trademark in the European Union and other countries.

ISBN 0-312-29339-9 hardback

Library of Congress Cataloging-in-Publication Data
Salacuse, Jeswald W.
The global negotiator : making, managing and mending deals around the world in the Twenty-first Century / by Jeswald W. Salacuse
    p.   cm.
  Includes bibliographical references.
  ISBN 0-312-29339-9
  1. Negotiation in business—Handbooks, manuals, ets.   I. Title.

HD58.6S246   2003
658.4'052—dc21

2002193099

A catalogue record for this book is available from the British Library.

Design by Letra Libre, Inc.

First edition: July 2003
10 9 8 7 6 5 4 3 2 1

Printed in the United States of America

In memory of Anne

CONTENTS

Part III
Global Deal Mending

PREFACE

The globalization of economic and business activity now more than ever before requires executives, lawyers, entrepreneurs, and officials to make deals with companies and organizations around the world, work productively with foreign partners and associates, and effectively handle disputes that inevitably arise with affiliates and governments in other countries. The basic tool for accomplishing each of these tasks is negotiation. Negotiation is the means to make deals, to manage them, and ultimately to mend them when conflicts arise. From this perspective, economic life in the twenty-first century demands that all of us become global negotiators.

The aim of this book is to provide guidance in the complex process of making, managing, and mending international business transactions. It draws on more than ten years of research conducted in a variety of settings in North America, Europe, Latin America, the Middle East, North Africa, and parts of Asia. The work was particularly informed by the twice-yearly, two-day executive seminar that Antonia Chayes, the late Abram Chayes, and I led under the auspices of the Program on Negotiation at Harvard Law School. During the decade of that seminar's existence, more than 1,200 senior international managers, lawyers, and officials shared their experiences and insights into the challenges of creating and managing international business relationships throughout the globe in many industries. It proved to be a rich source of information and ideas, a source that has informed this book from start to finish. In particular, many of the examples and anecdotes in the book came from participants in the seminar.

I am also grateful to my colleagues at the Program on Negotiation and at the Fletcher School of Law and Diplomacy for their thoughts on negotiation and international relations generally. I especially want to thank Joel Trachtman and Brian Ganson of the Fletcher School of Law and Diplomacy for reading and commenting on individual chapters, Lindsay Workman for helping to develop the bibliography, Josh Robbins for tracking down documentary sources, and my assistant, Lupita Ervin, for helping to prepare the index and final manuscript.

1

THE GLOBAL NEGOTIATOR

Why do all the tough problems seem to land on your desk?

Your company's product development division in Houston, Texas, has located a small manufacturer in Hungary that claims it can supply components at 35 percent less than what you are now paying your Dallas supplier, with whom you have had a relationship for over ten years. Your boss is pushing you to fly to Budapest to negotiate a long-term supply contract with the Hungarians. You don't know anything about Hungary and are worried about how to handle the Dallas supplier when you get back.

Or, your company and a Chinese enterprise have established a joint venture to manufacture and sell high-grade machine tools in China and Southeast Asia. The venture has clear mutual benefits, but you both have become cautious about sharing information. Your Chinese partner is withholding information about customer problems with products and requests for new product features. In response, your engineers have slowed the transfer of technology badly needed by the enterprise. Both of you are also fighting about advertising expenses. Your company wants to spend heavily on advertising, but the Chinese oppose additional advertising as unnecessary. On top of that, during your last visit to China, you met the new provincial governor, who took you aside at a cocktail party and suggested that the joint venture would have an easier time with provincial authorities if you sold a portion of your interest to one of his cronies.

Or, your company has begun construction on a resort hotel in Egypt near the pyramids after securing the necessary land from the government. Your company is financing the deal with a combination of its own money and loans from two London banks. So far the project has spent $15 million in construction costs. Last week, the Egyptian government, under pressure from foreign and domestic environmental groups fearful of the project's adverse impact on the area's archeological sites, revoked the land transfer and canceled the entire project. Your London banks are threatening to call the loan and to seek immediate repayment.

Although these problems have come at you from many different parts of the world and affect many different areas of business, they all have one thing in common: Their solution requires the effective use of negotiation. In order to deal productively with your potential Hungarian supplier and your current Texas supplier, your Chinese partner and the new governor, and the Egyptian government and your London banks, you will need to skillfully negotiate solutions to each of these difficult problems. You may already have significant experience negotiating deals with other businesses in your own city, state, or country. That experience will not help you much in Budapest, Beijing, and Cairo, where you will have to cope with unfamiliar political systems, cultures, languages, laws, bureaucratic traditions, and business practices. Today's expanding world of global business requires you to be a *global* negotiator.

The word *global*, aside from referring to the world, has another meaning: comprehensive. Being a global negotiator means not only making business deals in Budapest one week and in Beijing the next, but also effectively handling whole business relationships from start to finish. It means having the skills to deal comprehensively with the entire transaction from the first handshake with a potential foreign partner to the final liquidation of an international joint venture that has served its purpose. This book's goal is to help you gain those skills.

All international transactions are the product of a negotiation—the result of *deal making*. Deal making in global business requires executives to overcome many unfamiliar barriers not usually found in the U.S. setting, including differences in cultures, laws, bureaucratic traditions, ideologies, and government practices, as well as a perpetually unstable international political and monetary environment—precisely the challenges you will have to overcome to make a deal with a new supplier in Budapest.

Although some people believe that negotiations end when the participants agree on all the details and sign the contract, this view hardly ever reflects reality. In truth, an international deal is a *continuing negotiation* between the parties to the transaction as they seek to apply their contract to unforeseen situations and to adjust their relationship to a changing international environment. No contract, particularly in a long-term transaction, can predict all eventualities that the parties may encounter, nor can any negotiation achieve perfect understanding between the parties, especially when they come from different cultures. If the two sides do encounter changes in circumstances, misunderstandings, or problems not contemplated by their contract—for example, how much to spend on advertising in a joint venture in China—they will need to resort to negotiation, at least at first, to handle their difficulties. In short, negotiation is a fundamental tool for *managing* their deal.

And when the parties to a deal become embroiled in genuine conflict—for example, the cancellation of the resort hotel project in Egypt or the demand by London banks for premature loan repayment—negotiation may be the only realistic tool to resolve the controversy—particularly if the parties want to preserve their business relationship. In times of severe conflict, negotiation becomes a means to *mend* a broken deal.

In the life of any international deal, one may therefore identify three distinct stages when executives must rely on negotiation to achieve their goals:

- deal making,
- deal managing, and
- deal mending.

The aim of this book is to equip business executives, students, lawyers, and government officials to navigate each of these stages effectively. Whereas most business negotiation books end when the deal is made and the contract is signed, *The Global Negotiator* will guide the reader through the entire life of an international transaction.

This book is divided into three parts of unequal length. Part I, Global Deal Making, will discuss the challenges of and solutions to negotiating international business transactions in today's global environment. It will set out the seven important rules for preparing and conducting effective global deal making and suggest ways of overcoming the seven principal barriers to making deals abroad. Part II, Global Deal Managing, will discuss the complexities of profitably carrying out the deals that have been negotiated. It will focus particularly on handling power relationships with international business partners and on converting a signed contract into a productive working relationship. And finally, Part III, Global Deal Mending, will equip the reader with the knowledge, skills, and techniques to resolve conflicts that may threaten to destroy business transactions and relationships. In addition, the appendices to this book offer the global negotiators two important supports for carrying out their work: "The Global Negotiator's Checklist" guides the negotiation process and "A Primer on International Business Transactions" outlines the basic elements of common international deals.

Let's consider first the challenges of global deal making.

PART I

GLOBAL DEAL MAKING

2

NEGOTIATING DEALS,
CONTRACTS, AND RELATIONSHIPS

Deals don't just happen. They result from negotiations—usually long, hard negotiations that invariably consume considerable material, human, and emotional resources. The word "negotiation," after all, is derived from two Latin words, *neg* and *otium*, that literally mean "not leisure." The deal being proposed by your product development department with a new Hungarian supplier of components will take at least a week of your time and twenty or thirty thousand dollars of your company's money. Straightening out that troubled relationship with your Chinese joint-venture partner may cost even more.

Before we examine specific ways of solving these problems through negotiation, we should first have a general understanding of two basic concepts: negotiation and the deal. Just what are they, anyway?

NEGOTIATION MODELS

Negotiation is basically a *process of communication by which two or more persons seek to advance their individual interests through joint action.* The parties to a negotiation are sitting at the bargaining table because at least one side has decided that it can improve its situation in some way if both sides agree on a specific joint act, such as establishing a strategic alliance to produce cell phones, making a sales agreement to buy computer components, or transferring for a fee one party's communication technology to the other. Obviously, the other side is sitting at the same table because it too thinks that it has a chance to improve its own situation if it strikes a deal under the right conditions.

A negotiation is a process, a progressive movement toward a desired end. Succeeding in any negotiation requires a mastery of both the *substance* and the *process* of the transaction. Business negotiators sometimes become so enmeshed in substantive issues that they forget or neglect the process of creating and managing the deal. While substantive issues like capital contributions, payment terms, and performance guarantees are certainly important in successful deal making, effective negotiators must also pay attention to the negotiation process.

Most people tend to approach a negotiation with a model in mind of how the process should take place. The specific model they have in mind is important because it influences their actions at the negotiating table. There are three basic models of negotiation.

Model I: Negotiation as Compromise

For many executives, the process of negotiation is essentially one of *compromise*, of striking a deal somewhere between their initial offer and their counterpart's. Let's call this approach Model I. As they begin negotiations, each party has normally determined, but has not disclosed, a point beyond which it will not go to make a deal. For example, in the negotiation over the sale of a business, the seller may ask $10 million while having decided not to sell for anything less than $7 million. Similarly, a potential buyer may offer $5 million but has secretly determined not to pay more than $8 million. These undisclosed "reservation prices" may or may not change as the bargaining proceeds. As long as their reservation prices are not mutually exclusive (as would be the case, for example, if the buyer's maximum were $6 million and the seller's minimum were $8 million), the two sides have room to make a deal. They have what is called "a zone of possible agreement."

In a Model I negotiation, the two sides arrive at an agreement by a series of concessions that each makes until they reach a solution that both can accept. This is the market model of negotiation. As the following diagram shows, A starts at one extreme and B at the other. Over time, they may reduce their demands to the point that they eventually make a deal.

In the struggle to arrive at agreement, the parties see their negotiation as a "win-lose" process in which any gain for one side is a loss for the other. Every dollar gained by the seller in a market transaction is a dollar lost to the buyer. In this model of negotiation, which scholars call "distributive bargain-

Figure 2.1

MODEL I:
Negotiation as Compromise

A   B

→ DEAL ←

ing," the parties assume that their goals are incompatible, that they are struggling over how to divide a fixed pie, and that through a series of concessions and threats they will somehow arrive at an acceptable middle ground.

Model II: Negotiation as Domination

For some executives, negotiating a deal is combat, a means to dominate a business opponent. In this approach to negotiation (Model II), one side dreams up a deal and, using a variety of power plays and dirty tricks, tries to shove it down the throat of the other side, as in the following diagram.

Figure 2.2

MODEL II:
Negotiation as Domination

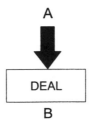

A

DEAL

B

Model II is really just a variation of Model I. In both models, the two sides see their interests as incompatible and truly believe they are struggling over a fixed pie. The principal difference between the models is the rough tactics used by one of the parties in Model II. Whereas Model I may be driven by agreed-upon norms or standards, Model II is invariably driven by power. Like extreme versions of boxing and football that verge on combat, Model II can be considered extreme negotiation.

Model III: Negotiation as Problem Solving

A third approach to negotiation conceives of the process not as compromise or combat, but as an exercise in problem solving. In Model III, the negotiators view their task as resolving a problem that they both share. They see negotiation as a process in which each can gain. In this form of negotiation, which is often called integrative bargaining, the participants consider themselves to have compatible goals. Rather than struggling over dividing a fixed pie, they search for ways to enlarge it so that both sides may satisfy their interests to the maximum extent possible. In this approach to negotiation, the parties begin by seeking to understand each other's interests and then try to fashion a deal that takes those interests into account and integrates those interests into a well-crafted transaction, as illustrated in the following diagram.

Figure 2.3

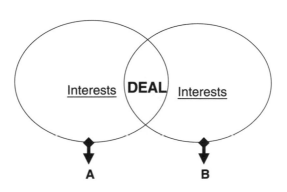

**MODEL III:
Negotiation as Joint Problem Solving**

Because understanding the parties' interests is central to the process, Model III has also been called interest-based negotiation. To arrive at an integrative solution, the parties' interests need not be identical. Instead, the parties need to recognize the extent to which their interests, though different, are compatible, or at least not mutually exclusive. All too often the two sides in a negotiation assume their interests are incompatible and therefore conduct the negotiation process from the start as an exercise in compromise, if not domination.

For example, in a case that took place in New York City, a wealthy man left his entire estate to be divided between his two daughters, Janet and Claire. The division of his property went smoothly until the two women faced the problem of deciding who would get their father's diamond ring, which he had worn all of his adult life. Both daughters wanted it. Compromise by cutting the ring in half was of course not a feasible solution. Following the pattern of many distributive negotiations, each sought to establish her right to the ring by asserting a norm or principle. Janet pointed to the fact that she had cared for their father in his old age and that she therefore rightfully should have the ring. Claire countered by claiming that years earlier their father had promised it to her. Relations between the two sisters became tense as each insisted on having the ring. Finally, in frustration Janet asked Claire a key question: "*Why* do you want the ring?" It was a key question because its purpose was to determine her sister's interests in the ring. Problem-solving negotiation begins with an understanding of interests. Claire replied: "Because it has a beautiful diamond and I would like the diamond. I thought I would make a pendant from it." Startled, Janet responded by saying: "That's not why I want the ring. I want it because it reminds me of our father." Claire's interest was in owning the diamond. Janet's interest was the ring's sentimental value. When the two sisters recognized that their interests were different but not necessarily incompatible, they began to explore mutually acceptable solutions to the problem of who should receive the ring. Finally, Janet proposed that Claire take the ring to a jeweler, have the diamond replaced with Janet's birthstone, return the ring to Janet, and keep the diamond. The solution allowed both sisters to achieve their interests.[1]

Joint problem solving is a "win-win" model of the negotiation process. Any negotiation has both competitive and cooperative aspects. Whereas

Models I and II emphasize the competitive aspects of negotiation, Model III stresses the cooperative aspects.

APPLYING THE MODELS

Individual negotiators may use any one of the three negotiation models, depending on their background, the industry in which they are working, and the type of deal they are trying to negotiate. For example, suppose you visit Kuala Lumpur to meet with a potential new supplier of components, either to supplement or to replace what you are receiving from one of your U.S. suppliers. You are impressed with the quality of the components produced, the efficiency of the manufacturer's factory, and the knowledge and attitude of the Malaysian managers. You proceed to negotiate a two-year purchase contract, but you become stuck on the price. The Malaysians are asking for $2 a component (which is still lower than what you are currently paying your U.S. supplier), but you are insisting on $1.50. You justify the lower price because of the increased risk of relying on a new, untested foreign supplier who is thousands of miles away from your plant. The Malaysians, on their side, insist on the higher price because of the risks in equipping their factory to produce a large shipment of components for a new customer who may or may not turn out to be reliable. In the typical win-lose fashion of Model I, the Malaysians come down to $1.95 and you increase your offer to $1.55. You are still forty cents apart. You are hoping to meet somewhere in the middle. You think they will come down some more. And they feel you certainly will sweeten the deal. Neither of you budges.

You become frustrated so you shift to Model II. You insist that you can't offer a penny more and you pound the table. When the Malaysians still insist on $1.95 for each component, you slam your briefcase closed, say there is no point in continuing the discussions, declare that you are leaving Kuala Lumpur that evening, and stomp out of the room, hoping that the Malaysians will call you at your hotel to make a concession on the price before you check out. Maybe they will, but then again maybe they won't. Your tactic not only risks losing you an advantageous deal, but even if the Malaysians accept your demand, you will not have laid a very positive foundation for the long-term relationship that will have to underpin a successful multiyear supply agreement.

Suppose that in your negotiations with the Malaysian managers, you had used a different approach, an approach founded on the idea that you and they had a common problem that you needed to work together to solve. This approach begins with an understanding of the interests of each of the parties. Suppose after spending some time talking with them, you learn that not only do they want to sell components to you, but they also have a strong interest in entering the American market and that their company manufactures other products besides the components you are negotiating about. This knowledge now gives you a means to devise some options that will help you bridge the gap caused by your difference over price. For example, in return for their acceptance of your offer of $1.55, at least on this first order, you might propose to help the Malaysian company enter the American market by offering to display some of its other products in your exhibits at the two major trade shows that you are planning to participate in during the next year. While the amount of space that the Malaysian products will take up will not be significant and will not cost you any more than you have already committed to pay for the exhibits, you think that their presence might even draw a few more visitors than usual to your exhibit, thus enhancing your own company's visibility. Recognizing that joining your exhibit free of charge will save them thousands of dollars compared to mounting their own, the Malaysians might well agree to lower their price for the components. In effect, the transaction you are engineering will result in substantial cost savings for the two companies, a win-win negotiation. The prospect of participating in your exhibits over the next year may also cause the Malaysian managers to devote extra care and attention to their relationship with you.

EVALUATING THE MODELS

Which negotiation model will bring you the best results? Certainly, individual negotiators will point to particular experiences when compromise or domination enabled them to make a sale or close a deal. But most negotiation scholars agree that, as a general rule, approaching an international business negotiation, particularly one of any duration, as an opportunity for joint problem solving is more likely to yield better results than viewing it as a win-lose exercise in compromise (Model I) or domination (Model II).[2]

Subsequent chapters will explain how to apply the problem-solving model of negotiation to your maximum advantage.

Compromise does not allow the parties to achieve their full potential. For example, if the parties in the Malaysian case mentioned above had been able to compromise on a price somewhere between $1.95 and $1.55, they would have missed the cost savings and future business opportunities that a wider business relationship between them would have generated.

While executives enjoy telling anecdotes about how they were able to dominate a negotiation and make a deal through various power plays, domination as an approach to negotiation has a high probability of hidden costs and failure either during deal making or later on when the transaction is implemented. Moreover, domination certainly does not create a solid foundation on which to base a long-term business relationship. For example, a U.S. multinational corporation used a variety of domination techniques in negotiating a joint venture with a small emerging-market company. As a result, throughout the life of the joint venture, the emerging-market company felt that it was much weaker than its partner and was afraid that it would be taken advantage of. Consequently, in all its dealings with the U.S. firm, it was extremely guarded and slow to reach agreement, an attitude that seriously hampered the development of the venture and ultimately led to its collapse. More generally, as will be seen in part III of this book, the incidence of *re*negotiation of deals is particularly high in international business. One factor that often leads to renegotiation of a contract is that one of the parties to the agreement feels that it was dominated and taken advantage of in the original negotiation. For example, host country governments have often successfully insisted on renegotiating investment contracts and mineral development agreements on the grounds that the conditions under which they were negotiated in the first place were unfair.[3]

Various factors determine whether individual negotiators will approach deal making as an exercise in compromise, domination, or joint problem solving. Among the most significant determinants are the context of the negotiation, the personalities of the negotiators, their culture, and their occupation.

The context of the negotiation and the nature of the transaction can influence a negotiator's attitudes toward the negotiating process. For example, an executive who is predisposed to approach a business negotiation as a problem-solving, integrative process may behave in a distributive, confrontational way when faced with a hostile counterpart at the negotiating table. Similarly, officials in developing countries, because of history or ideology, often consider negotiations with multinational corporations as win-lose competitions. In negotiating investment contracts, they may therefore view profits earned by the investor as automatic losses to the host country. As a result, they focus their efforts in the negotiation on limiting investor profit in contrast to discovering how to maximize benefits from the project for both the investor and the country. On the other hand, these same officials might conduct negotiations in their home villages with members of their ethnic group or clan in a more integrative, interest-based fashion.

A survey conducted by the author among more than three hundred persons from twelve different countries found wide differences among the cultures and occupations represented in the survey on the question of whether their general attitude toward negotiation was win-win or win-lose.[4] Among all respondents, approximately one-third had a predisposition to consider negotiations as a win-lose process, while two-thirds saw it as win-win. Gender appeared to have no influence on responses, for the distribution among men and among women was essentially the same—one third of the male respondents and one third of the female respondents considered negotiation to be a win-lose process. On the other hand, the study revealed wide differences among the cultures represented in the survey on this question. Whereas 100 percent of the Japanese viewed negotiation as a win-win process, only 36.8 percent of the Spanish stated a similar predisposition. The Chinese and Indians, the two other Asian cultures in this survey, also claimed that negotiation was for them win-win, and the French, alone among Europeans, took a similarly pronounced position on the question. The following table summarizes the results with respect to culture.

Figure 2.4

Negotiating Attitude: Win-Win or Win-Lose?

Win-Win (%):	Japan	China	Argentina	France	India	U.S.A.	U.K.	Mexico	Germany	Nigeria	Brazil	Spain
	100	82	81	80	78	71	59	50	55	47	44	37

An analysis of the responses by profession also revealed significant variations. Whereas only 14 percent of diplomatic and public service personnel and 19 percent of management and marketing persons considered negotiations to be a win-lose process, 58 percent of the lawyers and 60 percent of the military held this view. University students surveyed, who for comparative purposes can be considered to represent persons without significant negotiating experience and without a particular professional culture, also viewed negotiation as a win-lose process. The following table summarizes the results with respect to occupational background.

Figure 2.5

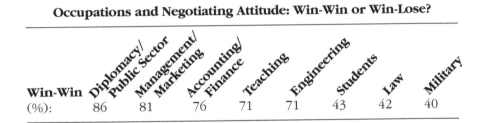

Win-Win (%):	Diplomacy/ Public Sector	Management/ Marketing	Accounting/ Finance	Teaching	Engineering	Students	Law	Military
	86	81	76	71	43	42	40	

Although the responses of men and women as a whole tended to be similar, the survey revealed significant differences according to gender within specific cultures. Thus, while only 20 percent of U.S. female respondents saw negotiation as a win-lose process, 50 percent of Spanish female respondents took this view.

None of the above information should be taken as absolute predictions as to how your counterpart will behave at the negotiating table. Rather, it is intended to make you aware of various factors that in a given negotiation may have a tendency to orient your discussions toward one negotiation model or another. In interpreting the survey results reported above and elsewhere in this book, you should bear in mind that the size of the group surveyed was relatively small, that the respondents' answers reflected only how they saw themselves (or would have liked others to see them) rather than their objectively observed negotiating behavior, and that attitudes in a given negotiation may be influenced by other factors beside culture, occupation, and gender.

PHASES OF THE NEGOTIATION PROCESS

Like other processes, negotiations tend to go through distinct phases. The effective negotiator understands those phases and recognizes that each calls for special skills, approaches, and resources. There are three basic phases: prenegotiation, conceptualization, and detail arrangement.

1. Prenegotiation.   In the first phase, which can be called prenegotiation, the parties to a potential deal determine whether they want to negotiate at all and, if so, what they will talk about, and how, when, and where they will do it. Much prenegotiation may happen in letters, telephone calls, and faxes even before the parties sit down together, but it may continue for many meetings thereafter. To take an illustration from diplomacy, despite years of contacts between the Arabs and the Israelis during their long conflict, the parties remained stalled in the prenegotiation phase until they decided to go to Madrid in 1991 to begin substantive discussions. In your own search for a new supplier of components in Southeast Asia, you may want to know much more about the Malaysian manufacturer before you actually undertake to negotiate a long-term purchase agreement. Information gathering and efforts by each of the parties to evaluate the other characterize the prenegotiation phase. It ends when both sides make a decision to negotiate a deal together, or when one informs the other, directly or indirectly, that it no longer wishes to continue discussions. If the parties do decide to enter into negotiations, their transition to the next stage of deal making may be evidenced by making an agenda for their talks and even signing a confidentiality agreement in which they promise not to divulge or to use for profit information that is exchanged during their substantive discussions.

As a general rule, executives from outside the United States tend to devote more time and attention to the prenegotiation phase than do Americans. Whereas Americans generally want to "dispense with the preliminaries" and to "get down to cases," most Asians, for example, view prenegotiation as an essential foundation to any business relationship; consequently they recognize the need to conduct prenegotiation with care before actually making a decision to undertake substantive negotiations. One of the consequences of this difference in approach is that Americans sometimes assume that discussions with Asian counterparts have passed from prenegotiation to a subsequent stage when in fact they have not. This type of misunderstanding can lead to suspicions of bad faith and ultimately result in total failure of the talks. It is therefore important to be sure that you and your counterparts are always in the same phase of the deal-making process. One way of making sure you both understand where you are in the process is by using written agendas, memoranda, and letters of intent to mark the various phases.

2. Conceptualization. In the second phase of the process, which might be called conceptualization, the parties seek to agree on a basic concept or premise upon which to build their deal. They attempt to establish the fundamental principles that will govern their future business relationship. For example, in the area of sales, is their relationship to be one of agency or of distributorship? In manufacturing, are they seeking to establish a joint venture to which both will contribute capital or will their relationship be a licensing arrangement? Even if the parties have agreed on the basic nature of their transaction, they will then need to find an acceptable formula for its structure. In one case involving the renegotiation of a long-term contract for the sale at a fixed price of electricity between a state power company in Ghana and a foreign-owned aluminum smelter, the parties, who were stymied on the question of price, only made progress when they agreed on the principle that the price of electricity under the contract would be "linked to the international price of energy." [5] Often the concept or underlying principle, once agreed upon, becomes encapsulated in a terse slogan or label. For example, in the Camp David negotiations between Egypt and Israel over the return of the Sinai, the basic concept of the deal was "land for security." And in the talks between China and the United Kingdom over the reversion of Hong Kong, the principle was "one country, two systems."

The conceptualization phase of negotiations is marked by the definition of the parties' interests, the advancement of proposals and counterproposals, and the exploration of options. The creativity of negotiators comes into play, as they seek to shape a basic concept and to find the precepts for their deal that will allow both sides to satisfy their interests. Once the parties have agreed, they may sign a letter of intent or similar document to record their understanding.

3. Detail Arrangement. The final phase is devoted to working out the details and implications of the agreed-upon concept. This phase relies heavily on technical expertise as the parties explore the problems of implementation.

Here, negotiators come to understand the full meaning of the old saying "the devil is in the details." For example, it is one thing to agree that the price of electricity should be linked to the international price of energy, but it is quite another to turn that into a formula for an effective pricing system that can be accurately and efficiently applied day-to-day throughout the life of the deal.

No negotiation is as neat and simple as this three-phase model suggests.[6] In the heat of discussion, the precise boundaries between the different phases may be unclear. Sometimes when the parties are unable to find an acceptable concept, they may try to agree on certain details in order to build confidence in one another and to give their talks the appearance, and perhaps the reality, of having momentum. Nonetheless, the accompanying diagram may serve as

Figure 2.6

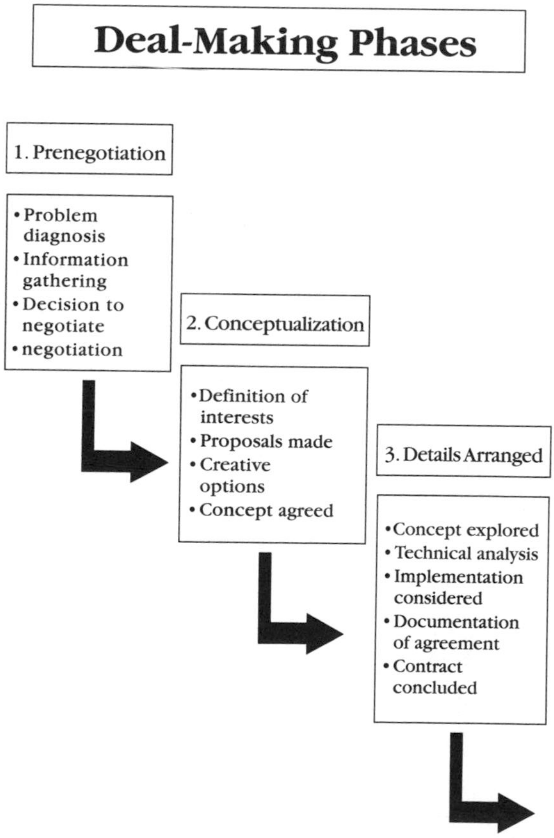

Deal-Making Phases

1. Prenegotiation

- Problem diagnosis
- Information gathering
- Decision to negotiate
- negotiation

2. Conceptualization

- Definition of interests
- Proposals made
- Creative options
- Concept agreed

3. Details Arranged

- Concept explored
- Technical analysis
- Implementation considered
- Documentation of agreement
- Contract concluded

a road map to give negotiators a sense of where they are in the deal-making process and what resources they need to make each phase a success.

THE DEAL: CONTRACT OR RELATIONSHIP?

Having arrived at a general understanding of negotiation, one must now try to come to grips with any negotiation's goal: the deal. But just what is a deal, anyway?

For many executives and lawyers, particularly in North America, the goal of a business negotiation, first and foremost, is achieving a signed contract between the parties. For them, the contract is a definitive set of rights and duties that strictly binds the two sides, controls their behavior in the future, and determines who does what, when, and how. According to this view, the parties' deal is their contract.

A different approach, often seen in Asia, is to consider the purpose of negotiation as the creation of a business relationship. This view recognizes that, just as a map is not a country but only an imperfect sketch thereof, a contract is not a business relationship. Although the contract that results from a negotiation may describe the relationship, the essence of the deal between the parties is their relationship, not their contract.

This difference in perspective about the negotiating goal requires business executives to ask a basic question as they approach their task: Just what is the deal that they are seeking? Is it a contract or a relationship? Although the answer to this question in transactions of any duration should be "both," negotiators too often concentrate on the contractual aspects of a deal and overlook the relational dimensions.

While signing a contract may be the single appropriate goal in negotiating an isolated business transaction or short-term arrangement, to approach the negotiation of a long-term transaction with that perspective alone may result in the failure to achieve the parties' objectives or to maximize their interests. Ultimately, a long-term alliance or partnership founded on contract alone may collapse.

In long-term transactions (such as joint ventures and strategic alliances), the parties are seeking to create a business relationship, a complex set of interactions characterized by cooperation and a degree of trust. A relationship implies a *connection* between the parties. Although a contract may be a necessary condition for a business relationship in some countries, it is never a sufficient condition for a business relationship in any country. An effective negotiator, while necessarily concerned about contractual provisions, should also work to lay a solid foundation for a relationship between the parties.

Accordingly, negotiators working on most deals should ask a variety of nonlegal and noncontractual questions: How well do the parties know one another? What is the nature of the personal chemistry between the two companies' leadership? To what extent do the two sides understand and respect each other's cultures, expectations, and goals? What mechanisms are in place to foster communications between the two sides after the contract is signed? To what extent is the proposed deal balanced and advantageous for both sides?

Although negotiating a productive business relationship is difficult in any context, it is particularly challenging when the parties come from different countries. Differences in the parties' cultures, legal systems, political regimes, and economic contexts complicate the creation of effective working relationships.

In the survey mentioned above, the author asked persons from twelve different countries as to whether they viewed the goal of a negotiation as a contract or a relationship. The respondents as a group were fairly evenly divided, with 54 percent viewing contract as a negotiating goal and 46 percent pursuing a relationship. Similarly while males had a slight preference for contract (57.3 percent) and females for relationship (52.5 percent), the difference was not significant, and certainly not as significant as the literature on gender might lead one to believe. On the other hand, the survey results revealed significant differences among both cultures and professions on this question. Thus, with respect to national cultures, only 26 percent of the Spanish respondents claimed that their primary goal in a negotiation was a relationship, compared to 67 percent of the Indians. On the other hand, the preference for a relationship was not as pronounced among the Chinese (54.5 percent) as one might have expected from the literature, and both the Japanese and the U.S. respondents appeared almost evenly divided on the question. Figure 2.7 summarizes the survey results on this issue among the twelve nationalities.

An analysis of responses on the basis of occupational background also revealed significant variations. For example, while 71 percent of the lawyers favored contract as a negotiating goal, 61 percent of those with management or marketing experience preferred relationships. Figure 2.8 summarizes the results.

Figure 2.7

Negotiating Goal: Contract or Relationship?

	Spain	France	Brazil	Japan	U.S.A.	Germany	U.K.	Nigeria	Argentina	China	Mexico	India
Contract (%):	74	70	67	55	54	54	47	47	46	45	42	33

Figure 2.8

Occupations and Negotiating Goal: Contract or Relationship?

	Law	Military	Engineering	Diplomacy/ Public Sector	Students	Accounting/ Finance	Teaching	Management/ Marketing
Contract (%):	71	60	52	50	49	43	43	39

Although for the group as a whole the responses by males and females did not reveal significant differences, one did find substantial variations between genders *within* certain cultures. Thus, whereas 66.7 percent of U.S. male respondents chose contract as a negotiating goal, 71.4 percent of the U.S. female respondents opted for relationship—a finding supported by studies on the impact of gender on negotiation.[7] On the other hand, 75 percent of French females and 66.7 percent of Spanish women chose contract, suggesting that gender roles in negotiation may be more influenced by culture than biology.

SEVEN RULES FOR CREATING THE FOUNDATION FOR A RELATIONSHIP

If the existence of a good working relationship is important to the success of the deal, a natural question is, How does a negotiator create a good relationship between the parties? The relationship will grow and develop after the deal is signed and the parties work together. Thus, relationship building will be very much a part of the deal-management phase, a subject treated in the second part of this book. Nonetheless, negotiators can do much during the deal-making phase to lay the foundation for a good relationship. The following are seven rules that global negotiators should consider in order to increase the chances that a good working relationship will develop between the parties.

1. Use prenegotiation fully and effectively.   Dealmakers should resist the temptation to rush through prenegotiation and to start talking about the deal as soon as possible. Instead, they should use the prenegotiation period of deal making to learn as much about the background, interests, and organizational culture of the other side as possible and to inform the other side of their own background, interests, and organization. This phase is vital if the parties are to know one another well. Knowing each other well is an important part of any foundation for a good relationship. In deals that will require substantial investments and close working relationships, the parties may even want to hire consultants or knowledgeable third parties to facilitate the process of getting to know one another thoroughly.

Executives often resist spending sufficient time on prenegotiation on the grounds that "time is money." Time is indeed money in the sense that it is a form of capital that must be invested to make any transaction profitable. To invest less time than is needed in a project is like investing less money than is required. Underinvestment increases the risk of failure. Consequently, you may save some time at the front of the deal by rushing through the preliminaries, but it will usually mean that you will have to spend more time later on to sort out the problems and misunderstandings that arise between you and the other company. In the mid-1990s when Enron's business still focused on the production of energy, the company was very proud of the fact that it signed a memorandum of understanding to build a $2 billion power plant in India five days after its negotiating team first entered the country. To justify its approach, a top Enron executive could not resist reminding the press that for Americans, time was money.[8] When a new Indian government came to power and cancelled the contract because of alleged irregularities, Enron executives had to spend nearly two years to renegotiate the deal and get it back on track.[9]

2. Recognize that a long-term business deal is a continuing negotiation.   Negotiations between parties do not stop when they sign their contract. Time and again, executives involved in the implementation of international transactions have given the author the same message: "Once the contract is signed, we put it in the drawer. After that what matters most is the relationship between us and our partner, and we are negotiating that relationship all the time." What this view means in practice is that many matters in the transaction, usually but not always of a minor nature, are subject to negotiation or renegotiation by the parties as part of the ongoing relationship, despite the fact that their contract contains no specific renegotiation clause. Many issues necessarily have to be left for a decision at a later time. For example, in a strategic alliance between two companies to produce a new product, it would be impossible and make no business sense for their contract to state the price at which the new product will be sold, the nature of the advertising campaign to promote it, or even the identity of the advertising agency that will design the campaign. Moreover, no deal-making negotiation can predict all eventualities that the parties may encounter, nor can it achieve perfect understanding between the parties, especially when they come from different cultures.

If change and uncertainty are constant risks in long-term transactions, what coping strategies are available to deal makers? One approach is for the two sides to consider the problem of renegotiation before, rather than after, they sign their contract. Both sides should recognize at the outset that the risk of changed circumstances is high in any long-term relationship. Unfortunately, most modern contracts deny the possibility of change. They therefore rarely provide for adjustments to meet altered circumstances. This assumption of contractual stability has proven false time and time again. For example, most mineral development contracts assume that the agreement will last for periods of from 15 to 99 years, but they rarely remain unchanged beyond a fraction of that time. One way to address this problem is to provide specifically in the contract for renegotiation at defined periods for issues that are particularly susceptible to changing circumstances. Rather than dismiss the possibility of renegotiation and then be forced to review the entire contract at a later time in an atmosphere of hostility between the partners, it is better to recognize the possibility of renegotiation at the outset and set down a clear framework within which to conduct the process. In short, recognize the possibility of redoing the deal, but control the process.

3. Consider a role for mediation or conciliation in the deal. Third parties—whether called mediators, conciliators, advisers, or something else—

can often assist in building and preserving business relations. For example, when some companies contemplate long-term relationships, such as strategic alliances requiring a high degree of cooperation, they may hire a consultant to develop and guide a program of relationship building that might include joint workshops, get-acquainted sessions, and retreats, all of which take place before the parties actually sit down to negotiate the terms of their contract. The consultant will facilitate and perhaps chair these meetings, conduct discussions of the negotiating process, point out potential pitfalls, and discuss with the parties ways to avoid possible problems. Once negotiations start, the consultant may continue to observe the process and be ready to intervene when the deal-making process encounters difficulties.[10]

After the deal has been signed, consultants, lawyers, and advisers may continue their association with one or both parties and informally assist as mediators in managing conflict that may arise in the execution of the transaction. In some cases, parties to a complex or long-term transaction may include specific provisions in their contract stipulating a process to manage conflict and to prevent it from causing a total breakdown of the deal. For example, the contract may state that if a dispute between the parties cannot be settled at the operational level, the two sides' senior managements will engage in negotiations to resolve it. Generally, top management officials, not directly embroiled in the particular conflict and with a broad view of the transaction and its relationship to their firms' overall strategies, may be in a better position to settle a dispute than persons at the operating level, who often have come to feel that they have a personal stake in "winning" the dispute.

The international construction industry has developed an important form of deal-managing mediation that employs a designated third person to resolve disputes that may arise in the course of a major construction project, such as a dam or a power plant. These projects typically include many parties, are highly technical and complex, and take a long time to complete. Possibilities for conflict are virtually endless, yet it is essential for all concerned that disputes not impede the progress of construction. The construction contract will therefore usually designate a consulting engineer, review board, permanent referee, or dispute adviser, with varying powers, to handle conflicts as they arise and in a way that will allow the construction work to continue. Sometimes, as in the case of a consulting engineer, the third person has the power to make a decision, which may later be challenged in arbitration or the courts; sometimes, as in the case of a dispute adviser, the third person plays the role of a mediator by engaging in fact-finding or by facilitating communication among the disputants.[11]

The use of dispute review boards or dispute advisers in construction contracts has proven to be a cost-effective means of settling disputes while permitting a continuation of construction projects in an expeditious manner. This mechanism would seem to have application in other areas. For example, in a complex multiparty strategic alliance, the parties might designate a person or organization to serve as a permanent mediator to assist them in managing conflicts that may arise in the course of their business relationship. Thus far, however, this device does not appear to have reached much beyond the construction industry.

4. Agree on regular meetings and contacts during the transaction. Organizational relationships depend on personal relationships. A solid working relationship between two companies requires effective relationships between their executives and employees, which in turn require regular meetings and contacts. Accordingly, before the deal is signed, the parties to a transaction should agree specifically on a schedule of regular meetings and contacts at appropriate levels within their two organizations and not assume that they will happen spontaneously. More than one joint venture has failed because the parties did not maintain adequate communications with each other once the deal was made.

5. Be specific about your interests both inside and outside of the transaction and encourage the other side to do the same. The development of a business relationship requires the two sides to understand each other's interests fully. During the deal-making process, they each need to explain clearly *why* they are making the deal, what they are hoping to achieve, and how their interests may change over time. Equally important, every company has interests outside of the transaction that may eventually compete with or subordinate its interests within the transaction. When that happens, the relationship between the two sides may suffer. For example, a pharmaceutical company may enter into a joint venture with another drug company to develop a new hypertension medicine. Once the drug is produced, each company may want to market it in a way that reinforces the marketing of its other pharmaceuticals. Here is a case in which they have a common interest within the transaction but potentially conflicting interests outside of it. To avoid damaging conflict later in their relationship, the two sides should make those interests clear to each other at the outset.

6. Each side should inform the other of its organizational culture.   Every company has its own organizational culture, its own way of making decisions and carrying out organizational tasks. For example, a U.S. publicly traded firm manufacturing high-tech medical devices has a distinctly different organizational culture from a family-owned medical supply distributor in Thailand. In the U.S. firm, committees make all major decisions after careful staff preparation and study. In the Thai company, the family patriarch decides everything and delegates little authority to his subordinates, all of whom are his sons and daughters. For the two companies to develop a business relationship in connection with a transaction, they both will need to understand how the other decides and acts according to its own organizational culture. For example, the Thai firm will come to understand why the U.S. company takes so long and needs so much information to make decisions, and the U.S. firm will come to appreciate that the Thai company can make quick decisions—except when the patriarch is out of town. The two sides should educate each other on their organizational cultures during the deal-making process. This knowledge is an important foundation stone for a business relationship between the parties.

7. Carefully define together how the deal will be executed.   Throughout the life of the transaction, the parties will have to make countless decisions about their transaction, regardless of the level of detail contained in their contract. Rather than assuming that the contract will serve as some sort of automatic instruction booklet for their deal, the parties during the deal-making process should talk about how they will decide issues that arise in the future. For example, in the event of late shipments under a long-term sales agreement, who in the buyer's organization will be responsible to contact which person in the seller's firm to work out the problem, and what authority will each person have to resolve the issue? Rather than hoping that problems will never arise, it is better when you are making the deal to acknowledge the possibilities of difficulties and then to develop a governance system to handle them.

3

SEVEN STEPS TO PREPARE
FOR GLOBAL DEAL MAKING

THE IMPORTANCE OF PREPARATION

The difference between a successful and an unsuccessful negotiation lies all too often in the quality of the parties' preparation. Business executives often fail to make a deal or to derive maximum benefit from their negotiation because one or both sides did not prepare effectively for their encounter. Probably the worst approach to a negotiation is the attitude "Let's hear what the other side has to say and *then* we'll decide how to deal with them." That view is like a general who leads an army onto the battlefield declaring, "Let's see what they throw at us and then we'll decide how to get organized." While flexibility and openness are certainly useful in a negotiation, it is nonetheless important to prepare for any deal-making session in a systematic and structured way. The following example, which one might call the "dance of the unprepared," illustrates the dangers of bad preparation.

South Beach Beverage Company, a successful producer of specialty soft drinks marketed under the name SoBe, decided to expand into the production of hard candies in flavors similar to its soft drinks. The problem was that while it owned the SoBe trademark for drinks, it did not own it for candy. Frank, the original owner of the SoBe trademark, had transferred it to the beverage company for stock and cash, but only for use in selling drinks, not candy. One day, John, the president of SoBe, called Frank, who lived in Montreal, Canada, and asked him to come to a meeting at John's office in Connecticut to discuss the company's possible purchase of the trademark for candies. Frank agreed and traveled to meet with John.

At the meeting, John, accompanied by two of his executives, began by saying, "Frank, we'd like to buy the SoBe trademark and we'd like to know how much you want for it."

Frank replied, "How much are you offering?"

John responded, "Look, we're serious. What do you want for the trademark?"

Frank countered, "No. I want to know what you are offering."

John replied, "Last year, you told me you'd be interested in selling. Now I want to know how much the trademark is going to cost us?"

Frank responded, "You asked for this meeting. So it's up to you to put an offer on the table."

As their conversation increasingly resembled a buyer and a seller haggling over a mango in a tropical market, John finally asked his two associates to step out into the hall with him so they could have a private conversation, leaving Frank to drink his coffee. After ten minutes, they came back into the room and John said: "Frank, we'll give you $100,000 for the trademark."

Frank reacted angrily. "That's ridiculous. The trademark is worth a lot more than that, and you know it. You must think I'm an idiot. You asked me to come all this way to play games? Forget it. I'm leaving." With that Frank slammed his briefcase shut and stomped out of John's office. As this book went to press, John and Frank had not yet renewed discussions, even though John still wanted to buy and Frank still wanted to sell.[1]

The fundamental reason for the failure of John's and Frank's negotiation was lack of effective preparation—by *both* sides. Their conversation was a dance of the unprepared. Had John taken the time to prepare a definite proposal based on objective criteria, Frank would not have walked out of the meeting, but would have considered it seriously. The proposal would have become the basis for discussion between the two of them. To give legitimacy and weight to his proposal, John might have linked it to objective market standards. For example, the proposal might have estimated the U.S. market for specialty candy at $300 million and might have estimated that after five years SoBe Candy had the potential to achieve 3 percent of the market, thereby yielding annual sales of $9 million. Using industry standards, a fair royalty on that amount would be, for example, 2 percent per year, which if discounted to present value might be worth $500,000. Frank might still have objected to the final figure as too low, but he would have had to base his discussions on the figures and assumptions in the study. He would not have walked out of the meeting. Equally important, a well-developed proposal would have signaled to Frank that John was taking Frank seriously and that there was a basis for the two of them to negotiate a solution to their problem. On his side, Frank might have gone through a similar exercise to prepare for the meeting with John.

Any proposal, particularly in an opening move, contains a variety of messages, both overt and subtle. It not only says what you think about the transaction, but it may also reveal what you think about the other side. In the SoBe case, John's unprepared opening move not only stated his views on the proposed purchase price, but it also conveyed what he thought about Frank. "He was telling me I was stupid," Frank later told the author. "That made me mad so I walked out." If John had prepared a studied proposal based on legitimate criteria and industry standards, Frank would not have concluded that John was belittling his intelligence.

SEVEN STEPS TO EFFECTIVE PREPARATION

To negotiate effectively, you have to prepare systematically. The aim of this chapter is to provide you with a method of effective preparation for global deal making. The following seven steps should guide your preparation. The "Global Negotiator's Checklist" in appendix A may give you additional help.

1. Determine your principal's goals and clarify your instructions and authority. In preparing for any negotiation, you must first of all determine your goals. What do you want from the negotiation? A clear definition of your negotiating goal will influence to a large extent your strategies and tactics in deal making.

Most of the time when we negotiate, we are negotiating for someone else.[2] In short, most negotiators are *agents*. Executives are agents for their corporations. Diplomats are agents for their governments. Lawyers are agents for their clients. Those corporations, governments, and clients are our *principals*, the organizations and persons for whom we are negotiating and to whom we are responsible.

Our ability as agents to make deals on behalf of somebody else depends first of all on understanding as clearly as possible our principal's goals and interests in the contemplated deal. In the SoBe case discussed earlier, Frank was a principal in the negotiations. He was negotiating for himself. Presumably he understood his goals and interests in negotiating a trademark deal with the beverage company. But suppose he had asked his lawyer, one of his employees, or a friend to negotiate for him. The lawyer, employee, or friend would first have to engage in a lengthy conversation with Frank to determine Frank's interests and goals in making the trademark deal before negotiating with John. An agent would have to obtain answers to many questions: Why does Frank want to make this deal? How does it relate to his other businesses? What other options for the trademark is Frank thinking about? What are his monetary goals? Does he want a continuing business relationship with South Beach Beverage Company or does he simply want to get as much money as he can as soon as possible and hope never to see John again? These are also the kinds of questions you will need to ask your own principal before you engage in global deal making on its behalf.

A second important element in a negotiating agent's preparation concerns the agent's authority and instructions from the principal. Authority refers to the agent's power to make legal obligations that bind the principal. Instructions refer to the kinds of deals that the agent may explore and tentatively agree to at the negotiating table. An agent may have very limited legal authority to bind a principal, but may have a broad set of instructions that gives great latitude to explore a wide variety of possibilities. For example, in many major negotiations, such as those relating to mergers, joint ventures, or direct foreign investments, both sides understand at the start that anything agreed at the negotiating table will have no binding legal effect until approved by the companies for whom the negotiators are working. On the other hand, the negotiators' instructions in those same negotiations may be sufficiently broad and clear to give assurance to all sides that whatever the negotiators agree to has a strong likelihood of acceptance by their respective principals.

A negotiator's authority and instructions are not simply handed down from on high like the stone tablets bearing the Ten Commandments. Instead, in most companies they are the product of a process that is itself a negotiation, an *internal* negotiation. For example, to formulate instructions for its executives to negotiate an agreement to establish a power plant in India, an energy company would need to conduct negotiations among a variety of internal departments—including finance, engineering, and legal, among others—in order to arrive at a common understanding of such important factors as the minimum acceptable rate of return on the project, the nature of legal guarantees required by the company, and the types of electrical generation technology that the company would be willing to transfer to India.

Often in determining an agent's authority and instructions for a negotiation, the agent plays a key role as adviser or counselor to the principal.[3] One of the reasons why a principal uses an agent in a negotiation is because of the agent's expertise in the substantive areas of business under discussion, as well as the agent's skill in carrying out the negotiation process. Because of that expertise and skill, negotiating agents are often able through advice to their principals to guide the formulation of their authority and instructions. In some cases—for example, trying to determine a maximum amount to be obtained from the negotiation—the principal may ask the agent's advice: "How much do you think we can get?" In other cases, when the principal's stated demands are extreme, the agent may have to deflate them by referring to the prevailing standards in a specific area of business as not justifying the principal's expectations. For example, if a CEO of an energy company wants to instruct a negotiator to obtain a minimum rate of return of 30 percent on the electrical generating station in India, the negotiator might advise the CEO that no Indian government has ever approved a project with that high a rate of return and that, in the negotiator's opinion, starting with such a high demand will not only meet quick rejection, but will also serve to sour relations permanently between the Indian government and the company.

2. Organize your team. The negotiation of a global deal is usually the work of a team, rather than one individual. Some members of the team sit at the negotiating table. Others remain in the background—in the company's home office or its local facility—but nevertheless support the negotiators at the table. Preparation for the negotiation requires the various members of the team to prepare together and to develop a coordinated plan of action.

The team should prepare for the negotiation before it leaves home. Negotiators should prepare well in advance as a team, rather than as individuals who come together for the first time to talk about a proposed deal on the plane taking them to the site of the negotiations. To facilitate coordination and communication among the team members, you may want to establish a space within a secure website where various documents related to the negotiation can be stored for consultation over the Internet. As part of their preparation, team members might engage in simulated negotiations and role-play to anticipate the situations they expect to meet.

Consider carefully the size and composition of your team.   The wrong people at the table can kill a deal, no matter how good it looks. Skilled and prepared negotiators, on the other hand, can turn a bad situation around. It is therefore important to select and prepare the negotiating team with care.

The size and expertise of the negotiating team will depend on the nature of the deal and the parties' cultural backgrounds. One or two persons with knowledge of sales can negotiate a simple machinery sales contract. Negotiating a joint venture to manufacture machinery, on the other hand, requires larger teams and a broader range of expertise. Some business cultures, such as the Chinese, tend to put together large negotiating teams, while others, like the American, tend to prefer small ones. In some cultures, the inclusion of a lawyer on the team may raise concerns on the other side as to possible future lawsuits and the sincerity of your intentions in building a working relationship. In many countries, a lawyer's primary function is to litigate disputes. In those cases, it may be better to keep your lawyer in the background or to refer to your attorney as an "advisor," "counselor," or "contract specialist."

The team should agree on a single spokesperson.   The effectiveness of a negotiating team can be severely diminished when more than one person speaks on its behalf. Several voices give several messages, a situation that confuses the other side and ultimately may lead it to question your side's credibility. While a team usually consists of specialists and technicians, the team leader should be a generalist with a broad vision, a person who can integrate the various technical requirements into a broad concept or premise that will become the basis for the deal. In one negotiation several years ago between an American construction company and a Turkish public-sector corporation for a contract to build a dam, both teams consisted only of specialists. Neither had a generalist. As a result, the technicians on each side argued about technical points. No one was capable of developing a general framework for the deal, so the talks ended after a week of fruitless bickering.

The team should allocate specific functions and tasks among its members.   To smooth the negotiation, specific team members should be given definite tasks relating to the deal-making process, including note taking, transportation arrangements, communicating with the home office, and arranging for an interpreter when deal making will be conducted in more than one language.

Select an appropriate interpreter. A negotiation team should hire its own interpreter. Except in cases where special reasons for trust exist, do not rely on the other side's interpreter unless someone on your team understands the language and can check the translation. Before hiring an interpreter, try to determine the individual's skill and experience from independent reliable sources. Before negotiations actually begin, meet with your interpreter to explain the nature of the deal you are trying to make. An interpreter may be an expert in languages but will need to be briefed on the nature of the business deal you are trying to negotiate. You should also explain what you want in the way of translation and why you want it. For example, if you want a word for word translation rather than a summary, make your requirements clear. In selecting an interpreter, guard against individuals who, because of personal interest or ego, try to take control of the negotiation or slant it in a particular way. This risk may be present if the interpreter also works as a middleman, agent, or business consultant. On the other hand, a skilled and knowledgeable interpreter can also help you to understand the culture and business practices of the country in which you are trying to make a deal.

3. Research the other side and the deal. Effective preparation requires knowing as much as possible about the deal that you hope to make and the party you hope to make it with, *before* you get to the negotiating table. To do this, you need to engage in some intensive research. For example, before flying to Cameroon in West Africa to negotiate a deal to build a pipeline, you should try to learn as much as possible about Cameroon's economy, political system, culture, and relationships with its neighbors. This vital knowledge will come not only from books, articles, and online sources, but also from talking to people who know the Cameroon environment. In this regard, you may want to engage a Cameroon consultant, adviser, or lawyer to assist in your preparations. The local U.S. consulate or the U.S. Department of Commerce may also provide valuable information. You will find a selective bibliography of useful published sources to aid your preparation to negotiate abroad at the end of this book.

As you will see in later chapters, negotiating a global deal requires a negotiator to understand and surmount obstacles not ordinarily encountered in negotiating a purely domestic transaction. These special barriers to global deal making include differences in culture, unfamiliar laws and regulations, government processes and bureaucratic traditions, all of which a negotiator should research before arriving at the negotiating table for the first time.

4. Determine your options and particularly your best option to the deal you hope to make. Try to estimate the other side's options. A critical step in preparing to negotiate is to determine options—yours and theirs. Your options fall into two categories: the options that you have in the event that negotiations fail and the options that you are willing to explore with the other side as a basis for the deal.

While determining what you will do if you do not make a deal may seem defeatist, it is nonetheless an important part of your preparation. In their book *Getting to YES*, Fisher, Ury and Patton stress the importance of defining your Best Alternative to a Negotiated Agreement, your BATNA.[4] Knowing your best alternative to a deal has several benefits. First, it gives you a standard against which to measure any proposal that the other side puts forward. Obviously, you do not want to accept any option at the negotiating table that is worse than what you can obtain elsewhere. Second, knowing your best alternative to the deal will often help to build your confidence at the negotiating table. Sometimes it may be possible to improve your best alternative to the deal, thereby increasing your confidence and negotiating power even more. Indeed, the power that a negotiator feels at the negotiating table is directly proportional to that person's evaluation of the best alternative to the deal. Third, if your alternative is particularly good, you may want to let the other side know it in hopes that it will persuade them to make a deal with you. For example, in the negotiations between Daimler-Benz and Chrysler over their proposed merger, Jergen Schrempp, chairman of Daimler-Benz, told Robert Eaton, chairman of Chrysler, that Daimler-Benz had also held talks with the Ford Motor Company about a possible merger. Although Schrempp was not particularly attracted to this option since it meant that Daimler-Benz would be dominated by Ford, he nonetheless revealed it to Eaton as a way of saying that if Chrysler, which had no other potential merger partner, did not make a deal with Daimler-Benz, Daimler-Benz would merge with Ford and Chrysler would be left with no one—a situation that Chrysler feared in an industry marked by overcapacity and increasing competition, an industry in which only the large automakers would survive. By revealing Daimler-Benz's BATNA, Schrempp moved Eaton toward the DaimlerChrysler merger.[5]

Your preparation should also try to estimate the options available to the other side, an exercise that requires you to put yourself in the place of your counterpart. Sometimes, when faced with adversaries that seem overwhelmingly powerful, a careful analysis of their options, particularly their BATNAs, may reveal that they are not as powerful as they first appear. In the preparation phase, you can only estimate the other side's options. Later, at the negotiating table, you will learn much more about their available options.

5. Define your interests and think about their interests. Businesses engage in negotiations in order to satisfy their interests. It is therefore important to define your interests clearly before you arrive at the negotiating table. We sometimes formulate positions without thinking hard about the interests that shape and drive those positions. For example, before beginning negotiations with a potential new supplier in Malaysia, you need to have clearly in mind *why* you are seeking a new supplier in Malaysia. Is it to lower costs? Is it to avoid overdependence on your current supplier in Dallas? Is it to develop a foothold in Southeast Asia? Is it to learn about the Malaysian market? If your interests are all of the above, then you should prioritize those interests to determine which are more important and which are less important to your business. The nature of those interests will determine the proposals you put forward and the ultimate deal you are willing to accept. For instance, if developing a foothold in Southeast Asia and diversifying suppliers is a primary interest, you might be more flexible on pricing than if your primary interest was simply to obtain components as cheaply as possible.

In addition to clarifying your interests as part of preparing to negotiate, you should also think about the other side's interests. Obviously, you will learn more about their interests at the negotiating table, but you ought also to try to estimate the interests that will be driving your counterpart once you sit down to negotiate. For example, if you are planning to negotiate to build a hotel in Egypt, you should try to estimate the interests of the Egyptian government in the deal. Those interests will certainly include the development of its tourist industry and increased opportunities to earn foreign exchange. But in view of certain segments of the Egyptian public's suspicion of foreign investment, it may also include a desire not to appear to have turned over the control of an important economic sector to foreigners. Recognition of that interest may help you to formulate proposals and to conduct negotiations in a way that will not offend traditional Egyptian sensitivities concerning foreign exploitation, and may thereby increase the prospect of a successful negotiation.

In contemplating interests, you should remember that in all likelihood you will be negotiating with an agent of the organization with which you are trying to make a deal. Agents have their own interests, as well as the interests of the principal, to pursue. In short, they may have a dual agenda. In its most extreme form, the agent's pursuit of personal interests can lead to demands for bribes and other forms of corruption. As you prepare for deal making, you should contemplate the possibility of requests for corrupt payments and develop strategies and tactics to deal with them. On the other hand, efforts to satisfy the personal interests of your counterparts across the negotiating table are not always illegal or unethical. Their desire for your respect, for favorable standing in the eyes of their superiors, and for positive recognition from colleagues in their organizations are personal interests that you should recognize and in appropriate ways help to satisfy as a means to pursue your company's interests in the negotiation. For example, if the lead negotiator on the other side is having difficulty understanding the financial technicalities of the deal you are proposing, it may be better to explain them in a private conversation than to lecture him in detail in front of the other side's whole team.

6. Identify the issues.   Your preparation needs to determine the precise issues that will arise during the course of the negotiations. Some issues, such as those relating to price, delivery dates, methods of payment, and performance specifications, will be obvious. Others may be less apparent. To understand the issues that may be important to the other side, it is helpful to put yourself in their place or to assign a member of your team to play the role of a negotiator for the other side. From this perspective, issues may be apparent that were not evident when you looked at the deal only from your vantage point. For example, in preparing to negotiate to establish a power plant in India to sell electricity to a state public utility, looking at the deal from the Indian point of view and particularly considering the country's traditional skepticism toward foreign investment may reveal that your lack of an Indian equity partner in the power project is likely to become a significant issue when you actually begin negotiations with the Indian government.

7. Formulate Mutually Beneficial Proposals in Advance. Before arriving at the negotiating table, you should prepare proposals that seem to meet the interests of both sides and could be a basis for an agreement. In the trademark case discussed earlier, neither John nor Frank had taken this step. As a result, the negotiations blew up in their faces. On the other hand, in negotiating with the U.S. Federal Trade Commission and European Union competition authorities in 2000 to obtain approval of their merger, AOL and Time Warner formulated possible options as to what they would divest in order to win the blessing of the two governmental agencies. Their divested selves would, however, still have to bring the merged entity the revenues that would make the merger advantageous; that is, the value of the merged entity had to be worth more than the value of AOL and Time Warner separately. In its discussions with the European authorities, AOL–Time Warner agreed to drop Time Warner's proposed acquisition of EMI (a large British music company) to prove to the European commission that it had no intention of dominating online music distribution. AOL–Time Warner anticipated the interests and concerns of the authorities on both continents and developed proposals in advance to meet them. As a result, both the United States and the European Union approved the merger.[6]

For many persons, the word "negotiation" evokes images of a process that goes through a fixed sequence of phases: The parties first state their positions and interests, then make concessions and adjustments, eventually reach an understanding, and finally write their agreement on paper. According to this view, the parties talk first and write last.

In certain situations, a negotiating team, as part of its preparation, may reverse this order by drafting a written proposed agreement *before* it actually meets with the other side. A common opening gambit in negotiations is for one party to present the other with a detailed document, known variously as a draft, model, prototype, or standard-form agreement, to serve as a basis for discussion. The presentation of a comprehensive draft agreement as a first step is a frequent practice in both business and diplomatic negotiations. Multinational corporations use draft contracts to sell jet aircraft, form joint ventures, and lend money. Governments seeking bilateral relations on trade and investment often launch negotiations by asking the other side to consider a draft treaty. Thus, in practice, negotiators often write first and then talk.

A draft or model agreement serves many purposes for the side presenting it. First, its preparation is an opportunity for the negotiators representing an organization to consult with important internal and external constituents in order to arrive at an acceptable negotiating position. For example, in preparing to negotiate an automotive joint venture in China, an international automaker might embody the consensus views of its finance, marketing, engineering, and legal departments in a draft memorandum of understanding that it would present as a basis of discussion to its potential Chinese partner. Before launching a program to negotiate bilateral investment treaties with developing countries in the 1980s, the United States government took nearly four years to reach a model treaty that was acceptable to concerned U.S. government agencies and departments.[7] This preliminary consultation is not only important preparation for the negotiations themselves, but it also gives the negotiators, whether for the international automaker or the U.S. government, some assurance that any deal that closely follows the draft will be approved by their home office.

Second, since companies and governments often contemplate similar arrangements with many different parties, a model agreement or standard form contract is an efficient means of informing potential negotiating partners about the type of transaction that the proposing party favors. Uniformity of contract language simplifies the administration of numerous similar transactions. It can also avoid later charges of discrimination that result in demands for renegotiation by countries or corporations who believe that others have received better treatment than they have. For many companies, beginning all negotiations with the same basic draft is generally seen as a cost-effective, efficient practice.

A third reason for preparing a formal draft agreement for submission in the negotiation is that it gives the proposing party a tactical advantage. Many experienced negotiators believe in the power of the first draft, that the person who controls the draft controls the negotiation. If the other side accepts the draft as the basis for the discussions, the presenter has, in effect, set the agenda for the talks and, more important, established the conceptual framework for the deal. To a large extent, the party submitting the draft fixes the terms of reference, while the other side (at least at the outset) is merely reacting to the draft's language, rather than advancing specific proposals of its own. Indeed, the party receiving the draft may be so preoccupied with countering the text that it neglects its own negotiating objectives and interests.

Although controlling the draft may allow you to control the negotiation, wise negotiators should be careful about applying this bit of conventional advice indiscriminately. Insistence on your own draft may enable you to dominate the negotiation at the beginning, but it may also obstruct agreement in the long run. Effective deal makers should focus on interests, not positions, should search for creative options for mutual gain, and should try to find a formula to accommodate competing goals. Insisting on one's own draft in a negotiation may frustrate these essential goals. For one thing, putting a draft on the table at an early stage in the negotiations may lock parties into bargaining positions, thereby obstructing a search for common interests and creative options. A draft or model agreement is, after all, nothing more than a detailed statement of a position. Then, too, if one of the functions of the early phase of a negotiation is to allow both sides to gather and share as much information as possible about one another, focusing at the outset on the draft is likely to hamper this vital process.

Although corporations may believe that their standard form contracts have universal application, they may in fact be inapplicable to particular local conditions or specific situations under discussion; consequently, unyielding insistence on their terms, especially in international deal making, may lead to results that are unsatisfactory for both sides. For example, the refusal by an American fast food company to change the language in its master franchise contract led to a business failure in Australia. The final contract, over the objections of the franchisee, retained the franchiser's standard language requiring the construction of top-quality snow-proof buildings. Since Melbourne, Australia, is not subject to heavy snows, the resulting construction costs to the franchisee placed an unnecessary and ultimately fatal burden on the Australian operation.[8]

Finally, since the party introducing the draft is usually in a superior bargaining position, the other side may view the presentation of the draft as an act of arrogance and a not-too-subtle signal of an unequal relationship between the parties. Consequently, placing a detailed draft contract on the table at the very beginning of the negotiation may instill suspicion and hostility in the other side, factors that at the very least will slow reaching an agreement and inhibit the development of an effective working relationship with the other side.

All of these reasons suggest that while the preparation of a draft, model, or prototype agreement may be important preparation for a negotiation, deal makers should not automatically introduce that document as an opening gambit in all negotiations. Instead, they should carefully analyze each situation to determine the appropriate time to present their draft in the negotiation process, if at all. They should also recognize that an inflexible insistence on the draft's terms is likely to prolong negotiation and may even derail any chance of an agreement.

4

SEVEN PRINCIPLES FOR GLOBAL DEAL MAKING

THE DEAL MAKER'S DILEMMA

After preparing carefully for a negotiation, a deal maker's next challenge is actually to use the negotiating process to make a deal with the other side. Negotiation is a *process*, a progressive movement toward a desired goal. In an international business negotiation, that goal is a deal. The job of the negotiators on both sides of the table is to manage the negotiation process over obstacles and around barriers to reach the goal.

Deal makers must pursue their companies' interests vigorously, but they also have to work together to overcome hurdles on the way to a deal. In any negotiation, negotiators need to do two things: to cooperate with each other to create value and to compete with each other to claim as large a share as possible of the value created.[1] For example, in negotiating a joint venture to build and operate an auto plant in China, an American negotiating team must cooperate with their Chinese counterparts to establish the enterprise, but they will also compete with them over a host of issues, such as profit sharing and royalty rates, in order to claim as many of the benefits from the venture as possible. The challenge for any negotiator in the deal-making process is to manage the continuing tension between the drive to compete and the need to cooperate. If deal makers compete too vigorously at the expense of cooperation, they risk losing the deal or failing to maximize the total gains from the negotiation. If, on the other hand, they cooperate at all costs, they risk obtaining less than the maximum benefit for their company. The dilemma always present in a deal maker's mind is: Will cooperating or competing with my counterpart best advance my interests?

At times the two sides at the negotiating table are like two persons in a canoe, who must combine their skills and strengths if they are to make headway against powerful currents, through dangerous rapids, and around hidden rocks. Alone, they can make no progress and probably will lose control. If one side paddles harder than the other, the canoe will go in circles. Unless they cooperate, they risk wrecking or overturning the canoe on the obstacles in the river. Similarly, unless global deal makers find ways of working together, their negotiations will founder on the many barriers encountered in putting together an international business transaction.

The problem for deal makers is to find a way to paddle the same canoe toward a common destination. Just as canoeists need a few basic rules to propel their canoe efficiently, so deal makers should follow a few basic principles to enable them to work together to advance the negotiating process. The purpose of this chapter is to provide those principles, to set down seven basic rules for making deals. They are:

1. Carefully plan your opening moves and make them fit your goals.
2. Work to build relationships with the other side.
3. Search for the other side's needs and interests and don't be afraid to reveal yours.
4. Always look to create value in a negotiation.
5. Rely on objective standards to justify your proposals and insist that the other side do the same.
6. Consider using third parties to help make the deal.
7. Plan effective implementation of the deal.

These seven rules may appear to be simple. But then so does paddling a canoe—until you get into the boat. The challenge is to apply them in the multitude of situations that you will face in making deals around the world.

OPENING MOVES

1. Carefully plan your opening moves and make them fit your goals. The old admonition that "you never get a second chance to make a first impression" underscores the importance of first impressions in interactions between persons. Just as first impressions in a job interview may mean the difference between being hired and being rejected, opening moves in a negotiation can influence the course of the discussion either positively or negatively for a long time afterward. Opening moves may even be the difference between making the deal and walking away empty-handed. As a result, you should carefully plan your opening moves in any negotiation.

Too often, negotiators approach the negotiating table with the attitude "I'll be tough at the start. If that doesn't work, I can always take a softer approach." The flaw in this tactic is that it assumes that your opening move will have no continuing effect on your counterpart once you have decided to adopt a softer approach. In fact, of course, an overly tough opening move not only communicates the nature of your demand, but it also communicates something about you as a person and your company as a future customer or partner. Thus, your counterpart may interpret your overly aggressive opening move as an indication that you and your company are unreasonable, arbitrary, rigid, and perhaps untrustworthy. Once they have formed that impression, it may be very difficult to persuade them to change that evaluation no matter how gentle you become in subsequent negotiating sessions.

Care in developing opening moves is particularly important in business negotiations among companies from different cultures. Culture profoundly influences how people think, communicate, perceive, and behave. It also affects the kinds of deals they make and the way they make them. As a result, an opening move that might be completely acceptable between two American executives may be highly offensive when an American uses it in a negotiation with a Chinese, Japanese, or German executive. For example, an American effort to talk about the substance of the deal at the very start of discussions may be seen as premature by Japanese negotiators who believe it is essential that the two companies first get to know one another before considering the specific terms of any proposed transaction.

The array of possible opening moves in a negotiation is often broader and more varied than one might assume at first glance. It is important to consider carefully the whole range of ways of starting a particular negotiation before deciding on the one to use. For example, suppose that your corporation, a multinational conglomerate manufacturing office products, discovers that a company in Taiwan is profitably producing a luxury pen under a trademark that you believe belongs to your corporation but which it has not used for several years. What should be your opening move with the Taiwanese company? You might send the Taiwanese a letter threatening a lawsuit and see what reaction it generates. Perhaps they will offer to buy the trademark or promise to stop using it. A second option, at the opposite end of the spectrum, is to ask for a meeting to discuss their use of a trademark that you believe belongs to you. The purpose here is to gather information about the company and the legality of its use of the trademark before you decide specifically how to deal with them. A third option is to request a meeting with the Taiwan company to discuss a possible sale or license of the trademark that they are using but which belongs to you. A fourth is to propose a partnership in which you and the Taiwanese company together would market pens with your trademark on a worldwide basis. A fifth option is to delay contacting the Taiwan company until you identify other possible companies in Asia that could manufacture the pen under your trademark. The purpose of this approach would be to improve your best alternative to a negotiated agreement (BATNA), a concept we discussed in the previous chapter, thus giving you added strength in any eventual negotiation with the Taiwanese company, as well as an option to pursue in case your discussions fail.[2]

The choice of a specific opening move in this case, and in any potential deal-making situation for that matter, will depend on your ultimate goal in the negotiation. If your goal is to preserve the trademark for your company's exclusive use at a future time, then perhaps threatening a lawsuit as an opening move may be appropriate. On the other hand, if you would consider a possible partnership or licensing arrangement with the Chinese company, threatening a lawsuit as your opening move will almost certainly prove counterproductive. If you are not yet sure of your goal because you do not know enough about your counterpart, it may be wise to shape your opening move as one of learning and of trying to get to know the other side, without committing yourself to one particular position or another.

International executives constantly stress the importance of relationships with counterparts as a condition for successful transactions. In negotiating almost any international deal, especially one of any duration, it is almost always important to plan for opening moves that will lay the foundation for a relationship between you and the other side. As discussed in chapter 2, whereas American executives often see the goal of negotiation as securing a contract, negotiators from many other countries view the purpose of a business negotiation as laying the foundation for a relationship. As a result, in negotiating a transaction of any significant duration, such as a joint venture or a long-term sales arrangement, it is usually wise to approach the negotiation as an exercise in relationship building and to plan your opening moves accordingly. Toward this end, you should fashion opening moves that show your willingness to learn about the other side and build rapport with executives from that company. Thus, instead of putting specific proposals forward as your opening move, you may want to wait until you and your counterpart have come to know one another and feel that a positive rapport exists between the two of you.

RELATIONSHIPS

2. Work to build relationships with the other side. A business relationship, so essential to the success of any significant transaction, is a complex set of interactions characterized by a degree of cooperation and trust between the parties. A relationship implies a *connection* between the parties. Rather than expect the relationship to emerge magically once the contract is signed, the two sides should seek to establish that necessary connection from the very start of negotiations.

Organizational relationships depend on personal relationships. A genuine relationship cannot exist between two corporations unless some of their executives have a relationship with one another. Moreover, to the extent that the negotiators themselves establish a positive relationship with each other, the negotiations are likely to proceed more smoothly and effectively than if no such relationship exists.

Relationship building should begin as soon as the two sides have contact with one another. As discussed in chapter 2, the negotiation of a deal tends to pass through three stages: prenegotiation, conceptualization, and detail arrangement. Prenegotiation, the initial phase in deal making, is a time when the parties determine whether they want to negotiate at all and if so, what they will negotiate about. Some executives often want to rush through the prenegotiation phase because they consider it a waste of time, a period when they are not doing business. That attitude can obstruct productive deals in the long run because any deal depends on a healthy relationship between the parties, and a healthy relationship begins during prenegotiation.

Relationship building requires first and foremost mutual knowledge by the parties. Thus in any negotiation, deal makers need to get to know each other. The hard and fast rule that some negotiators have of telling the other side as little as possible as a hard and fast rule is not conducive to relationship building or deal making. In other words, you need to get to know the other side and let the other side know you. A policy of "don't ask, don't tell," is not an effective rule for negotiating a business relationship. Indeed, deal makers should do just the reverse: ask and tell.

Ask

To build an effective working relationship, the negotiators must know something about each other, not just as executives but also as people. Relationship building may seem particularly difficult in an international negotiation because the negotiators at first may feel that they have very little in common, that they come not only from different countries but from different worlds. Yet even cultural differences, if approached wisely, can become a basis for building a relationship. By demonstrating sincere interest in the other side's culture, a negotiator can begin the process of getting to know the other side. So in a negotiation with a Thai business executive or a Chinese official, an American negotiator can begin relationship building by showing interest in, knowledge of, and respect for Thai or Chinese culture. Indeed, failure to show interest in or to ask about the culture of the other side can be easily interpreted as an act of cultural superiority and arrogance, a statement that the other side's culture is not significant or important. A negotiator seeking to build a relationship can begin to break down the wall created by cultural differences not by ignoring those differences but rather by encouraging the other side to talk about its culture.

A global negotiator should develop ways of inquiring about the other side's culture and of encouraging the other side to talk about its culture. Questions about culture, when framed in an uncritical way, are messages that say, "Your culture (and therefore you, your people, and your company) is interesting, important, and worth learning about." Invariably, sincere questions about another culture will elicit sincere answers. People like to talk about themselves, and a person's culture is very much a part of one's identity.

Tell

A further technique in relationship building is to find parallels or similarities between the two sides in the negotiation. Such parallels or similarities may exist between the two companies, the two cultures, or the two negotiators as individuals. For example, the discovery during the prenegotiation of a proposed joint venture that an American executive and his Swedish counterpart had both studied at the London School of Economics can serve as a first link in building a relationship between the two. Other kinds of shared human experience, both happy and tragic, can facilitate relationship building and ultimately deal making. Several years ago, in the midst of a particularly tense negotiation between Americans and Israelis, Prime Minister Golda Meir expressed deep sympathy to one of the U.S. negotiators' whose wife had recently died. Meir referred to the pain she had suffered upon the death of one of her own family members. That brief conversation between the two negotiators improved the negotiating atmosphere dramatically. Meir's expression of sympathy and her reference to a shared tragic experience served to build a relationship that led to more productive talks between the American and the Israeli negotiators.[3]

NEEDS AND INTERESTS

3. Search for the other side's needs and interests and don't be afraid to reveal yours.   The fundamental goal of all deal makers is to satisfy their interests and needs. Strangely enough, negotiators are often afraid to talk frankly about their interests and needs during the negotiation of a transaction. They will normally state positions forthrightly, but they either neglect or refuse to reveal the interests and needs behind those positions. For example, in the case of the two daughters quarreling over their dead father's ring, discussed in chapter 2, each stated a position: "I want the ring." But neither at first revealed the interests behind their positions. It was only when they divulged their interests that the two sisters were able to develop a creative, satisfactory solution to what at first appeared to be an intractable conflict. Similarly, it was only when the U.S. customer understood its Malaysian supplier's interest in penetrating the American market with its other products that a creative solution developed which allowed them to bridge what appeared to be a yawning chasm between them over price. As discussed earlier, problem-solving negotiation cannot take place until both sides understand each other's interests.

A determination of interests is as important to making a deal in international business as to resolving a conflict between two sisters over a ring. For example, suppose that you are negotiating a joint venture with an Asian company that insists adamantly on having a minimum of 51 percent of the equity in the new venture. Your company is equally insistent on having a 51 percent interest.

You and the Asian company have stated your positions on the issue, but you have not articulated your interests. The positions seem contradictory and irreconcilable, but an understanding of interests may allow creative problem solving to take place that will eventually lead to a mutually satisfactory solution. How do you manage the conversation at the negotiating table to arrive at those interests? It was suggested earlier that an important tool to determining interests is to ask the question "why?" Suppose that in answer to the question "Why do you want 51 percent of the equity?" each company responds, "So that we can control the joint venture." The interests still appear to be irreconcilable.

Determining interests is sometimes like peeling an onion. Having received an initial answer about interests, you need to probe deeper, to peel back another layer, in order to determine the interests that underlie the stated positions. In the case of the Asian joint venture, it is necessary to probe for the interests beneath each party's desire for control. One therefore needs to ask both parties why each one wants control of the enterprise.

Your company wants control of the venture in order to protect the technology that it plans to transfer to the joint-venture company. After some discussion, the Asian negotiators across the table mention that as a state-owned entity their corporation cannot be placed in a subservient position in a venture with a foreign company. So while your fundamental interest in controlling the joint venture is to protect your technology, one of their important interests seems to be national prestige. Although the interests of the two sides are different, they are not necessarily irreconcilable. Once the interests are known, the parties can engage in problem solving to create solutions that will at the same time protect your technology from unlawful appropriation and also protect the national prestige of the Asian state corporation. For example, the Asian company might contribute 51 percent and hold the position of chairman of the board of directors, but your company, with 49 percent of the equity, would hold another class of stock that would guarantee you one-half the seats on the board of directors, give you the ability to block any decision with which you disagree, and grant you the right to appoint the company's managing director responsible for day-to-day operations of the venture.[4]

Negotiators are sometimes reluctant to reveal their interests. They believe that revealing information about their interests will weaken them in the negotiation and will allow the other side to exploit them. But in the cases we mentioned earlier, the parties would not have found a solution had they not at some point revealed their real interests about why they each wanted the ring or why they each wanted a 51 percent interest in the joint venture. It was only when they revealed their interests that genuine problem solving could begin.

But what if the other side does not tell you its interests? What are you supposed to do then? Throughout the negotiation, a skilled deal maker constantly needs to delve behind stated positions in order to determine the other side's real needs and interests. In the search for interests, the question is the deal maker's most powerful tool—particularly questions that begin with the word "why." So in the conflict about the ring between the two sisters, interests were revealed only when one of them asked, "Why do you want the ring?" In the conflict between two potential joint-venture partners, their interests became clear only when they fully answered the question "Why do you want 51 percent?"

Although the question is a vital tool, a deal maker should not always accept the other side's responses literally. You will need to evaluate their words and actions against your knowledge of the country's culture, history, ideology, and political system. For example, the fact that a government controls the foreign company with which you are negotiating should indicate that among its various interests national prestige and political concerns will probably have a high priority. On the other hand, those interests will probably have less importance for a privately owned Asian company. Knowing that your counterpart is owned by the state will be helpful in interpreting its insistence on control of the new joint venture.

Sometimes your questions to the other side may elicit no response or incomplete answers. In that case, a tactic to try to understand their interests is to speculate with them on what you think their interests are in the hope that your speculations will result in a conversation about genuine interests. For example, in the case of the conflict over the ring, if one sister had refused to say why she wanted the ring, the other might respond: "Well, since you won't tell me why you want the ring, I can only guess that you want it in order to sell it for its cash value." That might have provoked the other to correct the false impression by saying, "No, I want the ring because I like the diamond."

While you are trying to dig out the interests of the other side, it is well to remember that problem-solving negotiation is a *mutual* process that requires knowledge of *both* sides' interests. Thus, it is as important for you to reveal your interests as for you to determine the interests of the other side. Indeed, an effective way to encourage the other side to talk about its interests is for you to talk about yours.

VALUE CREATION

4. Always look for ways to create value in a negotiation.   Many people see a negotiation as a struggle in which their task is to obtain as much value for themselves as possible. For them, a negotiation is, basically, a distributive process. The parties are fighting over a pie whose size is fixed, and each side is seeking to obtain for itself as big a slice as possible. For example, one tendency is to see the negotiation between the Malaysian manufacturer and the American purchaser of components as a struggle by one to pay as little value as possible for the components and by the other to obtain as much value as possible for them. Certainly, every negotiation involves issues of distribution over which the parties must struggle. Discussion about the price of the goods to be purchased, the amount of capital to be contributed to a joint venture, the interest rate to be charged by a lender, and the royalty rate to be paid by a trademark licensee are all examples of issues involving the distribution value. Every additional dollar gained by one side in the negotiation of these issues is a dollar lost by the other side.

To focus only on these distributive questions ignores an equally important aspect of any negotiation: the creation of value. The negotiation of any deal is an opportunity to create value, to make the pie bigger, to enlarge the total amount of resources from which the parties will ultimately benefit. Often the parties in a deal-making negotiation focus so intently on distributing value that they miss opportunities to create value and thus in the end have to settle for less individually than they might have otherwise. For example, in the negotiation between the Malaysian manufacturer and the American buyer of components mentioned earlier, if the two parties had concerned themselves only with struggling over the price of the components, they would have missed the opportunity to create value by allowing the Malaysian manufacturer to exhibit some of its goods in the American's space at the trade show. By doing so, the two companies created value in the sense that the American paid a lower price for the components and the Malaysian gained a low-cost means to introduce its goods to the American market.

Value creation in negotiation begins with a vision by both sides that the essence of deal making is not just a struggle over distributing money and resources but is first and foremost an opportunity to create wealth, and that the task of deal makers is to extract the maximum amount of value presented by the encounter between the two sides. Too often, deal makers arrive at a contract that does not maximize the potential economic benefits that the encounter presents. Suppose two persons were negotiating over the division of 100 pennies in a bowl and, after long negotiation, walked away in triumph since each agreed to allow the other to take 25 pennies. It is obvious that the two negotiators did not maximize the value since they left 50 pennies in the bowl, hardly what one would describe as a very good deal. The difference between a business negotiation and the example of pennies in the bowl is that while we know at the outset the exact number of pennies in the bowl, we do not know at the outset the exact amount of value that can be created by joining two companies in a business transaction. One of the basic purposes of a negotiation is to exchange information and ideas that will allow the parties to see the various opportunities to create value from their encounter.

The challenge for deal makers is to use the negotiation to create the maximum amount of value from their encounter. How should they proceed to attain this objective? What techniques should they use to avoid leaving value untapped at the negotiating table like so many pennies left in a bowl?

Value creation in a negotiation begins with fostering a favorable atmosphere for problem solving. At the outset, through words and actions, negotiators need to make it clear to each other that they see the process of deal making not as combat or struggle but as an effort to find a mutually acceptable solution to a problem that they both share. They need to do their utmost throughout the deal-making phase to maintain an atmosphere of problem solving despite the tensions and conflicts that inevitably arise during the course of any business negotiation.

OBJECTIVE STANDARDS

5. Rely on objective standards to justify your proposals and insist that the other side do the same.   In any deal-making session, each party is seeking to advance its interests. While both sides may have a common interest in working together, their interests will ordinarily conflict on a variety of individual issues affecting the relationship that they are trying to negotiate. For example, in a negotiation between a Japanese company and a Vietnamese enterprise to form a joint venture to manufacture high-definition television sets in Vietnam, both companies have a common interest in structuring a successful manufacturing operation. Nonetheless, they face difficult and potentially contentious issues on a host of matters where their interests seem to conflict, including profit distribution, capital contributions, control over management, and the royalty rate to be paid by the joint venture for the technology and know-how to be transferred by the Japanese company.

The Japanese company will want to secure as high a royalty rate as possible for its technology, while the Vietnamese, knowing that a high royalty rate will only diminish the joint venture's profits, will seek as low a rate as possible. One effective way to resolve such potentially contentious issues is for the parties to agree on a standard, norm, principle, or objective criteria to regulate the matter in question. Linking a proposal to an agreed-upon standard makes that proposal much more persuasive than if the proposal is simply based on the desire of the party to obtain as much as it can from the other side. Thus, the Japanese are more likely to be more effective at the negotiating table if they justify their demand for a 5 percent royalty of gross revenues by indicating that 5 percent is the prevailing rate in the electronics industry in Southeast Asia than by simply asserting that a 5 percent royalty is company policy. The use of an accepted industry standard also tells the Vietnamese that they are not likely to receive a better rate from another foreign company.

Just as the use of a standard to justify a proposal will make you more persuasive at the negotiating table, your own insistence that the other side also use an objective standard will also help you to shape a deal that is in your interests. For example, the Vietnamese, faced with a Japanese demand for a 5 percent royalty rate because it is company policy, should ask what the basis is for that company policy to determine if it is rooted in any kind of an objective standard or is merely another way of saying "we want 5 percent because we want 5 percent."

A standard used in a negotiation may have its basis in a variety of sources: precedent, prevailing practice in an industry or country, a legal or moral principle, an independent expert opinion, custom, market value, a cost-of-living index, the prime rate, or the standards of a particular profession, to name just a few. Obviously, a party will select a standard that advances its interests. Nonetheless, the use of standards in the process of deal making tends to give a quality of rationality to discussions, which facilitates arriving at an agreement.

Using standards to resolve contentious issues will not only facilitate agreement at the table but will also help negotiators on the other side of the table to convince their superiors that the deal they have made is fair and in the best interests of their own organization. It is good to remember that agents on behalf of their organizations conduct virtually all significant international business negotiations and that those agents must convince their superiors to accept the deals they have made. In persuading their superiors of the fairness of a deal, negotiators will often rely on standards that have been agreed upon at the negotiating table. So the Vietnamese negotiators of the high-definition television joint venture will convince the leaders of their organization that a 5 percent royalty rate on transferred technology is fair by demonstrating that it is no more than the prevailing rate in Southeast Asia in similar projects or that the Japanese company is also receiving 5 percent on a similar project in Malaysia.

Many international business deals affect important public interests and therefore must also be defended to the public. Here too, the existence of a standard is important in making such a defense. For example, opponents of privatization or of big foreign investment projects often challenge them on the ground that they are unfair, exploitative, or a give-away of national assets. To defend the deal to the public, a government may employ the same standards used by negotiators at the bargaining table. The absence of a convincing standard, on the other hand, makes the public defense of such transactions difficult. For instance in the early 1990s, Enron, a large U.S. energy company, agreed to develop a $2 billion electrical generating plant in India and made a contract to sell electricity for twenty years to a state utility at a tariff that was high by Indian standards and was subject to continuing escalation during the life of the contract. The result gave Enron an expected rate of return on equity of over 25 percent on the project. In the negotiations, the Indian government considered that rate to be too high and argued that 20 percent was more reasonable. Enron originally insisted on 26.52 percent, claiming that given the risks involved and the prevailing market expectations for similar projects, the projected rate of return was proper, and that even 30 percent would be appropriate. Although the negotiations nearly collapsed over the issue, the two sides finally agreed on a rate of 25.22 percent, which certain government officials still considered too high. Almost from its inception, the project was subject to ferocious public attacks on the grounds that it was unfair, exploitative, and would be paid for on the backs of the poor. Defenders of the project were not able to present a clear and convincing standard to show that the project was fair. Ultimately, an opposition political party that had made criticism of the project the centerpiece of its election campaign came to power and canceled the contract, forcing Enron to renegotiate the power tariff.[5]

In some areas of international business, appropriate standards to guide negotiators on specific issues may be fairly well established. For example, in an international sale of goods, it is a generally accepted principle that the buyer is to pay by a confirmed, irrevocable letter of credit. In other areas, because of differences in cultures and national business practices, two or more conflicting standards may apply. Here, the negotiators must use their ingenuity and creativity to devise a rule or norm that will satisfy or at least not offend the underlying values implicit in the conflicting norms. Suppose, for instance, that in the sale of equipment on credit, the practice in the seller's country is to charge interest on the outstanding balance, but the buyer's country, following strict Islamic law, forbids the payment of interest. Rather than allow these two conflicting standards to obstruct deal making, the parties might agree to a price that accounts for the fact that the sale is being made on credit terms. Another approach is to label the portion of each payment attributable to interest as "administrative fees" to compensate the seller for the added administrative burden that a sale on credit entails. Or, the parties might wish to structure the transaction as an equipment lease for a specific period of time, with the ownership of the equipment transferring to the seller only after the final lease payment is made.

In some situations, no specific standard may exist that covers the transaction in question. One may encounter this problem in developing countries that have had little experience with certain kinds of complex transactions or whose societies are in a significant state of transition, perhaps from a command economy to a market economy. In this situation, negotiators may seek analogies from other fields or other countries in order to find a mutually acceptable standard that is applicable to their transaction. For example, during the 1960s, the Saudi Arabian government made a series of construction contracts with foreign and domestic private companies to undertake works near its border with Yemen. When hostilities with Yemen broke out, Saudi Arabia ordered a stoppage of the construction work for reasons of national security.

The construction companies demanded compensation from the Saudi government and the two sides entered into negotiations to resolve the problem. The country had not previously faced a similar situation. On the one hand, the Saudi government had not caused the hostilities, had acted in what it judged were the best interests of the country, and was willing to allow construction to continue once the military situation was secure. On the other hand, the companies had sustained a loss by not being allowed to complete the work so that they could be compensated. Ultimately, the parties negotiated a settlement by applying the principle of French administrative law known as the act of the prince doctrine (*la théorie du fait du prince*).[6] This principle holds that when a public contracting authority makes the conditions for the execution of one of its contracts more difficult than expected because of its own actions, the public authority must indemnify the private party for any injury sustained as a result. The Saudi negotiators, who had all been trained in Egyptian law schools where they had learned French administrative law, knew the act of the prince doctrine and therefore accepted it as the standard in the negotiation. The foreign companies also knew it and accepted it as the standard since it met their interests in the negotiation.

THIRD PARTIES

6. Consider using third parties to help make the deal. The usual model of an international business negotiation is that of representatives of two companies from different countries sitting alone in a room in face-to-face discussions to shape the terms of a commercial contract. While many transactions take place in that manner, many others require the services of one or more third parties to facilitate the deal-making process. These individuals perform many different tasks in helping to make the deal and they have many different names: adviser, agent, broker, investment banker, and consultant, among others. If mediation can be defined as helping two parties to reach an agreement, then these individuals may be called deal-making mediators.

Despite the variety of labels and tasks, the contribution of these deal-making mediators to the deal-making process can be grouped into three areas: procedural activities, communication activities, and substantive activities. Procedural activities may include bringing the parties together initially, arranging meetings, chairing meetings, and organizing the negotiation agenda. Communication functions include transmitting messages in various

formats between the parties, interpreting statements, and maintaining channels of communication between the parties. And substantive functions relate
to helping the parties actually shape their deal, including determining the
parties' priorities and interests, making suggestions and recommendations,
and proposing solutions that resolve differences.

In many situations, the presence of a third party can mean the difference
between making a deal or failing at the negotiating table. Global deal makers
should therefore consider the kind of help they will need in making international transactions and how and when they will use it. The following examples illustrate ways that third parties may assist in making global deals.

Deal-Making Mediators in Hollywood

The acquisition in 1991 by Matsushita Electric Industrial Company of Japan,
one of the world's largest electronics manufacturers, of MCA, one of the
biggest U.S. entertainment companies, for over $6 billion illustrates the use
of mediators in the deal-making process. Matsushita had determined that its
future growth was dependent on obtaining a source of films, television programs, and music—what it termed "software"—to complement its consumer
electronic "hardware" products. Matsushita knew that it could find a source
of software within the U.S. entertainment industry, but it also recognized
that it was virtually ignorant of that industry and its practices. It therefore
engaged Michael Ovitz, the founder and head of Creative Artists Agency, one
of the most powerful talent agencies in Hollywood, to help it.[7]

After forming a team to assist in the task, Ovitz, fascinated by Asian cultures and a consultant to Sony when it bought Columbia Pictures, first ex-
tensively briefed the Japanese over several months, sometimes in secret
meetings in Hawaii, on the nature of the U.S. entertainment industry. He
then proceeded to propose three possible candidates for acquisition, one of
which was MCA. Ultimately, Matsushita chose MCA, but it was Ovitz, not
Matsushita executives, who initiated conversations with the MCA leadership, men whom Ovitz knew well. Indeed, Ovitz assumed the task of actually
conducting the negotiations for Matsushita. At one point in the discussions,
he moved constantly between the Japanese team of executives in one suite of
offices in New York City and the MCA team in another building, a process
that one observer described as "shuttle diplomacy." Although Matsushita
may have considered him their agent in the talks, Ovitz seems to have con-

sidered himself both a representative of Matsushita and a mediator between the two sides.

Because of the vast cultural and temperamental differences between the Japanese and American companies, Ovitz's strategy was to limit the actual interactions of the two parties to a bare minimum. During the first six weeks of negotiations, the Japanese and Americans met face-to-face only once. All other interactions took place through Ovitz. He felt that to bring the parties together too soon would create obstacles that would inevitably derail the deal. He was concerned not only by the vast differences in culture between the two companies but also by the greatly differing personalities in their top managements. The Japanese executives, reserved and somewhat self-effacing, placed a high value on the appearance if not the reality of modesty, while MCA's president was an extremely assertive and volatile personality. Like any mediator, Ovitz's own interests may also have influenced his choice of strategy. His status in the entertainment industry would only be heightened by making a giant new entrant into Hollywood dependent on him and by the public image that he had been the key to arranging one of the biggest deals in the industry's history. It should also be noted that Ovitz's primary interest was in making the deal happen, and only secondarily in creating a foundation that would result in a profitable long-term acquisition for Matsushita.

Although Ovitz launched the deal-making process and moved it a significant distance, he was not able to bring it to completion alone. Eventually the talks stalled over the issue of price, and meetings between the two sides ceased. At this point, a second deal-making mediator entered the scene to make a crucial contribution. At the start of the negotiation, Matsushita and MCA together had engaged Robert Strauss, a politically powerful Washington lawyer who had been at various times U.S. ambassador to the Soviet Union and U.S. trade representative, as "counselor to the transaction." Strauss, a member of the MCA board of directors and a close friend of its chairman, was also friendly with the Matsushita leadership and did legal and lobbying work in Washington for the Japanese company. In effect, his strong personal and business relationships with the two sides led them to appoint him to represent them both. Although his letter of appointment merely stated that Strauss was to "co-ordinate certain government relations matters," and even excluded his participation in the negotiations themselves, it appears that both MCA and Matsushita felt that he might be useful in other, unspecified ways.

When the talks stalled on the question of price, Strauss's close relationship to the two sides allowed him to act as a trusted conduit of communication, and he facilitated a meeting between the top MCA and Matsushita executives that ultimately resulted in an agreement on what Masushita would have to pay to acquire the American company. In arranging that meeting over some fifteen hours, he gained an understanding of the pricing parameters acceptable to each side and then communicated them to the other party. The Japanese, at that point, apparently had greater trust in Strauss, particularly because of his former role as a high U.S. government official, concerning the delicate issue of price than they did in Ovitz who, they sensed, had a dominant interest in simply getting the deal done regardless of the price the Japanese would have to pay. In the end, as a result of that meeting, the two sides reached an agreement allowing Matsushita to acquire MCA.

The Matsushita-MCA case shows clearly how two mediators facilitated the deal-making process, a deal that the parties probably would not have achieved by themselves. The factors that allowed Ovitz and Strauss to play successful roles were their knowledge of the two companies and their industries, their personal relationships with the leadership of the two sides, their respective reputations, the trust that they engendered, and their skills and experience as negotiators. On the other hand, although Matsushita did succeed in purchasing MCA, the acquisition proved to be troubling and ultimately a disastrous financial loss for the Japanese company. One may ask whether Ovitz's strategy of keeping the two sides apart during negotiations so that they did not come to know one another contributed to this unfortunate result. It prevented the two sides from truly understanding the vast gulf that separated them and therefore from realizing the enormity—and perhaps impossibility—of the task of merging two such different organizations into a single coordinated and profitable enterprise.

Other Deal-Making Mediators

An opposite mediating approach from that employed by Ovitz is the use of consultants to begin building a relationship between the parties *before* they have signed a contract and, indeed, before they have actually begun negotiations. When some companies contemplate long-term relationships, such as a strategic alliance, that will require a high degree of cooperation, they may hire a consultant to develop and guide a program of relationship building, which might include joint workshops, get-acquainted sessions, and retreats to take place before the parties actually sit down to negotiate the terms of their contract. The consultant will facilitate and perhaps chair these meetings, conduct discussions of the negotiating process, make the parties recognize potential pitfalls, and discuss with them ways to avoid possible problems. Once negotiations start, the consultant may continue to observe the process and be ready to intervene when the deal-making process encounters difficulties.[8]

Not all mediators in an international business negotiation have the reputation and prestige of a Robert Strauss or a Michael Ovitz, or receive specific authorization to engage in relationship building. Sometimes persons involved in the negotiation because of their technical expertise or specialized knowledge may assume a mediating function and thus help the parties reach agreement. For example, while language interpreters ordinarily have a limited role, they may facilitate understanding by explaining cultural practices that seem to complicate discussions or by finding linguistic formulas that lead to agreement, formulas that the parties would not be able to arrive at on their own. Similarly, local lawyers or accountants engaged by a foreign party to advise on law or accounting practices in connection with international negotiation may assume a mediating role in the deal-making process by serving as a conduit between the parties, by suggesting approaches that meet the other side's cultural practices, by explaining why one party is behaving in a particular way, and by proposing solutions that are likely to gain agreement from the other side.

In some situations, a third party with influence over the other side can be helpful in resolving a conflict that stands in the way of making a deal. In one case, Reebok, the internationally known manufacturer of athletic footwear and clothing, wanted to begin talks with one of its distributors to renegotiate an existing contract to reduce the amount of its local advertising commitments. When the distributor refused such a change, Reebok asked the president of a noncompeting manufacturer, whose products were also handled by the distributor, to intervene to help settle the matter. That president had an interest in seeing the dispute settled because he feared that a protracted conflict with Reebok would weaken the distributor and thereby make the distributor less effective in handling the president's own brands. He therefore held a series of conversations with the distributor that ultimately led to a satisfactory settlement of the dispute with Reebok.[9]

EFFECTIVE IMPLEMENTATION

7. Plan effective implementation of the deal.   A deal is a prediction. A negotiation is always about the future. The parties to a deal use their contract and its enforcement mechanisms to assure that specified acts will take place in the days, weeks, months, and years ahead. An American electrical equipment manufacturer will deliver a promised generator to Bangladesh in six months' time. A Brazilian borrower will repay its loan to a New York bank in five years. A French mining company with a concession in Niger will be able to take minerals out of the country over the next fifteen years. For any of these things to happen, the parties during their negotiation have to plan for effective implementation of their deal.

Many transactions encounter significant problems in the field because the deal makers at the negotiating table did not plan for effective implementation. Sometimes the reason for this failure is that the negotiators do not have significant experience in transaction implementation or lack strong incentives to focus on implementation problems, particularly if those problems risk preventing a deal from being closed. For example, a major automobile manufacturer adopted a firm policy of creating international joint ventures to produce cars and trucks in key markets around the world. It therefore established specialized joint-venture negotiating teams whose only function was to negotiate such venture deals. When it came time to implement the deals that the teams had negotiated, the automaker invariably encountered serious problems. The cause of the problems, it was discovered, was that the deal-making teams had not considered important implementation issues in depth, and in many cases when they did foresee implementation questions, they glossed over them or left the solution ambiguous in order to close the deal. The reasons for this state of affairs were not only that none of the negotiating teams had operational experience with joint ventures but also that the team as a whole had no incentive to focus on implementation issues seriously because no team member would in any way be involved in implementing the joint ventures. Consequently, since the automaker evaluated its negotiating team members on the basis of the number of joint ventures concluded and not on how successfully they turned out, the deal-making teams had no incentive to be concerned with implementation issues. Thus, a first rule of effective implementation planning in a negotiation is to be sure that at least one member of the negotiating team has experience in implementation and that the team as a whole has an incentive for the transaction to be implemented effectively.

Effective planning requires accurate predictions about the future: the two sides individually and jointly have to envision the future. To try to see the future together, negotiators may use a variety of techniques that are helpful, but by no means certain. Indeed, in some cases, individual techniques may result in differing visions of the future. Four of the more important techniques are trend projection, analogical forecasting, simulation, and scenario building.

1. Trend Projection

This technique assumes that certain trends that have been happening in the past will continue, and that the duration and speed of those trends can be projected into the future. Thus, detecting a growing demand for oil in the early 1970s, specialists in world oil markets projected a trend of rising oil prices for the remainder of the decade. On the basis of that projection, negotiators made deals for tankers and refineries. At the same time, projecting growing inflation rates throughout the world, they financed this expansion through debt that they estimated could be paid off in cheaper dollars in the years ahead. But the simple projection of trends can become a trap, particularly if negotiators fail to see the emergence of forces and factors that may divert a trend or even stop it dead in its tracks. Many deal makers in the late 1970s predicted that oil prices could only go higher and that the world could expect to buy oil for $100 a barrel within a few years. What these analysts failed to see, of course, was that increased oil prices would encourage widespread energy conservation and a major, successful effort to find new sources of oil—both of which served to slow, and eventually, to stop the trend of rising oil prices.

2. Analogical Forecasting

Another technique for predicting the future of a particular situation is to look for a similar situation in the past, and thus create an analogy between the prior event and what might happen in similar circumstances. An experienced executive negotiating to build a telecommunications facility in Indonesia prior to the fall of President Suharto in 1998 saw a close similarity between that country's tense political climate and the conditions in Eastern Europe prior to the end of

communism ten years before, and therefore decided to adopt a series of delaying tactics until the Indonesian situation becomes more stable.

Analogies are important tools for the global negotiator. Generally speaking, the more experienced the negotiator, the more analogies available to
draw on. The principal trap in using this technique is to make sure that you
are relying on the right past experience to formulate a plan for a future action. Many times, past and present situations will seem identical, but the
analogy fails to provide sound guidance because the negotiator does not see
important distinguishing characteristics between earlier experience and the
case at hand. Analogical forecasting is an important tool for any negotiator,
but it is important to be sure that you are using the right analogy.

3. Simulation

Through simulation, negotiators attempt to create the initial stages of a situation, induce their team members or the other side to imagine themselves in
that circumstance, and then to ask what might happen. In a more technically
sophisticated setting, using computers, a negotiator might simulate a situation
and then introduce variables to determine what the result might be if the parties behaved in a particular way. The use of a graphic simulation is a powerful
method for getting the other side to think about and to understand the consequences of a given course of action. For example, during the highly complex
negotiations for the Law of the Sea Treaty involving more than a hundred
countries, the conference leadership used a computer program developed by
MIT to show the delegates the financial consequences of various proposals.
Many developing-nation delegates assumed that high fees imposed on sea bed
mining would not deter companies from mining activities. The MIT computer program demonstrated clearly at what point the fee level would prevent
companies from prospecting for minerals on the ocean floor.[10] Deal makers in
complex negotiations should consider developing similar computer programs
in order to formulate strong proposals and to demonstrate to their counterparts the consequences of their own proposals on the transaction.

4. Scenario Building

Because a situation may evolve in many different ways depending on what
the participants may do, one technique of trying to ascertain the future is to

build scenarios of the various ways that a situation might unfold and then evaluate the probability of each scenario actually happening. For example, suppose an American oil company and a Venezuelan state corporation are negotiating a joint venture for the exploration and production of petroleum. One of the issues they confront is the question of the right of each party to withdraw profits from the enterprise. The American company would like to withdraw them without restriction but the Venezuelan corporation is insisting that they be used only for reinvestment in Venezuela. The two finally compromise on a general principal that each side may withdraw profits in special situations. Through scenario building, they envision a variety of situations in which profit withdrawal will and will not be permitted. Through this process, each side will gain a clear understanding of their options and what actions will be permitted.

BALANCING CONTRACTUAL
STABILITY AND CHANGE

A goal sought by all sides in any negotiation is contractual stability—the assurance that the terms of their agreement will be respected in the future. At the same time, the parties know that during the period of their agreement unforeseen events may arise to change drastically the balance of benefits originally contemplated. Consequently, a fundamental challenge in deal making is to achieve contractual stability and at the same time allow the parties to deal with changing circumstances in the future. The traditional approach to resolving this dilemma is for the parties during their original negotiation to attempt to anticipate all possible contingencies and to provide detailed solutions for them in their agreement.

Despite the belief of lawyers in their own abilities to capture that agreement in lengthy and detailed contracts, in practice, a written contract, particularly one for long-term arrangements, can only achieve that goal imperfectly, largely for three reasons. First, the parties to long-term agreements are inherently incapable of predicting all of the events and conditions that may affect their transactions in the future because that would require perfect foresight. Second, the transaction costs of making contracts limit the resources that the parties are willing to devote to the contracting process and thus further restrict the ability of the parties to make a contract that perfectly reflects their understanding. Third, even if the parties have the requisite foresight and resources to draft a perfect contract, they have no assurance that a court will interpret their contract exactly as they intended. In international transactions, the problem of accurately negotiating and articulating the parties' intent in a long-term arrangement is particularly difficult because of their different cultures, business practices, ideologies, political systems and laws—factors that often impede a true common understanding and inhibit the development of an effective working relationship.

Another solution to the problem of balancing the imperatives of stability and change is for the contract itself to authorize the parties to renegotiate key elements of their relationship upon the occurrence of specified events or circumstances. In view of the impossibility of predicting all possible future contingencies, the inclusion in the agreement of some type of renegotiation clause would appear to be a useful device to give needed flexibility to long-term agreements. In fact, however, western organizations rarely use them.

The traditional reluctance to use renegotiation clauses stems from a variety of factors, both legal and practical. First is the concern among lawyers that renegotiation clauses are merely "agreements to agree" and therefore may be unenforceable. However, the courts have held that a renegotiation clause in an existing contract with definite terms as to how the parties are to conduct the renegotiation process is sufficiently specific to be enforceable. The required certainty would be further satisfied by specifying the precise events that give rise to the obligation to renegotiate and by specifically providing for the timing, locale, and conditions of the renegotiation process.

Practical considerations have also led western executives to view renegotiation clauses with suspicion on the grounds that they increase uncertainty and risk in transactions and offend western concepts of the sanctity of contract. Their presence in a contract also creates a risk that one of the parties will use a renegotiation clause as a lever to force changes in provisions that, strictly speaking, are not open to revision. The challenges of drafting these provisions and the heightened risks to contractual stability by renegotiation clauses that have yet to be tested in the courts are additional factors that have deterred their use in long-term contracts.

Despite these potential pitfalls, the inclusion of a renegotiation clause may actually contribute to transactional stability in certain situations. First, in cases in which significant changes in circumstances may result in severe, unexpected financial hardship, a renegotiation clause may permit the parties to avoid default and the attendant risk of litigation and forced renegotiations. During the original negotiations, it may be wiser for the parties to recognize the risk of changed circumstances and create within the contract a process to deal with them rather than to try to predict all eventualities and then be subject to the uncertainty of court decisions when those predictions prove flawed.

A second situation in which a renegotiation clause may be helpful occurs in cases when the parties, by virtue of their different cultures, understand and perceive the basis of their transaction in fundamentally different ways. For example, Western notions of business transactions as founded on law and contract often clash with Asian conceptions of business arrangements as based on personal relationships. In Asia, executives often consider the essence of a business deal to be the relationship between the parties rather than the written contract, which in their view can only describe that relationship imperfectly and incompletely. They may also assume that any long-term business relationship includes an implicit, fundamental principle: In times of change, parties in a business relationship should decide together how to cope with that change and adjust their relationship accordingly. In long-term business transactions between a western and Asian firm, the Western party may view the transaction as set in the concrete of a lengthy and detailed contract without the possibility of modification, while the Asian side may see the transaction as floating on the parties' fluid personal relationships, which always have within them an implicit commitment to renegotiate the terms of the transaction in the event of unforeseen happenings. In long-term transactions, such as a joint venture between Asian and Western companies whose success depends on close and continuing cooperation, it may be wise to recognize this difference of viewpoint at the outset of negotiations and attempt to find some middle ground. A renegotiation clause may represent such middle ground between total contractual rigidity on the one hand and complete relational flexibility on the other. It recognizes the possibility of redoing the deal but controls the renegotiation process. A renegotiation clause, then, may give stability to an arrangement whose long-term nature creates a high risk of instability. Chapter 12 will survey the various types of renegotiation provisions used in international transactions.

PLANNING FOR DISPUTES

The potential for conflict is a constant in all human transactions. International business transactions are no exception. Despite the flush of good feeling from having successfully negotiated an agreement, the parties at the negotiating table should plan for the possibility of conflict and put in place mechanisms that will help to resolve at least possible cost conflicts arising in the future.

In most international business contracts, it is standard procedure today to specify the law that governs the contract and the court that has jurisdiction to hear disputes arising under it. In negotiating this issue, each side obviously would like the courts of its own country to hear such disputes and would like to avoid the other's courts due to fears of bias. In order to find a neutral decision maker for possible future disputes that may arise from their negotiated transactions, businesses and governments throughout the world are increasingly choosing international commercial arbitration to the exclusion of national courts.

Arbitration, an age-old process of resolving disputes, is found in one form or another in most cultures. While it has many variations, basically it is a process whereby two persons agree to submit a present or future dispute to a third person and further agree that they will carry out that third person's decisions. Most international business contracts (except for loan agreements) today contain a clause that should a dispute arise between the parties (even if one of the parties is a government or state corporation), they will not go to court but will refer the matter to an arbitrator or arbitrators, usually located in a third country, to hear the dispute and make a decision. In many cases, the parties elect to submit disputes to three arbitrators—one chosen by each side and a third selected by the two appointed arbitrators.

In addition to assuring neutrality, arbitration avoids the uncertainty of going to court and the further possibility that the court systems of two or more countries may become involved. Moreover, because the parties often choose the arbitrators (who are to act independently, not as representatives), they have greater assurance that the arbitration panel will have appropriate international business expertise than if they leave the matter to the ordinary national courts of law. In addition, since arbitration proceedings are private, the parties can avoid unwanted publicity. Privacy may tend to protect business secrets and create an atmosphere favoring a negotiated settlement.

Arbitration is of two types: institutional and ad hoc. In institutional arbitration, the parties select a specific institution to administer their arbitration proceeding. Many institutions exist around the world to handle arbitration. The best known include the International Chamber of Commerce, the American Arbitration Association, the London Court of Arbitration, the Stockholm Chamber of Commerce, and the Zurich Chamber of Commerce. Each has its own rules and procedures. In an ad hoc arbitration, the parties themselves administer the arbitration according to rules that they have agreed upon.

Institutional arbitration has several advantages over ad hoc arbitration. First, the institution selected has a tested set of rules and procedures to govern the arbitration. Second, it has an administrative organization to assist in managing the proceeding. Third, unless the parties otherwise agree, the arbitration institution appoints the arbitrators from its own lists of experts and makes other necessary decisions to advance the arbitration. In addition, the arbitration institution, for a fee, can provide hearing rooms, secretarial services, translation facilities, and other support services. The primary disadvantage of institutional arbitration is cost. The fees charged for administering the arbitration can be substantial. Ad hoc arbitration may therefore be cheaper than institutional arbitration.

Arbitration is not "palm tree justice." The arbitrators follow definite procedures and are required to apply the law in making their decision. Arbitration is, however, private justice. This means that the parties, not the state treasury, must finance it. Therefore, the parties have to pay not only for their lawyers but also for the arbitrators and the institution selected to administer the proceedings.

Having negotiated an arbitration clause into a deal, a business executive may well ask, In the event of a dispute, what will make the other side respect that clause? And even if they do go to arbitration, what will make a party accept an adverse arbitration decision? The answer to these two questions is to be found in an international treaty, the United Nations Convention on the Recognition and Enforcement of Foreign Arbitral Awards, a treaty ratified by more than a hundred countries. The courts of the ratifying countries are required to enforce foreign arbitration agreements and foreign arbitration awards. If an American company has a long-term supply contract with a Nigerian enterprise providing for arbitration in Paris, and the arbitrator makes an award in favor of the American company, that company can enforce the award in the courts of any country that has signed the agreement and in which the Nigerian enterprise has assets.

While international arbitration has important advantages over litigation in national courts, it is by no means an ideal form of dispute settlement. International commercial arbitration is much like litigation in that it is expensive, adversarial, and (in many cases) lengthy. It usually results in the dissolution of the business relationship, not in its reconstruction. Consequently, while using international arbitration as a dispute resolution of last resort, negotiators planning implementation of their transaction ought also to consider other, intermediate measures, such as mediators, or dispute resolution advisers, that will perhaps facilitate settlement of the conflict without the expense and delay of litigation.

One particular type of mediator worthy of note is the dispute review board, which was used in constructing both the Channel Tunnel between England and France and the new Hong Kong Airport and is now required by the World Bank for any construction project having a cost of more than $50 million that it finances. Under this procedure, a three-member board is created at the start of the project. One member of the board is appointed by the project owner and a second by the lead contractor. The third member is then selected either by the other two members or by mutual agreement between the owner and the contractor. The board functions according to rules set down in the construction contract and generally is empowered to examine all disputes and to make recommendations to the parties concerning settlement. If the parties to a dispute do not object to a recommendation, it becomes binding. If, however, they are dissatisfied, they may proceed to arbitration, litigation, or another form of mandatory dispute settlement. [11]

More generally, in considering implementation problems and conflict resolution, deal makers might agree to use mediation in the event of a future dispute before they try other means of dispute settlement such as courts and arbitration. Recognizing the damaging effect of arbitration on business relationships, some companies agree in their contract to attempt mediation or conciliation before invoking arbitration. Many arbitration institutions, such as the International Chamber of Commerce and the International Centre for Settlement of Investment Disputes, offer a service known as conciliation, which is normally governed by a set of rules. Generally in institutional conciliation, a party to a dispute addresses a request for conciliation to an administering institution, such as the International Chamber of Commerce. If the institution concerned secures the agreement of the other disputant, it will appoint a conciliator. While the conciliator has broad discretion to conduct the process, in practice this person will invite both sides to state their views of the dispute and will then make a report proposing an appropriate settlement. The parties may reject the report and proceed to arbitration or they may accept it. In many cases, they will use the conciliator's report as a basis for a negotiated settlement.

Conciliation in international business disputes tends to be rights-based in its approach, affording the parties a third person's evaluation of their respective rights and obligations. Conciliators do not usually adopt a problem-solving or relationship-building approach to resolving the dispute between the parties. The process is confidential and completely voluntary; either party may withdraw from conciliation at any time. In practice, few disputants in international business avail themselves of conciliation. Nonetheless, in view of the shortcomings of arbitration and litigation as dispute settlement mechanisms, parties negotiating business relationships should consider including in their contracts from the outset mechanisms such as dispute advisers to help in the problem of deal management, and they might also commit themselves to try mediation or conciliation before they take the usually irrevocable step of submitting their disputes to arbitration.

5

SEVEN SPECIAL BARRIERS
TO GLOBAL DEAL MAKING

Negotiating any deal risks hitting barriers. One side gets locked into a position and refuses to look at other options. The negotiators come to dislike each other and let their personal feelings interfere with the talks. One team thinks the other is hiding information or lying. The members of both teams start bickering among themselves. The skilled negotiator must find ways of dealing with these barriers. The principles discussed in previous chapters are designed to help with that task.

Negotiators meet these obstacles whether they are making a deal to build a factory in their hometown or to create a timbering joint venture in Indonesia. But when deal makers negotiate international transactions, they also face other, special barriers that they do not usually encounter in making domestic business deals. The internationally inexperienced negotiator is often unprepared to tackle them. As a result, these special barriers frequently block proposed international transactions.

To illustrate the point, let us take a simple example. Houston Glue Company, a manufacturer located in Houston, Texas, makes and distributes a powerful adhesive under the trademark MegaGlue. The basic component of MegaGlue is a chemical known as cyanoacrylate. One of Houston Glue's suppliers of cyanoacrylate is Dallas Adhesive Company, a family-owned business located in Dallas, Texas. Last year, Houston Glue negotiated a five-year contract with Dallas Adhesive for the supply of cyanoacrylate at $1 a pound. The market demand for MegaGlue has expanded rapidly so Houston Glue is looking for an additional supplier of cyanoacrylate and has identified Budapest Adhesive Co., a recently privatized enterprise in Budapest, Hungary, which has proposed to sell cyanoacrylate to Houston Glue, f.o.b. (free on board) Budapest, for 250 forints a pound at a time when $1 U.S. equals 250 forints. Here we have two similar business deals involving the same product at roughly the same price, but the process of negotiating and making these two transactions raises distinctly different problems.

Put yourself in the place of the Houston Glue Company executive who successfully negotiated the deal with Dallas last year and is now contemplating the negotiation of a similar long-term supply agreement with Budapest. In both situations, you will need to prepare effectively, to understand the other side's interests, to develop creative options, and to apply the other principles that chapters 3 and 4 discuss. But in addition, you will need to know how to cope with special barriers that were not faced in negotiating the Dallas deal. Seven of those special barriers facing global negotiators are particularly important.

1. The first and perhaps most obvious barrier is the *negotiating environment.* The parties negotiating an international deal are usually located at a great distance from each other in different countries. Even in this age of instant global communication and high-speed travel, distance and geographic unfamiliarity still complicate the planning and execution of negotiations. One side usually has to travel to the other side's turf to negotiate. For the visitor, whether a Hungarian in Dallas or a Texan in Budapest, that turf is a foreign environment and that foreignness is a potential barrier to deal making. In contrast, the negotiating environment for the deal between Houston Glue and Dallas Adhesive would not have created significant problems since negotiators on both sides would have understood and felt comfortable in that environment, whether their discussions took place in Dallas or in Houston.

2. *Culture* is a second barrier to making deals. International business transactions not only cross national boundaries, they also cross cultures. Culture is a powerful factor shaping how people think, communicate, and behave. It also affects the way they negotiate. Cultural differences between negotiators can create barriers that can block a deal. So negotiators for Dallas Glue and Budapest Adhesive are likely to approach their task from two widely different cultures, whereas those for Houston Glue and Dallas Adhesive will not encounter similar obstacles since they share a common culture.

3. Even the most bland and self-effacing negotiator has an ideology. In the international arena, business negotiators encounter and must be prepared to deal with ideologies vastly different from their own. Whereas Dallas and

Houston negotiators probably share a common ideology, the Dallas and Budapest deal makers may face ideological differences, particularly in view of Hungary's history as a communist country. *Ideology*, then, is the third barrier to negotiating global deals.

4. The fourth barrier to international business negotiations is *foreign organizations and bureaucracies*. In virtually all negotiations, global negotiators are seeking to make deals with organizations. To do that successfully, they must understand how those organizations function and know how to work with them effectively. Whereas the Dallas and Houston negotiators will fairly quickly and easily come to understand how each other's organization makes decisions, the Dallas and Budapest deal makers will probably have to devote significant time and attention to this issue.

5. By engaging in international business, a company enters into a world of many laws and political systems. That can mean the difference between success and failure in a negotiation. *Foreign laws and governments* are a fifth barrier in global deal making. The deal between Dallas and Houston will involve only Texas law and potentially only Texas courts. On the other hand, a transaction between Dallas and Budapest will bring the parties into contact with at least two foreign legal and governmental systems.

6. Unlike purely domestic deals, international transactions take place in a world of many currencies and monetary systems. Global deals cross monetary boundaries just as they cross political, cultural, and ideological lines. So although the transaction between Dallas and Houston will involve only dollars, a Dallas-Budapest deal will raise issues of dollars and forints, the currencies of the two countries concerned. *Multiple money*, the sixth barrier in international business negotiations, is always present in global deal making, and it has proven to be insurmountable on several occasions.

7. The seventh special barrier to global deal making is the risk of *instability and sudden change* so common to the international system itself. Change, of course, is a fact of life, and sudden changes in circumstances are to be found in both domestic and international business. Still, the type and magnitude of change in the international arena appears far greater than in the U.S. domestic setting. The war in Afghanistan, the end of communism in Eastern Europe, the fall of the shah of Iran, and the closing of the Suez Canal are just a few examples of events that had wide and serious consequences for international business deals.

The special barriers, then, that all global negotiators must face are:

1. negotiating environment
2. culture
3. ideology
4. foreign organizations and bureaucracies
5. foreign laws and governments
6. multiple money
7. instability and sudden change

These special barriers have a twofold impact on global deal making. First, they increase the risk of failure—the risk that the two sides will not agree, the risk that their agreement will be more apparent than real, the risk that any agreement they make will not last. Second, these barriers usually lengthen the time it takes to arrive at a deal. As a rule, an international deal takes longer to conclude than does a purely domestic transaction of the same variety. McDonald's negotiated for nearly ten years to open its first hamburger restaurant in Moscow, and IBM needed almost two years to secure an agreement to build a computer plant in Mexico. As a result, global negotiators must have patience and be prepared to commit an amount of time that would seem excessive in negotiating a purely domestic transaction in the United States.

Let's now look at each of these barriers to see what they are made of and how a negotiator can climb over, burrow under, and go around them. Better yet, let's discover how negotiators can work together to tear them down.

6

SPECIAL BARRIER NO. 1:
THE NEGOTIATING ENVIRONMENT

Negotiations do not happen in a vacuum. They take place in a specific environment, and the elements of that environment—place, time, surroundings, and people—can profoundly influence the course of discussions. In international deal making, the negotiating environment can be a particular barrier because for one of the parties that environment is distinctly foreign. So while Houston Glue Company executives would not be especially concerned about the negotiating environment in Dallas, a place with which they are generally familiar, they most definitely would have to plan for and study the negotiating environment in Budapest, a place they do not know at all. At its worst, an encounter between a visiting business executive and a foreign environment can produce culture shock, a phenomenon that can incapacitate the visitor and lead a usually dynamic executive to withdraw from contact with other persons, to feel confused, and to become excessively concerned about his health.[1] As a result, the visitor may refuse to eat any local food, no matter how well cooked, avoid meetings with more than two persons at a time, and feel compelled to wash his hands every ten minutes.

Even for experienced deal makers immune to culture shock, negotiating in a strange and unfamiliar environment creates pressures and constraints that, if not managed effectively, may slow progress drastically, prevent a good agreement, and worst of all, cause the visiting team to pack its bags and go home without a deal. The negotiating environment, like so many other factors in global deal making, confronts an executive with a series of choices and questions. The first and most basic environmental question is where to negotiate.

YOUR PLACE OR MINE?

The negotiating environment is determined largely by the negotiators' decision on the site for the talks. Site selection is never a casual response to the question "Your place or mine?" International negotiators often deliberate long and hard about *where* they will negotiate because they assume—usually with good reason—that the location they choose will have consequences for the ensuing process and, ultimately, its result. Generally, parties to a proposed business deal have four options in choosing a site: your place, my place, some other place, or (as a result of advances in international communications) no specific place. Let us consider the advantages and disadvantages of each of these choices.

My Place

Athletes know that the home field or home court advantage is often the difference between winning and losing. Similarly, most people probably would prefer to hold negotiations on their own territory, rather than on the other side's. The benefits of negotiating at home are many. First, negotiating on your own territory gives you the advantage of familiarity with the negotiating environment. Your opponents, not you, run the risk of culture shock. They, not you, must cope with unfamiliar foods, strange customs, and a foreign language. You know where everything is located, ranging from telephones and rest rooms to reliable secretarial services and secure areas for private consultation. You need not devote valuable time and energy to getting to know the negotiating environment.

Second, negotiating at home also gives you the possibility of controlling the physical environment, including the selection and arrangement of the negotiating room, the seating of the participants at the bargaining table, and the nature and timing of hospitality and social events. Negotiators with the home field advantage often use this power to manipulate the negotiating environment in their favor. Playing host in a negotiation also gives you an opportunity to impress the other team with your organization and to make its members feel indebted to you for your hospitality—factors that may make them more cooperative in the talks. In addition, it protects you from the other side's unfair manipulation of the negotiating environment in its favor, for example, by forcing you to labor through the first few negotiating sessions under the debilitating effects of a long airplane ride, compounded on arrival by elaborate, late-night entertainment organized by the host.

Negotiating at home also gives you easy access to your own experts for needed advice and to superiors for special authorization and consultation. If the other side, during a sales contract negotiation, asks for special financing terms, a negotiation at home allows you to obtain a quick yes or no from your financial vice president. And if the financial department needs persuading, you are in a much better arm-twisting position if you are on the spot than if you have to do it by telephone or e-mail from five thousand miles and six time zones away.

Finally, negotiating at home is cheaper. Transporting a two-person negotiating team to Tokyo or Seoul and maintaining them in a hotel for a week can easily cost $15,000. Negotiating at home not only saves money, it also saves executive time. Host negotiators can usually continue to handle other job demands while participating in a negotiation; a visiting U.S. negotiator in China cannot do the same, despite the marvels of e-mail, fax machines, and satellite telephones. Another disadvantage is that visiting negotiators are away from their personal lives—from family, friends, hobbies, and daily routine. The longer one is away, the stronger the emotional drive to conclude the negotiations and return home.

The desire to return home and the costs in time and money of negotiating abroad can put pressure on visiting executives to make a deal (or break off talks) more quickly than they might if they were negotiating in their own country. Sometimes the other side may exploit this situation by deliberately or inadvertently creating delays that run up costs and increase pressures. Many executives set a date for negotiations with their opposite numbers in a foreign capital only to be told on arrival that a key manager or government official has been called out of the country at the last minute and that the visitor should be patient for a few days until his return. Indeed, these types of delays occur so often that the experienced negotiators take account of them in arranging their travel plans and schedules. One American banker visiting Cameroon to negotiate a loan failed to take account of this factor in obtaining a visa. He calculated that the negotiation would take a week, so he asked for only a seven-day visa. Because of the importance of the deal and the progress the parties were suddenly making, he decided to stay on until he realized that his visa was set to expire the next day and it would take a week to obtain an extension. He had to make a second trip to Africa to close the deal.

While a host may deliberately cause delays to put pressure on the other party, unexpected events can also prolong negotiations. Hosts may not appreciate the significance of these events to the visitors because they are unaware that the visiting executives are working under inflexible time limits or because their cultural background leads them to attach less importance to time. For these reasons, experienced negotiators, in arranging a meeting, make very clear to their hosts the precise date of their departure, even going so far as to specify their exact departure time and flight number. Some even *understate* the length of time they are prepared to stay in the country. As a general rule, if visiting negotiators, after encountering delays, feel increased pressure to make concessions so that they may return home or go on to other business, it is better to leave as planned and agree with the other side to continue negotiations at another specified time and place.

Sometimes visiting negotiators representing the side with the greater power in a deal set a fixed departure date in order to pressure the host to sign a contract. During nine years of residence in Africa and the Middle East, the author observed executives of multinational corporations use this tactic many times in their negotiations with developing countries that were poorly served by international airlines. They would arrive on a Sunday nights, hold general discussions on Monday and Tuesday, and present a draft agreement on Wednesday, expressing strong hope that a contract could be signed by the time their plane left on Friday morning. This tactic amounted to an ultimatum, although the source of the ultimatum appeared to be the airline rather than the multinational corporation. An ultimatum, though common, is rarely an effective negotiating device. Here too, rather than make a hasty agreement, it is better for the developing country to defer signing and propose to continue discussions at a later time.

Your Place

Negotiating on the other side's territory seems to offer only disadvantages: It is costly; the environment is unfamiliar and uncontrollable; lines of communication to the home office are long, uncertain, and insecure. On the other hand, in most international deals in which you are in the position of a seller, it is only by going to the other side's country that you can bring your product, service, or business needs to the other side's attention. The choice of site also has symbolic value. The visiting negotiators are usually those who are

the moving force behind the proposed deal. By going to the other side's territory, you show your seriousness of intent and your strong desire to make a
deal. This symbolic act may be important in persuading the other side that
your company is the one to deal with.

Beyond symbolism, the most important reason of all for negotiating on
the other side's territory is *to learn*. An international business negotiation
serves many purposes, but one of the most significant, yet unappreciated, is
that it gives each side an opportunity to learn about the other, about their
businesses, about the conditions in which they must operate. In this respect,
comparisons of a negotiation to a sporting event, with allusions to home field
advantage, are false. Executives engaged in making a deal are rarely in the
type of competition that ends abruptly when they finish the ninth inning or
the fourth quarter. Instead, they are laying the foundation for a continuing
relationship, and the successful management of that relationship depends
crucially on how much they know about one another. The need for learning
is particularly acute in global deal making since the parties usually come from
different cultures, political systems, and business orientations. (Indeed, according to some studies, culture shock itself is not a psychological disorder
but rather the lack of learned skills need to cope with a new and different environment.[2]) As a result, the effective global deal maker sees a negotiation as
an opportunity to learn, and the best way to learn is to visit the other side's
territory to conduct the negotiations.

In some cases, negotiating in another country is the only way to make a
deal quickly because the other side's negotiators cannot travel easily. Government officials in many developing countries are not permitted to travel
abroad without completing lengthy procedures, and even then they may not
be able to secure the funds to pay for the trip. So if you want a deal any time
soon, you are the one who must get on the airplane. Then there is the problem of the negotiator who has more authority at home than abroad. If your
opposite number is in that position, it may be better to make the trip yourself. For example, in one negotiation between an American oil company and
a Congolese government corporation, then-president Mobutu insisted on
being informed of developments and on making all decisions. At the end of
each day's negotiating session, the Congolese negotiators briefed the president's advisers, who then briefed the president. By the following morning,
the Congolese negotiators had received their instructions for the day. Within
a relatively short time, the two sides signed a contract.[3] Had the negotiations

been held in New York instead of Kinshasa, it is doubtful that the two sides would have reached an agreement as quickly as they did.

In global deal making, then, the answer to the question "Your place or mine?" is never automatic. It requires careful study of the negotiation in which you are engaged. But in some situations, a good solution to the site selection question is for the two sides to agree at the outset of their talks to alternate rounds of their negotiation between the two countries, a solution that is particularly appropriate if the negotiations are expected to stretch over a long period of time and the parties contemplate a continuing relationship. For example, in negotiating a joint venture between a U.S. manufacturer and Egyptian investors to build a dry-cell battery plant in Cairo, the two sides, recognizing that the discussions will require several sessions, might agree to alternate their discussions between New York and Cairo, or at least that *some* portion of their talks take place in the United States. Alternating sites allows the Egyptians and the Americans to share the costs and burdens of being host and guest. It also reduces the incentive to take unfair advantage of one's position as host since the other side will have the opportunity to act similarly in the next negotiating session. Most important, moving the negotiations between the two countries assures that both sides will have the opportunity to learn about each other's business and home environment, knowledge that is essential to effective deal making and to building a long-term business relationship.

And even though you are visiting the country, you can still play host by holding negotiations in a place, such as a hotel conference room, that you can select and control.

Finally, whenever for whatever reason you are negotiating in new and unfamiliar territory, it is always wise to arrive a couple of days before the negotiations begin to familiarize yourself with the negotiating environment in which you will be operating.

Some Other Place

The choice of a neutral, third country for negotiation has a certain superficial attraction. Each side gains no special advantage or disadvantage as a result of the location of the talks. At the same time, it has a worst-of-both-worlds quality, for it effectively limits the ability of each side to learn much about the other. Whatever inhibits learning inhibits deal making.

Nonetheless, the choice of a third country may be useful if additional learning is not important to advancing the transaction and if other advantages, such as reduced cost or increased convenience of time, are to be gained. For example, a U.S. manufacturer and a Nigerian distributor, after several negotiating sessions in each other's country, may find it convenient to meet in London to put the finishing touches on the deal. Moreover, negotiating in a third country takes the members of both teams away from their daily preoccupations and forces them to focus on the task at hand. It was precisely for that reason that in one auto negotiation between the U.S. and Japanese governments, the two delegations met in Hong Kong, instead of either Washington or Tokyo. Also, if the purpose of the negotiation is to settle a severe business conflict, such as a dispute between joint-venture partners over profit distribution or between foreign investors in a nationalized industry and an expropriating government, a third country may be the best place to hold discussions. In situations of conflict, negotiating in the territory of either party may make visitors feel they are under pressure or even duress. In the case of a nationalization, both sides may prefer a third country—the investor because it does not want to negotiate in hostile climate, and the government because it would prefer to reach an agreement with the investors quietly and away from the scrutiny of local media and the demands of radical pressure groups at home.

No Place

Rather than chose one site over another, global negotiators can consider the option of avoiding face-to-face meetings entirely. Instead, whether they are in New York and Tokyo or Los Angeles and London, they can use technology to communicate with one another. E-mail, satellite telephone, fax, and video teleconferencing offer low-cost convenient ways to make global deals. Global negotiators are using them with increasing frequency in innovative ways. For example, some negotiators in particularly important deals create secure websites on which documents and other information can be stored for easy consultation by both sides at any time. Communications technology has also vastly simplified and improved the ability of negotiators away from the home office to consult with their home office for advice and instructions as negotiations proceed. E-mail in particular enables negotiators in widely different time zones to conduct efficient negotiations and consultations in situations in which such communications by telephone would require one side to participate in the middle of the night or at a highly inconvenient time.

While communication technologies are important supports for global deal making, they are not satisfactory substitutes for face-to-face negotiations in all transactions. Their principal defect is that they do not enable the parties to learn as much about each other as they would in a meeting around a conference table. In effect, e-mail, faxes, and telephone calls, if relied upon exclusively, compel the parties to negotiate with incomplete information.

An important part of any face-to-face meeting is nonverbal communication—body language, such as slight but meaningful gestures and shrugs. We gain full understanding of a person's meaning from more than their words. Moreover, sensing nuances of their reactions to our own words through feedback allows us to rapidly adjust our own communications to meet their concerns. Video teleconferencing, e-mails, and even telephone calls convey such information poorly, if at all. There is also evidence to suggest that telecommunications technology, when used alone, may encourage lying and the delivery of messages that are impetuous and insensitive to the other side's feelings.

Equally important, the parties in telecommunication negotiations are limited to what they see on the screen and hear over the line. Valuable information about the other side's business environment is not conveyed at all. That can be gained only by a visit to the other side's facilities and through direct, personal contacts with your counterparts in the other company. In addition, e-mail and even video teleconferencing allow only a formal, somewhat stilted style of communications. They eliminate opportunities for productive socializing—a drink before dinner, a game of tennis at the end of the day, even a simple coffee break—occasions for negotiators to get to know one another better and to work out problems privately that may have stymied them in formal negotiations. In short, the use of telecommunications alone to negotiate deals does not allow the development of the kind of sound business relationships that are so necessary to the success of long-term transactions.

For these reasons, it would seem that electronic negotiation is best used in two types of situations: (1) relatively simple transactions, such as the sale of a standard commodity, in which the two sides can gain sufficient knowledge through information exchanged by e-mail, fax, telephone, or video conferencing; and (2) negotiations in which the parties already know each other well and preferably have agreed upon a basic set of rules about the use of electronic communications in making deals. This is one reason that companies tend to use their video conferencing facilities almost exclusively within their own organizations or with established business partners, rather than for negotiations with outsiders.

Until the world gains more accurate, comprehensive, and sensitive communications technologies than it now has, global deal making will require a location of some sort for at least part of the negotiation. Like Archimedes who claimed he could lift the world with a lever if only he had a place to stand, global negotiators need a place to sit together to do business.

YOUR TIME OR MINE?

The negotiating environment is not only affected by place; it is also influenced by time. In any country there are good times and bad times to negotiate. Deal making is usually difficult during holidays, vacations, and cultural events. For example, Ramadan, the month when Muslims fast from sunrise until dusk, is generally not the best time to make deals in the Middle East. In France, August, the traditional month for vacations, is an extremely difficult time to get French executives to sit at a bargaining table. And most experienced non-American negotiators have learned that in the United States the weeks between Thanksgiving and New Year's Day are not the best time to gain the full attention of American managers.

Since holidays, national celebrations, and vacation periods vary from country to country and from culture to culture, it is important to know the other side's calendar in planning for negotiations, regardless of where discussions are to take place. One of the most frustrating yet all too common experiences is for a deal maker to arrive in the country for negotiations only to find that it is the eve of a four-day national holiday, such as the Spring Festival (New Year) in China. Not only are there no negotiations for four days, but also a visitor's ability to learn about the country is severely limited because all business and government offices are closed and useful informants are occupied with family and friends. Most of the time, you can avoid this problem by studying the local calendar. But not always. In the Muslim world and many parts of Asia, holidays are determined by locally observed lunar movements. Thus, the same Muslim holiday may fall on different dates in different countries. In other countries, holidays are fixed on an annual basis, such as the bank holidays in France that are determined annually through negotiations between the banks and their employees' union. Some countries, particularly developing nations, have a disconcerting tendency to create surprise holidays, as happened in the Congo when President Mobutu's wife died and he declared a five-day period of national mourning that brought the country to a standstill. The vagaries of local holidays not only have implications for planning negotiations but may also have significant consequences for implementing transactions. The existence of an unexpected holiday can complicate or even prevent promised deliveries and payments.[4]

Understanding local time requires more than learning the country's calendar. Time, and particularly the appreciation and meaning of time, is also affected by local culture. The significance of a fixed starting time for negotiations may vary from country to country. In Japan, if negotiations are scheduled to begin at 10:00 A.M., Japanese negotiators expect your team to be ready at precisely ten. In Nigeria, a ten o'clock starting time is only an approximation. Failure to arrive precisely at the time specified is to be expected. Similarly, the appropriate length of negotiating sessions and whether a negotiation is progressing "too slowly" or whether the response to a proposal has taken "too long" may vary depending on the culture of the negotiator. Americans may interpret the slow pace of discussions as evidence that the other side is dragging its feet and is not seriously interested in making a deal. But Japanese negotiators, who need to consult many persons within their company each step of the way and are intent on building a long-term relationship with your firm, may consider the pace of the same negotiations as perfectly appropriate. It is therefore important to understand that the other side may have a concept of time different from yours, and you should adjust your negotiating techniques accordingly.

While negotiations taking place in a particular environment are affected by the realities of local time, visiting negotiators also remain subject to daily schedules, annual calendars, and conceptions of time prevailing in their home countries. In effect, they must operate on both local and home time. American executives who conduct negotiations in Tokyo on local time often consult with their New York office on home time. Because of the difference in time zones, American negotiators in Japan can call the home office for discussions only after 10 P.M. Tokyo time. For negotiations involving Middle Eastern countries—where Friday is a traditional day of rest—and the United States—where offices are closed Saturdays and Sundays—the fact that offices of the two countries are functioning simultaneously only four days a week can affect the progress of discussions. If a document is faxed from New York to Riyadh on Thursday morning, the earliest someone in New York may expect to see a response from Saudi Arabia is on Monday.

E-mail has greatly facilitated the task of consultation between widely different time zones. Nonetheless, experienced negotiators may also handle the problem by arranging to consult with their associates in the United States at their homes after normal business hours. Another technique is to designate a specific person in the home office to backstop the deal and to agree on definite times during the day when you will contact each other.

Despite adjustment to local time by visiting negotiators, their home office remains firmly tied to its usual conceptions of time in judging the progress of any negotiation. Using home standards, it often challenges its negotiators on the slow pace of the talks. So visiting executives may feel squeezed between local conceptions of time in which they are negotiating and home conceptions of time to which they must respond as employees. As a result, global deal makers often have to conduct two sets of negotiations simultaneously—one with the other side to speed up the process and one with the home office to convince them that good progress is being made. A Japanese negotiator in the United States often has just the reverse task: to speed up decision making in Tokyo corporate headquarters while convincing American counterparts that the talks are making meaningful progress.

Even though negotiations are conducted on your territory, knowing the calendar and conceptions of time of the other side can be useful. It facilitates scheduling negotiating meetings, gives you insights into the time pressures felt by the other side, and enables you to evaluate the progress of the talks. Although Ramadan may not be a good time to visit certain Islamic countries for negotiations, it may be a good time to invite negotiators from those countries to come to your country for negotiations. Seeking to avoid the fasting rigors enforced by strong social pressures and sometimes by law, they may readily accept an invitation to go abroad during Ramadan. Similarly, knowing that a traditional festival is scheduled to take place the following week in the other side's home country may lead you to propose new concessions in hopes of securing prompt approval so that the visiting team may return home in time to celebrate the holiday with their families.

7

SPECIAL BARRIER NO. 2: CULTURE

Although negotiating a purely domestic business deal and negotiating an international transaction have much in common, the factor that is almost always present in an international negotiation and generally absent from a domestic negotiation is a difference in culture among the parties. International business transactions cross cultures as well as borders. Culture profoundly influences how people think, communicate, and behave. It also affects the kinds of deals they make and the way they make them. Differences in culture between business executives—for example, between a Chinese public sector plant manager in Shanghai and an American division head of a family company in Cleveland—may therefore create barriers that impede or completely stymie the negotiating process.

THE MEANING OF CULTURE

What do we mean by culture? Culture consists of the socially transmitted behavior patterns, attitudes, norms, and values of a given community. Persons from that community use the elements of their culture to interpret their surroundings and guide their interactions with other persons. When executives from Houston Glue Company and Dallas Adhesive Co. negotiate their deal, they rely on their common culture to interpret each other's statements and actions. But when persons from two different cultures—for example, executives from Houston Glue and Budapest Adhesive—meet for the first time, they do not share a common pool of information and assumptions to interpret each other's statements, actions, and intentions. When a Hollywood film producer and a New York agent for a movie star agree to "do lunch and talk contract," they both know that they will be discussing a detailed document covering not only salary, but billing, advertising, rehearsal time, dressing room facilities, and a host of other matters peculiar to the U.S. entertainment industry. If, after the first martini, the agent says, "We want a gross deal," the producer understands immediately that the film star is seeking a portion of the film's gross revenues before deduction of expenses. And when the producer replies, "Nicholson he's not!" the agent knows that he has to convince the producer that his client is indeed in the category of performers like Jack Nicholson whose reputations command a percentage of gross revenues. Without adequate background knowledge, a person from another country—perhaps a bilingual French executive or an Argentinean rancher with excellent English—would find it difficult to understand the exchange between the producer and the agent because words like "gross deal" and even "contract" gain full meaning only when interpreted in light of the business culture of the U.S. entertainment industry. In many cases, words are just a code that you cannot understand unless you know the context and the background. Culture is an important part of the background and context of any deal.

Culture can therefore be seen as a kind of language, a "silent language" that the parties need in addition to the language they are speaking if they are to arrive at a genuine understanding.[1] Culture serves as a type of social adhesive that binds a group of people together and gives them a distinct identity as a community. It may also give them a sense that they are a community different from other communities.

Culture and nationality are not always the same thing. Within Nigeria, for example, the culture of the Ibos of the largely Christian southeastern part of the country and that of the Hausas of the mainly Muslim north are different and distinct. Similarly, individual corporations and professions may have their own organizational or professional cultures whose norms and behavior patterns may predominate in certain respects over the ethnic or national cultures of their members. For example, a continuing concern in both domestic and cross-border mergers is the problem of blending the cultures of two companies after the deal has been signed, a difficult challenge even for firms from the same culture. While cultural values, attitudes, and behavior patterns may appear permanently embedded in a group, particularly in the context of an encounter between two different cultures, culture is in fact dynamic. It is constantly changing.

And finally, in considering culture's role in international negotiations and relationships, it is important to remember that the world has a staggering diversity of cultures. While executives sometimes speak of Asian culture as if it were homogeneous, in reality, Asia has many different and distinct cultures, from India to Laos, from Korea to Indonesia. Each has its own values and practices that may differ markedly from those prevailing in another Asian country—or indeed, in another part of the same country. The negotiating style of Koreans, for example, is not the same as that of the Lao. And even within countries that from outward appearances seem to have a fairly uniform cultural identity, significant regional differences may exist, such as in France between the business communities of Paris and of the *Midi*.

THE ELEMENTS OF CULTURE

One may conceive of the four cultural elements mentioned in the definition above—behavior, attitudes, norms, and values—as forming a series of concentric circles, like the layers of an onion.

Figure 7.1

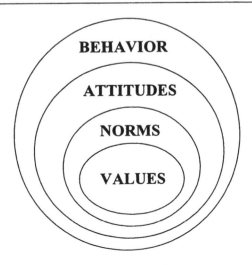

Culture as an Onion

BEHAVIOR

ATTITUDES

NORMS

VALUES

The process of understanding the culture of a counterpart in a negotiation is similar to peeling an onion. The outermost layer is behavior, the words and actions of one's counterpart. This is the layer that a deal maker first perceives in an intercultural negotiation. A second, inner layer consists of the attitudes of persons from that culture toward specific events and phenomena—for example, attitudes about beginning meetings punctually or the appropriate format of presentations. Attitudes may become evident to a counterpart in an intercultural negotiation only after protracted discussions. Next are norms, the rules to be followed in specific situations. Here, a negotiator may come to realize that a counterpart's seemingly rigid insistence on punctuality is not merely a personal idiosyncrasy but is based on a firm rule derived from that person's culture.

The innermost layer—the core—consists of values. One of the essential characteristics of a value is the belief by an individual or a group that a specific conduct is personally or socially preferable to an opposite conduct.[2] The way meetings are conducted, representatives chosen, and persons rewarded are usually based on certain values that are important to the culture of the individuals involved. Differences in values are often difficult for negotiators to detect and understand. Indeed, the parties to an international negotiation may discover their value differences only after they have signed the contract and have begun to work together. Once discovered, differences in cultural values between partners in an international joint venture may lead to severe conflict and ultimately the failure of their enterprise, a factor that may explain why many international ventures have a short life.

In their valuable book *The Seven Cultures of Capitalism*, Charles Hampden-Turner and Alfons Trompenaars report on the results of an extensive survey among 15,000 executives and employees from all over the world concerning their attitudes toward such basic management tasks as group decision making, hiring, rewarding employees, and making and applying rules. The authors found sharp differences that could only be explained by the respondents' differing cultural values. For example, with respect to group decision making, a wide variation among cultures existed as to whether they preferred to choose a person to represent a group by *consensus* (i.e., members of the group should meet and discuss candidates until almost everybody agrees on the same person) or by *adversarial democracy* (i.e., the group members should meet, nominate persons, vote and choose the person with a majority of votes, even if there is strong minority opposition). While 84.4 percent of the Japanese opted for consensus, only 37.7 percent of the Americans did so. One can imagine that this difference in cultural values about decision making, if not managed properly, might lead to conflict between Japanese and American joint-venture partners. The differences on this issue ought not to be viewed as a matter of East versus West. The Germans, who place a high value on social solidarity, favored consensus by 69 percent, as did a strong majority of the Dutch, Belgian, and French executives surveyed. On the other hand, only 35 percent the Italians, whose fractious political culture has resulted in fifty governments in fifty years, preferred consensus.[3]

Other kinds of value conflicts may arise in making, managing and mending global deals—for example, between individualism prized by Americans and communitarianism embodied in many Asian cultures, about whether it is more important to consider individual talent or the ability to fit into the organization when hiring an employee, about whether to reward persons on the basis of group performance or individual achievement only, and about whether an organization should favor or frown on the hiring of relatives of its executives. Differences in cultural values present themselves in international business transactions and relationships time after time and day after day, and they may ultimately turn what appeared to be a harmonious negotiation or business relationship into a continuing source of conflict between the parties.

Once the conflict surfaces, it may be exacerbated by the way the parties try to cope with it. One unfortunate tendency is for each side to extol its own cultural values and to denigrate those of the other side. For example, Americans, with their high store on individualism, will tend to see their value system positively. They would see themselves as supporting individual rights and human freedom, as putting the individual above the tyranny of the group, as knowing that a group prospers only when individuals prosper, and as efficient. Persons coming from cultures where communitarian values are prized will see themselves as unselfish, humane, for group interests and rights, and as knowing that the individual prospers only when the group prospers. Yet Americans, when confronted with a communitarian culture, may tend to ascribe to it only negative characteristics. So Americans, reacting to Japanese values in a decision to retain a fifteen-year employee whose performance has declined, might consider their Japanese counterparts as tolerant of freeloaders, giving in to the tyranny of the group, weak, and inefficient. On the other hand, the Japanese would probably characterize the Americans as ignoring the contributions and needs of the group, lacking loyalty, inhumane, and selfish. This kind of confrontational approach to negotiating cultural differences will only lead to increased conflict between the parties, conflict that can damage both the transaction and their relationship. In any negotiation, it is therefore important for negotiators to understand the values inherent in the culture of their counterparts and not to characterize those values in a negative way.

CULTURE'S IMPACT ON DEAL MAKING

Differences in culture between deal makers can obstruct negotiations in many ways. First, they can create misunderstandings in communication. If one American executive responds to another American's proposal by saying, "That's difficult," the response, interpreted against American culture and business practice, probably means that the door is still open for further discussion, that perhaps the other side should sweeten its offer. In some other cultures, for example, many in Asia, people may be reluctant to say a direct and emphatic "no," even when that is their intention. So when a Japanese negotiator in response to a proposal says, "That is difficult," he is clearly indicating that the proposal is unacceptable. "It is difficult," means "no" to the Japanese, but "maybe" to the American.

Second, cultural differences create difficulties not only in understanding words but also in interpreting actions. While Americans and Canadians may find it perfectly appropriate to conduct business discussions at lunch, Brazilian and Mexican executives may consider serious business negotiations to be totally out of place in that setting. Thus, there can be sharp cultural differences as to when and where deal making is appropriate.

Most Westerners expect a prompt answer when they make a statement or ask a question. The Japanese, on the other hand, tend to take longer to respond. As a result, negotiations with Japanese representatives are sometimes punctuated with periods of silence that seem excruciating to an American. For the Japanese, the period of silence is normal, an appropriate time to reflect on what has been said. The fact that they may not be speaking in their native language lengthens even more the time needed to respond.

From their own cultural perspective, Americans may interpret the Japanese silence as rudeness, lack of understanding, or a cunning tactic to get the Americans to reveal themselves. Rather than wait for a response, the American tendency is to fill the void with words by asking questions, offering further explanations, or merely repeating what they have already said. This response to silence may confuse the Japanese, who are made to feel that they are being bombarded by questions and proposals without being given adequate time to respond to any of them.

On the other hand, Latin Americans, who place a high value on verbal agility, have a tendency to respond quickly. Indeed, they may answer a point once they have understood it even though the other side has not finished speaking. While inexperienced American negotiators are sometimes confused by Japanese delays in responding, they can become equally agitated in negotiations with Brazilians by what Americans consider constant interruptions.

Third, cultural considerations also influence the form and substance of the deal you are trying to make. For example, when McDonald's began to franchise its operations in Asia, it considered itself to be selling not only hamburgers but, as one of its senior executives told the author, "an American experience." It was therefore reluctant to change its traditional American menu. Its franchisee in Thailand pressed hard for permission to sell noodles, a dish traditionally served on auspicious occasions like birthdays. McDonald's finally relented, and sales increased at its Thai restaurants as a result.

More substantively, differences in culture will invariably require changes in products, management systems, and personnel practices. For example, in Thailand, the relationship between manager and employee is more hierarchical than it is in the United States. Workers are motivated by a desire to please the manager, but they, in turn, expect their managers to sense their personal problems and be ready to help with them. Elsewhere, for example in Australia, employees neither expect nor want managers to become involved with their personal problems. Thus an Australian project in Thailand would need to change its concept of employee relations because of the local culture.

And finally, culture can influence negotiating style—the way persons from different cultures conduct themselves in a negotiation and make deals. Research indicates fairly clearly that negotiation practices differ from culture to culture.[4] Indeed, culture may influence how persons conceive of the very nature and function of negotiation. Studies of negotiating styles are abundant;[5] some focus on describing and analyzing the negotiating styles of particular groups. The practitioner's fascination with cultural negotiating styles seems to have spawned a distinct literary genre: the "Negotiating with . . ." literature. Numerous books and articles bearing such titles as "Negotiating with the Japanese," "Negotiating with the Arabs," and "Negotiating with the

Chinese" seek to lead the novice through the intricacies of negotiating in specified cultures. (For a bibliography of some of this work, see the appendix in this book.) Another approach to studying negotiating styles is cross-cultural and comparative, seeking to identify certain basic elements in negotiating styles and to determine how they are reflected in various cultures. The remainder of this chapter adopts this approach.

TEN WAYS THAT CULTURE AFFECTS DEAL MAKING

The great diversity of the world's cultures makes it impossible for any negotiator, no matter how skilled and experienced, to understand fully all the cultures that may be encountered. How then should an executive prepare to cope with culture in making deals in Singapore this week and Seoul the next? The following checklist identifies ten crucial areas where cultural differences may arise during the negotiation process. Knowledge of these ten factors may enable you to understand your counterpart and to anticipate possible misunderstandings.

1. Negotiating Goal: Contract or Relationship?

As we saw in chapter 2, negotiators from different cultures may tend to view the very purpose of a negotiation differently. For deal makers from some cultures, the goal of a business negotiation, first and foremost, is usually to arrive at a signed contract between the parties. American lawyers tend to represent this approach. For them, a signed contract is a definitive set of rights and duties that strictly binds the two sides, an attitude succinctly summed up in the statement "a deal is a deal."

Other cultures tend to consider that the goal of a negotiation is not a signed contract but the creation of a relationship between the two sides. Although the written contract expresses the relationship, the essence of the deal is the relationship itself. The difference in approach may explain why certain Asian negotiators, whose negotiating goal is often the creation of a relationship, tend to give more time and effort to prenegotiation, while Americans usually want to rush through this first phase in deal making. The activities of prenegotiation, whereby the parties seek to get to know one another thoroughly, are a crucial foundation for a good business relationship. They may seem less important when the goal is merely a contract.

It is therefore important to determine how your counterparts view the purpose of your negotiation. If relationship negotiators sit on the other side of the table, you need to be aware that merely convincing them of your ability to deliver on a low-cost contract may not be enough to land you the deal. You may also have to convince them, from the very first meeting, that your two organizations have the potential to build a rewarding relationship over the long term. On the other hand, if the other side is basically a contract deal maker, trying to build a relationship may be a waste of time and energy.

2. Negotiating Attitude: Win-Lose or Win-Win?

Chapter 2 also showed that because of differences in culture or personality, or both, business persons appear to approach deal making with one of two basic attitudes: that a negotiation is either a process in which both can gain (win-win) or a struggle in which, of necessity, one side wins and the other side loses (win-lose). Win-win negotiators see deal making as a collaborative and problem-solving process; win-lose negotiators see it as confrontational. In the latter situation, the parties see their goals as incompatible; in the former they consider themselves to have compatible goals. As you enter negotiations, it is important to know which type of negotiator is sitting across the table from you.

The presence of a win-lose negotiator on the other side of the table can impede deal making. Searching constantly for the negative implications of every proposal while failing to evaluate the positive side, this type of negotiator may simply take a position and refuse to budge. How should you negotiate with a win-lose deal maker?

First, without appearing to condescend, explain fully the nature of the proposed transaction. Do not assume that the other side has the same degree of business and financial knowledge as you do. Part of the intransigence may stem from a lack of understanding of the deal and an unwillingness to show ignorance. For example, in Asia the range of business acumen varies dramatically from the highly sophisticated negotiators of Hong Kong to the much less experienced business people in Laos.

Second, try to discover the other side's real interests. What do they really want out of the deal? Negotiators who encourage the other side to provide information about themselves, their interests, and their preferences generally achieve better results in understanding interests than those who do not. Earlier chapters have stressed the importance of understanding interests in order to reach agreement. In an international negotiation, cultural attitudes toward business secrecy complicate the process. Many foreign companies attach a much greater importance to the secrecy of a broad range of business information than do American corporations, which have to contend daily with the disclosure requirements of U.S. law and business practices. For example, although the salary of the CEO of a U.S. publicly traded corporation is a matter of public record, the salary of the president of a French corporation is a tightly kept secret. Although cultural differences among negotiators on what is and what is not considered secret can complicate information exchange, one principle that all cultures seem to respect is reciprocity. If you are open and provide information easily, the other side will be led to provide you with information. Your own openness may be the best way to get persons across the table to open up.

Third, to understand the other side's interests, you need to know something about its history and culture. China's troubled history of relations with the West and its justified pride in its own culture and accomplishments may cause joint-venture negotiations that place the Chinese party in a visible, second-class position to fail.

And finally, once you have identified the other side's interests, you have to develop proposals directed at satisfying those interests. Here, creativity and innovation are essential. In one negotiation between Bechtel, an international construction firm, and a foreign manufacturing corporation for the construction of an electrical cogeneration plant, the foreign negotiators insisted that if the plant did not operate at a specified standard, Bechtel would have to dismantle the entire plant and take it away. Bechtel was unwilling to make that guarantee. As the negotiations appeared to disintegrate, Bechtel negotiators understood that the real interest of the foreign corporation was not in having a cogeneration plant, but in having a reliable supply of electricity. They therefore proposed that, if the plant were defective, Bechtel would take it over and run it, provided that the purchaser agreed to buy all the electricity it produced. Ultimately, the two sides struck a deal on this basis.[6]

3. Personal Style: Informal or Formal?

Personal style concerns the way a negotiator talks to others, uses titles, dresses, speaks, and interacts with other persons. Culture strongly influences the personal style of negotiators. It has been observed, for example, that Germans have a more formal style than Americans.[7] A negotiator with a formal style insists on addressing counterparts by their titles, avoids personal anecdotes, and refrains from questions touching on the private or family life of members of the other negotiating team. An informal style negotiator tries to start the discussion on a first-name basis, quickly seeks to develop a personal, friendly relationship with the other team, and may take off his jacket and roll up his sleeves when deal making begins in earnest. Each culture has its own formalities that have special meanings within that culture. They are another means of communication among the persons sharing that culture, another form of adhesive that binds them together as a community. For an American or a Spaniard, calling someone by the first name is an act of friendship and therefore a good thing. For a Japanese or an Egyptian, the use of the first name at a first meeting is an act of disrespect and therefore a bad thing.

In the author's survey of negotiating styles among 310 professionals of twelve nationalities, a majority of the respondents within each cultural group, except for the Nigerians, claimed to have an informal negotiating style; however, the strength of this view varied considerably. While nearly 83 percent of the Americans considered themselves to have an informal negotiating style, only 54 percent of the Chinese, 53 percent of the Spanish, and 58 percent of the Mexicans took a similar view. Among the four European cultures represented in the survey, the French were the strongest in claiming an informal style (80 percent). Although both the Germans and the Japanese have a reputation for formality, only slightly more than one-quarter of the respondents in these two groups believed they had a formal negotiating style. Differences in cultures with respect to interpreting the meaning of the terms "formal" and "informal" may have influenced this result.

Figure 7.2

Personal Style: Formal or Informal?

	Nigeria	Spain	China	Mexico	U.K.	Argentina	Germany	Japan	India	Brazil	France	U.S.A.
Formal (%):	53	47	46	42	35	35	27	27	22	22	20	17

Negotiators in foreign cultures must respect appropriate formalities. As a general rule, it is always safer to adopt a formal posture and move to an informal stance, if the situation warrants it, than to assume an informal style too quickly.

4. Communication: Direct or Indirect?

Methods of communication vary among cultures. Some emphasize direct and simple methods of communication; others rely heavily on indirect and complex methods. The latter may use circumlocutions, figurative forms of speech, facial expressions, gestures, and other kinds of body language. In a culture that values directness, such as the American or the Israeli, you can expect to receive a clear and definite response to your proposals and questions. In cultures that rely on indirect communication, such as the Japanese, reaction to your proposals may be gained by interpreting seemingly vague comments, gestures, and other signs. What you will not receive at a first meeting is a definite commitment or rejection.

The confrontation of these styles of communication in the same negotiation can lead to friction. For example, the indirect ways Japanese negotiators express disapproval have often led foreign business executives to believe that their proposals were still under consideration when in fact the Japanese side had rejected them. In the Camp David negotiations that led to a peace treaty between Egypt and Israel, the Israeli preference for direct forms of communication and the Egyptian tendency to favor indirect forms sometimes exacerbated relations between the two sides. The Egyptians interpreted Israeli directness as aggressiveness and, therefore, an insult. The Israelis viewed Egyptian indirectness with impatience and suspected them of insincerity, of not saying what they meant.

In the author's survey, respondents in all the cultural groups by a high margin claimed to have a direct form of communication. Their organizational culture, their international experience, and their interpretation of the words "direct" and "indirect" may have strongly influenced their responses to the questionnaire. It is worth noting, however, that the two cultural groups with the largest percentage of persons claiming an indirect style were the Japanese and the French. The following table summarizes survey results on this question.

Figure 7.3

Communication Style: Direct or Indirect?												

	Japan	France	China	U.K.	Brazil	India	Germany	U.S.A.	Argentina	Spain	Mexico	Nigeria
Indirect (%):	27	20	18	12	11	11	9	5	4	0	0	0

5. Sensitivity to Time: High or Low?

Discussions of national negotiating styles invariably treat a particular culture's attitudes toward time. It is said that Germans are always punctual, Latinos are habitually late, Japanese negotiate slowly, and Americans are quick to make a deal. Commentators sometimes claim that some cultures value time more than others, but this observation may not be an accurate characterization of the situation. Rather, negotiators may value differently the amount of time devoted to and measured against the goal pursued. For Americans, the deal is a signed contract and time is money, so they want to make a deal quickly. Americans therefore try to reduce formalities to a minimum and get down to business quickly. The Japanese and other Asians, whose goal is to create a relationship rather than simply sign a contract, need to invest time in the negotiating process so that the parties can get to know one another well and determine whether they wish to embark on a long-term relationship. They may view with suspicion aggressive attempts to shorten the negotiating time as efforts to hide something. For example, in one case that received significant media attention in the mid-1990s, a long-term electricity supply contract between an Enron subsidiary, the Dabhol Power Company, and the Maharashtra state government in India was subject to significant challenge and was ultimately cancelled on the grounds that it was concluded in "unseemly haste" and had been subject to "fast track procedures" that circumvented established practice for developing such projects in the past. Important segments of the Indian public automatically assumed that the government had failed to protect the public interest because the negotiations were so quick. In the company's defense, Rebecca Mark, chairman and CEO of Enron International, pointed out to the press: "We were extremely concerned with time, because time is money for us."[8]

This difference between the Indian and U.S. attitudes toward time was clearly revealed in the author's survey that asked 310 professionals whether they had a low or high sensitivity to time. Among all nationalities, the Indians had the largest percentage of persons who considered themselves to have a low sensitivity to time, as table 7.4 shows.

Although a majority of the respondents from all the cultural groups surveyed claimed to have a high sensitivity to time, the strength of the minority view on this question varied considerably among the groups. In addition to the Indians, the French, the Germans, and the Mexicans included a substantial percentage of respondents asserting a low sensitivity to time.

Figure 7.4

Time Sensitivity: High or Low?

	India	France	Germany	Mexico	Spain	Argentina	U.S.A.	Japan	China	Nigeria	U.K.	Brazil
Low **(%):**	44	40	36	33	21	15	15	9	9	7	6	0

6. Emotionalism: High or Low?

Accounts of negotiating behavior in other cultures almost always point to a particular group's tendency to act emotionally. According to the stereotype, Latin Americans show their emotions at the negotiating table, while the Japanese and many other Asians hide their feelings. Obviously, individual personality plays a role here. There are passive Latinos and hot-headed Japanese. Nonetheless, various cultures have different rules as to the appropriateness and form of displaying emotions, and these rules are brought to the negotiating table as well. Deal makers should seek to learn them.

In the author's survey, Latin Americans and the Spanish were the cultural groups that ranked themselves highest with respect to emotionalism in a clearly statistically significant fashion. Among Europeans, the Germans and English ranked as least emotional, while among Asians the Japanese held that position, but to a lesser degree. The following table summarizes the results with regard to emotionalism.

Figure 7.5

	Brazil	Argentina	Mexico	Spain	China	U.S.A.	Nigeria	France	India	Japan	U.K.	Germany

Emotionalism: High or Low?

	Brazil	Argentina	Mexico	Spain	China	U.S.A.	Nigeria	France	India	Japan	U.K.	Germany
High (%):	89	85	83	79	73	74	60	60	56	55	47	36

7. Form of Agreement: General or Specific?

Whether a negotiator's goal is a contract or a relationship, the negotiated transactions in almost all cases will be embodied in some sort of written agreement. Cultural factors influence the form of the written agreement that the parties make. Generally, Americans prefer very detailed contracts that attempt to anticipate all possible circumstances and eventualities, no matter how unlikely. Why? Because the deal is the contract itself, and one must refer to the contract to handle new situations that may arise. Other cultures, such as the Chinese, prefer a contract in the form of general principles rather than detailed rules. Why? Because it is claimed that the essence of the deal is the relationship between the parties. If unexpected circumstances arise, the parties should look to their relationship, not the contract, to solve the problem. So, in some cases, a Chinese negotiator may interpret the American drive to stipulate all contingencies as evidence of lack of confidence in the stability of the underlying relationship.

Among all respondents in the author's survey, 78 percent preferred specific agreements while only 22 percent preferred general agreements. Male and female participants responded in roughly the same proportions. The survey found that a majority of respondents in each cultural group preferred specific agreements to general agreements. This result may be attributed in part to the relatively large number of lawyers among the respondents, as well as to the fact that multinational corporate practice favors specific agreements and many of the respondents, regardless of nationality, had experience with such firms. The survey responses on this point may have been a case in which professional or organizational culture dominated national cultural traits. On the other hand, the degree of intensity of responses on the question varied considerably among cultural groups. While only 11 percent of the English

favored general agreements, 45.5 percent of the Japanese and of the Germans
claimed to do so.

Figure 7.6

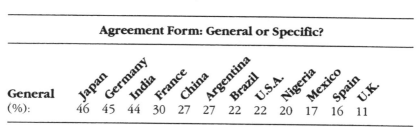

Agreement Form: General or Specific?											
	Japan	Germany	India	France	China	Argentina	Brazil	U.S.A.	Nigeria	Mexico	Spain	U.K.
General (%):	46	45	44	30	27	27	22	22	20	17	16	11

Occupational groups demonstrated wider variations, a finding that supports the notion that professional culture may dominate national culture on
this question. For example, while 100 percent of the respondents with military backgrounds preferred specific agreements, only 64 percent of management and marketing persons and of diplomats and civil servants had a similar
inclination,[9] as table 7.7 indicates:

Figure 7.7

Occupations and Agreement Form: General or Specific?							
	Military	Students	Accounting/ Finance	Law	Engineering	Teaching	Diplomacy/ Public Sector	Management/ Marketing
Specific (%):	100	92	86	84	74	71	64	64

Some experienced executives argue that differences over the form of an
agreement are caused more by unequal bargaining power between the parties
than by culture. In a situation of unequal bargaining power, the stronger
party always seeks a detailed agreement to "lock up the deal" in all its possible dimensions, while the weaker party prefers a general agreement to give it
room to "wiggle out" of adverse circumstances that are bound to occur. A
Chinese commune, as the weaker party in a negotiation with a multinational
corporation, will seek a general agreement as a way of protecting itself
against an uncertain future. According to this view, it is context, not culture,
that determines this negotiating trait.

8. Building an Agreement: Bottom Up or Top Down?

Related to the form of the agreement is the question of whether negotiating a business deal is an *inductive* or a *deductive* process. Does it start from an agreement on general principles and proceed to specific items, or does it begin with an agreement on specifics, such as price, delivery date, and product quality, the sum total of which becomes the contract? Different cultures tend to emphasize one approach over the other. Some observers believe that the French prefer to begin with agreement on general principles, while Americans tend to seek agreement first on specifics. For Americans, negotiating a deal is basically making a series of compromises and trade-offs on a long list of particulars. For the French, the essence is to agree on basic principles that will guide and indeed determine the negotiation process afterward. The general principles become the framework upon which the contract is built.

A further difference in negotiating style is seen in the dichotomy between the building-down approach and the building-up approach. In the building down approach, the negotiator begins by presenting the maximum deal if the other side accepts all the stated conditions. In the building-up approach, one side begins by proposing a minimum deal that can be broadened and increased as the other party accepts additional conditions. According to many observers, Americans tend to favor the building-down approach, while the Japanese tend to prefer the building-up style.

The survey of negotiating styles found that the French, the Argentineans, and the Indians tended to view deal making as a top-down (deductive process); while the Japanese, the Mexicans and the Brazilians tended to see it as a bottom-up (inductive) process. The results among the twelve groups were as follows.

Figure 7.8

Style of Building Agreement: Top-Down or Bottom-Up											
	India	Argentina	France	U.K.	China	Germany	U.S.A.	Nigeria	Spain	Japan	Brazil	Mexico
Top-Down (%):	74	70	67	54	54	54	47	47	46	45	42	33

9. Team Organization: One Leader or Group Consensus?

In any negotiation, it is important to know how the other side is organized, who has the authority to make commitments, and how decisions are made. Culture is one important factor that affects how executives organize themselves to negotiate a deal. Some cultures emphasize the individual while others stress the group. These values may influence the organization of each side in a negotiation.

One extreme is the negotiating team with a supreme leader who has complete authority to decide all matters. Many American teams tend to follow this approach. Other cultures, notably the Japanese and the Chinese, stress team negotiation and consensus decision making. When you negotiate with such a team, it may not be apparent who is the leader and who has the authority to commit the side. In the first type, the negotiating team is usually small; in the second it is often large. For example, in negotiations in China on a major deal, it would not be uncommon for the Americans to arrive at the table with three people and for the Chinese to show up with ten. Similarly, the one-leader team is usually prepared to make commitments more quickly than a negotiating team organized on the basis of consensus. As a result, the consensus type of organization usually takes more time to negotiate a deal.

Among all respondents in the author's survey, 59 percent tended to prefer one leader while 41 percent preferred a more consensus form of organization. Male and female respondents tended to follow this same distribution. On the other hand, the various cultural groups showed a wide variety of preferences on the question of team organization. The group with the strongest preference for consensus organization was the French. Many studies have noted French individualism.[10] Perhaps a consensus arrangement in the individual French person's eyes is the best way to protect that individualism. Despite the Japanese reputation for consensus arrangements, only 45 percent of the Japanese respondents claimed to prefer a negotiating team based on consensus. The Brazilians, the Chinese, and the Mexicans to a far greater degree than any other groups preferred one-person leadership, a reflection perhaps of the political traditions of those countries. The results of the survey on this point are summarized in table 7.9.

Occupational groups also revealed significant differences. For example, while 100 percent of the military respondents preferred a single leader for a negotiating team, only 43 percent of the accountants expressed a similar view, as is indicated in figure 7.10.

Within cultures, male and female respondents to this question demonstrated significant differences. Thus, 78 percent of American male respondents preferred a one-leader team organization, but only 35 percent of the female respondents expressed a similar preference. On the other hand, the small sample indicated that among Nigerians, 80 percent of the men preferred consensus arrangements while 80 percent of the women opted for one leader. In addition, a majority of the Japanese, Chinese, French, Spanish, Argentineans, and Brazilian women all preferred a one-leader approach to team organization.

Figure 7.9

Team Organization: One Leader or Consensus?

	Brazil	China	Mexico	U.K.	U.S.A.	Spain	Argentina	Germany	Japan	India	Nigeria	France
One Leader (%):	100	91	91	65	63	58	58	55	55	44	40	40

Figure 7.10

Occupations and Team Organization: One Leader or Consensus?

	Military	Engineering	Teaching	Students	Management/ Marketing	Law	Diplomacy/ Public Sector	Accounting/ Finance
One Leader (%):	100	68	62	62	61	56	50	43

10. Risk Taking: High or Low?

Research supports the conclusion that certain cultures are more risk averse than others.[11] In deal making, the negotiators' cultures can affect the willingness of one side to take risks—to divulge information, to try new approaches, and to tolerate uncertainties in a proposed course of action. The Japanese, with their emphasis on requiring large amounts of information and their intricate group decision-making process, tend to be risk averse. Americans, by comparison, are risk takers.

Among all respondents in the author's survey, approximately 70 percent claimed a tendency toward risk taking while only 30 percent characterized themselves as low risk takers. Here too, the distribution among men and women was similar and tended to follow that of all respondents as a group. Among cultures, the responses to this question showed significant variations. The Japanese are said to be highly risk averse in negotiations, and this tendency was affirmed by the survey which found Japanese respondents to be the most risk averse of the twelve cultures. Americans in the survey, by comparison, considered themselves to be risk takers, but an even higher percentage of the French, the British, and the Indians claimed to be risk takers. Figure 7.11 summarizes the survey results with respect to risk.

The survey also found significant differences among professional groups. For example, although 100 percent of the military respondents considered themselves to be high risk takers in negotiations, only 36 percent of the diplomats and civil servants characterized themselves similarly (see figure 7.12).

Generally, a large majority of males within each cultural group considered themselves high risk takers, with the exception of the Japanese (12.5 percent), the Spanish (39 percent) and the Mexicans (44 percent). Female re-

Figure 7.11

Risk Taking: High or Low?

	France	India	U.K.	China	U.S.A.	Nigeria	Argentina	Germany	Brazil	Mexico	Spain	Japan
High (%):	90	89	88	82	78	73	73	72	56	50	47	18

Figure 7.12

Occupations and Risk Taking: High or Low?									
	Military	Accounting/Finance	Engineering	Management/Marketing	Students	Teaching	Law	Diplomacy/Public Sector	
High (%):	100	81	77	75	72	67	66	36	

spondents who registered a higher percentage of risking taking than males from the same culture were U.S. women (86 percent), Spanish women (67 percent), and Mexican women (67 percent).

Faced with a risk-averse counterpart, how should a deal maker proceed? The following are a few steps to consider:

1. Don't rush the negotiating process. A negotiation that is moving too fast for one of the parties only heightens that person's perception of the risks in the proposed deal.
2. Devote attention to proposing rules and mechanisms that will reduce the apparent risks in the deal for the other side.
3. Make sure that your counterpart has sufficient information about you, your company, and the proposed deal.
4. Focus your efforts on building a relationship and fostering trust between the parties.
5. Consider restructuring the deal so that the deal proceeds step by step in a series of increments rather than all at once.

NEGOTIATING STYLES: A FRAMEWORK

Negotiating styles, like personalities, have a wide range of variation. The ten negotiating traits discussed above can be placed on a spectrum or continuum, as illustrated in the following chart. Its purpose is to identify specific negotiating traits affected by culture and to show the possible variation that each trait or factor may take. With this knowledge, a deal maker may be better able to understand the negotiating styles and approaches of counterparts from other cultures. Equally important, it may help negotiators determine how their own styles appear to those same counterparts.

Figure 7.13

The Impact of Culture on Negotiation

Negotiation Factors	Range of Cultural Responses
Goal	Contract ◄──────► Relationship
Attitudes	Win-Lose ◄──────► Win-Win
Personal Styles	Informal ◄──────► Formal
Communications	Direct ◄──────► Indirect
Time Sensitivity	High ◄──────► Low
Emotionalism	High ◄──────► Low
Agreement Form	Specific ◄──────► General
Agreement Building	Bottom Up ◄──────► Top Down
Team Organization	One Leader ◄──────► Consensus
Risk Taking	High ◄──────► Low

OVERCOMING CULTURAL DIFFERENCES IN DEAL MAKING

In view of the importance of cultural differences in international negotiations and transactions, how should negotiators cope with them? The following are a few simple rules.

Rule No. 1: Learn the Other Side's Culture

In any negotiation, it is important to learn something about the other side's culture. Ideally, learning a culture other than your own requires several years of study, mastery of the local language, and prolonged residence in the country of that culture. An American faced with the task of negotiating a strategic alliance with a Thai company in Bangkok in two weeks' time cannot, of course, master Thai culture that fast. At best, the negotiator can learn enough to cope with some of the principal effects that Thai culture may have on making the deal.

History is an important window on a country's culture. So at the very least, the American should read a history of modern Thailand. If time permits, an executive might consult anthropological studies, reports on the current political situation, and accounts, if any, on negotiating with the Thais.

Consultation with persons who have had significant business experience in Thailand can also be helpful. International banks and transnational corporations may be excellent sources of advice on the impact of Thai culture on business. The U.S. Department of State and the American Embassy or consulate may also advise you on negotiating business deals in Thailand. Another source of advice may be a university with a Southeast Asian studies program. Finally, if you have hired a Thai lawyer, business consultant or interpreter to work on the deal with you, that person can also explain how the local culture affects the negotiating process, communications between the parties, the structure of the transaction, and the execution of the deal itself.

Rule No. 2: Don't Stereotype

If rule number one in an international negotiation is know the other side's culture, rule number two is avoid over-reliance on that knowledge. Not all Japanese evade giving a direct negative answer. Not all Germans tell you specifically what they think of a proposal. In short, negotiators who enter foreign cultures should be careful not to allow cultural stereotypes to determine their relations with local business people. Foreign business executives and lawyers will be offended if they feel you are not treating them as individuals but rather as cultural robots of a particular ethnic group. In addition to giving offense, cultural stereotypes can be misleading. Many times the other side simply does not run true to the negotiating form suggested by books, articles, and consultants. The reason, of course, is that other forces besides culture may influence a person's negotiating behavior. Specifically, these forces may include the negotiator's personality and experience, the organization represented, and the context of the particular negotiation in question.

Rule No. 3: Be Aware of Your Own Culture and How Others May Perceive It

Using the negotiating style framework and other guides, you should become aware of the basic elements of your own negotiating style and how your cultural values influence your approach to deal making, deal managing, and deal mending. For example, if you are highly sensitive to time during a negotiation and consider that time is money, you should be aware of that tendency and of the fact that it may cause friction with negotiators from cultures in which time does not have the same importance.

Rule No. 4: Find Ways to Bridge the Culture Gap

Generally, executives and lawyers who confront a culture different from their own tend to view it in one of three ways: an obstacle, a weapon, or a fortress. At the operational level, cultural differences are hardly ever seen as positive.

The conventional view among most American executives is that cultural differences are an obstacle to agreement and effective joint action. They therefore search for ways to overcome the obstacle. But a different culture in a business setting can become more than an obstacle; it can be seen as a weapon, particularly when a dominant party tries to impose its culture on the other side. For example, foreign counterparts may consider American lawyers' insistence on structuring a transaction "the way we do it in the United States" as the use of American culture as a weapon.

Faced with a culture that it perceives as a weapon, a party to a business deal may become defensive and try to use its own culture as a fortress to protect itself from what it perceives as a cultural onslaught. The Japanese have often adopted this approach when confronted with American demands to open their markets. France's drive to limit the use of English in advertising is a defensive response to what it considered to be the weapon of Anglo-Saxon culture. Groups fearful of globalization often raise their culture as a fortress to prevent incursion of foreign businesses whose practices are culturally threatening.

It may be helpful to try to think of cultural differences in yet another way. Differences in cultures tend to isolate individuals and groups from each other. In short, cultural differences create a gap between persons and organizations. The effective negotiators should seek to find ways to bridge that gap. Negotiators need to think of themselves as bridge builders. Often the action that people take when confronted with cultural differences serves only to widen the gap. In China, for example, an expatriate manager whose company was having problems with the Customs Department sent a middle-level employee to handle the matter, as he would have done if he had faced the same problem in the United States. In China, however, this approach failed. For reasons of saving face, high-level Chinese officials in the Customs Department refused to meet with the company representative and instead delegated an officer at a correspondingly low level to meet with him. As a result, the problem became the subject of interminable meetings but was never solved.

Bridges are often vital links between countries. Accordingly, effective joint action among persons and organizations of differing cultures requires a bridge over the culture gulf. One way to build that bridge is by using culture itself. If culture is indeed the glue that binds together a particular group of people, the creative use of culture between persons of different backgrounds is often a way to link those on opposite sides of the gap. The essence of the technique is to create community with the other side. Basically, there are four types of cultural bridge building that a deal maker should consider when confronted with a culture gap in a negotiation or transaction.

Bridge the gap using the other side's culture.   One technique for bridging the gap is for a negotiator or manager to use elements of the other side's culture in their communications with that side. In international business, negotiators often try to use or identify with the other side's culture in order to build a relationship. For example, when President Anwar Sadat of Egypt negotiated with Sudanese officials, he always made a point of telling them that his mother had been born in the Sudan. He was thus using a common cultural thread to build a relationship with his counterparts. In effect, he was saying: "Like you, I am Sudanese, so we have common cultural ties. I understand you and I value your culture. Therefore you can trust me." Similarly, an African American managing a joint venture in Nigeria stressed his African heritage to build relationships with Nigerian counterparts. And an Italian American negotiating a sales contract in Rome emphasized his Italian background as a way of bridging the cultural gap that he perceived.

In his memoir, *Turmoil and Triumph*, former U.S. Secretary of State George Shultz gives a graphic example of how a Russian counterpart used American culture to build a bridge to the Americans during the Reykjavik summit. In an early meeting with Shultz, Marshal Sergei Akhromeyev, then deputy minister of defense, remarked that he was "one of the last of the Mohicans," meaning that he was the last of the Soviet World War II commanders still in service. When Shultz asked Akhromeyev where he learned the expression "last of the Mohicans," Akhromeyev replied that he had been raised on the tales of the American writer James Fenimore Cooper. The answer had an immediate impact of Shultz. It led him to conclude that

Akhromeyev was more open and ready for conversation than previous Soviet negotiators, that he was a man with a sense of history and an awareness of the American way, and that he was a person the Americans could deal with. "Literature can build bridges," Shultz wrote.[12]

Bridge the gap using your own culture.   A second general approach to bridging the culture gap is to persuade or induce the other side to adopt elements of your culture. Successful implementation of this approach requires time and education. For example, in order to give a common culture to a joint venture, an American partner incurred significant costs by sending its foreign partner's executives to schools and training programs in the United States and then assigning them for short periods to the U.S. partner's own operations. The danger in this technique is that your foreign counterpart will view your culture as a weapon and therefore use its own culture as a fortress, creating the potential for heightened conflict.

Bridge with a combination of both cultures.   A third approach to dealing with the culture gap is to build a bridge using elements from the cultures of both sides. In effect, culture bridging takes place on both sides of the gap and hopefully results in the construction of a solid integrated structure. The challenge in this approach is to identify the most important elements of each culture and to find ways of blending them into a consistent, harmonious whole that will allow business to be done effectively.

Bridge with a third culture.   A final method of dealing with the culture gap is to build a bridge relying on a third culture that belongs to neither of the parties. Thus, for example, in a difficult negotiation between an American executive and a Chinese manager, both discovered that they had a great appreciation of French culture since they had both studied in France in their youth. They began to converse in French, and their common love of France enabled them to build a strong personal relationship. They used a third culture to bridge the gap between China and America.

A variation of this approach is to use a common professional culture to overcome national cultural differences. As the survey results indicated, sometimes the professional cultures of negotiators on certain issues appear stronger than their national cultures. This finding suggests that when companies from two different cultures face strong cultural differences at the negotiating table, they should seek to find a common culture in the professional backgrounds of the negotiators on both sides of the table. Thus, lawyers may be able to build relationships with lawyers and engineers with engineers. If an engineer on the other team seems to be creating an obstacle and is resistant to an agreement, it may be wise to select one of your own engineers, rather than one of your lawyers, to deal with him and to build a bridge over the cultural divide between the two companies.

8

SPECIAL BARRIER NO. 3: IDEOLOGY

Deal makers take not only their cultures to the negotiating table but also their political beliefs. Probe deeply enough into the mind of even the most apolitical executive, and you will find an ideology, a more or less systematic body of beliefs about how society ought to work and what program of action it should follow. Far from being political baggage, ideologies define right and wrong, direct human conduct toward specific goals, and inspire social change. Communism, capitalism, socialism, nationalism, Islamic fundamentalism, fascism, Peronism, Maoism, and Nasserism are just a few ideologies that the world has had to contend with over the last century. Throughout that time, numerous conflicting ideologies have also been a constant feature of the international business scene.

U.S. managers, whether they are Republicans or Democrats, generally share a more or less common ideology, so ideological differences rarely complicate domestic deal making. Once Americans enter the global business arena, however, they encounter ideologies vastly different from their own. Ideological differences can therefore become a barrier to global deal making. This chapter examines the nature of that barrier, its impact on the negotiation process, and some ways of overcoming it. As a general rule, global negotiators should try to avoid ideology at the bargaining table.

THE ELEMENTS OF IDEOLOGY

Ideology is deadly serious business. Whether it is socialism or capitalism, communism or Islamic fundamentalism, ideology gives authoritative answers to some basic questions. What should be the relationship between the individual and the community? How should that relationship be guaranteed and enforced? How should the means of producing goods and services be organized and governed? What should be the role of the state in the lives of its citizens? How should the state and its citizens treat the citizens of other states?

No two ideologies answer all these questions precisely alike. Each ideology has its own explanation of what is good and bad in society; each has its own approach to fixing social ills. The answers they offer are essential background in putting together any business deal.

Some U.S. managers tend to think of ideologies in sweeping general categories—capitalism, socialism, nationalism—that are much too broad to guide deal makers in specific countries abroad. Existing ideologies in a particular country have usually been shaped to meet that country's particular needs. The socialism of China is different from that of North Korea, and the capitalism of the United States is different from that of Canada.

Numerous factors shape and influence a particular ideology. Internal factors, such as a country's geography, demography, culture, and resources are powerful forces shaping an ideology. Thus, Germany's ideology of a social democratic economy with its concept of "codetermination" that grants labor a formal role in the management of large corporations is a product of communitarian values in its culture and a reaction to its history of Nazism and the consequences of two world wars. Similarly, Latin America's history of outside domination has prompted the strong nationalist ideologies that one finds throughout that continent.

Ideology may be identified with a particular culture or nationality but it is distinct from both. Some countries with a more or less unified culture are nevertheless ideologically divided. France, for example, has two basic ideological tendencies—one left and one right—that date back to the French Revolution of 1789. As a result, there is no single French ideology, although a single French nationality and broad culture do exist. And in many Arab countries, like Egypt, one can find the ideologies of Western capitalism, Arab socialism, and Islamic fundamentalism sitting side by side (however uneasily) in the same office or on the same negotiating team. And even if a country has officially abandoned an ideology, individual managers may still hold to it. For instance, although Eastern European countries have dismantled their communist systems, some managers and workers continue to cling to certain elements of a communist ideology.

IDEOLOGY AND THE DEAL'S
PROCESS AND SUBSTANCE

Ideology has a dual impact on global deals: It affects the negotiation process and it influences the nature of the transaction ultimately agreed upon. Ideological differences between the two sides can complicate the deal-making process in numerous ways.

First, ideologies have an adversarial quality. They have their good guys and bad guys, friends and foes, right and wrong ways. Ideological differences at the negotiating table can thus increase mistrust between the parties and raise suspicions about the other side's intentions, honesty, and reliability. As a result, the parties may come to see themselves not as jointly engaged in solving a business problem but as ideological adversaries to be watched very carefully.

Second, ideological differences can complicate communications between negotiators. The use of ideological jargon may seem natural and right to a person holding that ideology, but it is often provocative to the other side. A U.S. executive may consider "free enterprise," "profit," and "private property," to be unquestionably good things; however, an Indian government official or Chinese manager may consider them more ambivalently.

Third, ideology may lead negotiators to take hard-and-fast positions. As a result, ideological differences may obstruct the process of shaping an agreement by precluding the exploration of mutual interests and the development of creative options to advance them. In negotiating the privatization of a state-owned telecommunications company in a developing country, the local government may insist on retaining a 51 percent ownership for reasons of nationalism requiring that enterprises be under local control. Although the purpose behind its position on ownership is to assure local control, ideology may prevent the government from exploring ways to control the enterprise without owning 51 percent of its shares, for example, by retaining a "golden share" that in effect gives the government a veto over major decisions.

Ideology can also complicate the substance of the deal itself and relations between the parties once they have signed the contract. Three areas of ideological difference often faced by U.S. negotiators are private investment, profit, and individual rights and incentives. Americans tend to view private investment as a positive good, a force to create wealth, jobs, useful products, and income; however, people in many other countries look at investment more circumspectly. For them investment—particularly foreign investment—has its benefits and its costs, and host governments seek to maximize the benefits and minimize the costs to the country through governmental regulation. More generally, in the minds of many managers, foreign investment in their countries represents the prospect of selling out to foreign capital and of being controlled by foreigners.

Profit, too, has different ideological interpretations. For U.S. managers, profits result from growth and are good because they can be reinvested to yield further profits. In other countries, the profits that one person gains are seen as wealth taken from somebody else. Indeed, ideological differences on this question may go to the very purpose of a corporation. For example, many U.S. companies have made building shareholder value a priority, a recognition that a fundamental purpose of a corporation is to increase the wealth of its owners, the shareholders. Some multinational companies that have made explicit statements in favor of shareholder value in the United States have been less open about the concept in their European affiliates for fear of antagonizing European governments, labor unions, and environmental groups that strongly believe that a corporation must advance their interests as stakeholders in addition to increasing the wealth of its shareholders. When asked about this difference in approach, the CEO of a French company with a listed U.S. affiliate, responded: "I drive differently in the U. S. than I do in France. I also don't manage in the same way."[1]

Similarly, American ideology stresses the rights of the individual, but other nationalities, like the Chinese, emphasize the rights of the group. For example, in certain joint ventures in China, the U.S. approach to rewarding high-performing workers with incentive packages has clashed with communist ideology that stresses equal treatment of workers.

Aside from these individual issues, the ideology of nationalism is a constant theme, sometimes muted, sometimes blatant, in many if not most international business negotiations. Its presence at the bargaining table is basically defensive—to thwart a proposal that might harm perceived national interests. It can take many forms. Sometimes, as in Japan, it is a general but unstated barrier to foreign penetration of the local market. In other places, such as in Latin America, it may be embodied in a specific law or doctrine, such as the Calvo doctrine that prohibits local companies from agreeing to submit their business disputes to international arbitration because this would give foreigners the privilege of avoiding local courts.

DEALING WITH IDEOLOGIES

How should you deal with the barrier of ideology at the negotiating table? The basic strategy to follow is avoidance. No matter how long and hard you argue about ideological issues, you will certainly not change the other side's beliefs, and they will not change yours. Therefore if you want to succeed as a global negotiator, you should do your best to duck ideological matters.

That piece of advice is not as easy to put into practice as it sounds. The following eight simple rules may help you overcome ideological barriers at the negotiating table.

1. Know your own ideology.   American executives tend to think of themselves as pragmatists. They have viewpoints, even philosophies. But few self-respecting corporate executives believe they have an ideology. The ideologies are on the other side of the table. They, not we, are the zealots and the fanatics.

That belief is a self-delusion. We all have ideologies. We all have answers to the basic questions raised earlier in the chapter, questions that every ideology tries to answer. And even if our political beliefs seem to us to be obvious and eternal truths, acknowledged by mankind as laws of nature, those beliefs will inevitably appear to be an ideology to somebody on the other side of the negotiation table. You should also try to understand how the other side views the ideology that you hold.

2. Once you understand your own ideology, don't preach it.   You are at the table to make deals, not converts. Trumpeting your own ideology may antagonize the other side. At the very least, in a socialist country your gratuitous praise of "free enterprise" will be interpreted as criticism of that country's prevailing ideology. Do not transform a business negotiation into an ideological struggle. Even in these days, when capitalism seems to have triumphed over other economic systems, becoming a missionary for capitalism, rather than focusing on your job as a business negotiator, may lose you a deal in the end. Your prospective business partner may find your preaching annoying and condescending and may come to believe that it would be a constant irritant in a long-term relationship.

3. Know the other side's ideology and take it seriously.   Ideology, like culture, gives you important insights into the other side. You should therefore seek to understand that ideology and how it came about.

One way you can begin to gain that knowledge is by reading a modern political history of the country in which you want to do business. Local newspapers and magazines and discussions with embassy officials and your consultants can also be extremely helpful. Of course, members of the other negotiating team, often in social conversation, may provide important information on the prevailing ideology in the country, as well as on their own political beliefs.

Understanding the other side's ideology helps you understand the other side's interests, and an understanding of interests is essential in shaping an acceptable deal. In the old Soviet Union, Coca Cola wanted to set up a bottling plant and distribution network. The prevailing ideology in the country at the time stressed the importance of the group over the individual and the need to develop industrial capacity at the expense of consumer goods. Soft drinks hardly seemed to fit the country's ideological priorities. Indeed, one government official dismissed the product as a "useless drink." Eventually, the two sides struck a deal, but not on the basis that the drink would quench the local population's thirst. Instead, the U.S. negotiators justified the project on the grounds that it would contribute to the country's industrial development. They restructured the project to include a heavy training component for local workers and managers, as well as a farm that would grow certain of the drink's ingredients. In addition, Coke promised to make efforts to persuade other American companies to consider investments in the country.[2]

Americans not only believe that they themselves have no ideology, but they also tend to think that the proclaimed ideologies of other persons are not genuine. For many U.S. executives, ideological statements merely justify interests. They assume that foreign business executives and officials just parrot the ideological line to get along with their governments, that nobody actually believes that stuff.

It is dangerous to arrive at the negotiating table with that attitude. It is far better to assume that negotiators on the other side of the table believe the ideological statements they are making—at least until you have direct evidence that they don't.

4. Look for ideological divisions on the other side.   In negotiating any deal you have to be concerned about the other side's ideology at three different levels: personal, organizational, and national. Specifically, you need to determine: (1) the ideology of the persons with whom you are negotiating; (2) the ideology of the organization with whom you hope to make a deal; and (3) the ideology prevailing in the country in which you want to do business.

In many but not all instances, the ideologies at the three levels are the same. But it sometimes happens that the personal, organizational, and national ideologies of the other side are different, even inconsistent. These differences in ideology may either facilitate or complicate deal making. For example, if a foreign executive with whom you are negotiating is clearly not sympathetic to his country's prevailing socialist ideology, the opportunity to make a deal may be greater than if he were a genuine socialist. However, if the country has a declared open-door policy toward foreign investment, but the official with whom you are negotiating holds strong nationalist and socialist views, making a deal on a foreign investment project may prove difficult.

U.S. companies discovered the problem created by ideological diversity in the 1970s, when Egypt, under President Anwar Sadat, actively tried to promote foreign investment. Despite favorable policies and laws, prospective investors in Egypt encountered significant barriers in government agencies and corporations. Officials in those organizations had formed a set of beliefs known as Arab socialism during the previous twenty years under the rule of President Gamal Abdel Nasser. As a result, they came to view foreign investors as a threat to Egypt's sovereignty and public sector. The arrival of a new president with new laws and policies did not cause them to put aside those beliefs. Regardless of Sadat's speeches inviting foreign capital to Egypt, many Egyptian officials continued to bring their old ideology to the negotiating table and thereby obstructed deal making. To counter this situation, American companies sought to shift negotiations to a higher level in the bureaucracy, where they hoped to find an ideology more in tune with what they were hearing from President Sadat.

5. Avoid discussion of ideological positions, and focus instead on interests. If a country has taken a strong ideological position on an issue— say, the predominance of public sector enterprise over that of the private sector in the field of energy—it does little good to try to persuade officials of that country that its position is wrong. Rather, try to determine the goals that the other side is pursuing through that ideological position, and then seek to propose options that will enable it to achieve those goals. In the case of the soft drink plant, it would have been confrontational and counterproductive for the U.S. company to try to persuade the Soviet government to provide more goods to consumers. Instead, the U.S. investor identified the country's interests in developing its industrial capacity and convinced the government that the soft drink plant, distribution system, and farm would help the country advance its interests.

6. Look for gaps between ideology and reality.   As we saw in Eastern Europe as the cold war ended, reality changes faster than ideology. With that change, a gap develops between the two as ideology's explanation of society and its proposed solutions seem more and more inadequate. Eventually, when the gap becomes too great, the prevailing ideology is abandoned or reformed. Thus, when communism became less and less relevant to the problems of East Germany, it was discarded as that country's prevailing ideology.

Similarly, as deal makers come to know a country, they should seek to identify gaps between ideology and the realities of the local business and economic environment. The existence of large gaps may suggest areas in which official ideology is less of an obstacle to deal making. For example, if the ideology of the state stresses the importance of the group over the individual but the role of the individual is increasing in the society, opportunities for business deals in consumer goods may arise. Then, too, the existence of big gaps between official ideology and the social realities may mean that major political changes will soon take place.

7. Try to structure deals around ideological obstacles.   Often ideological principles crystallize in laws, rules, and institutions that threaten to block deals. Nationalism requires that all resources belong to the state and that no one else may own them. Islamic fundamentalism prohibits interest payments on loans. Egyptian socialism demands that workers participate both in the management and the profits of an enterprise. Each of these principles can be an obstacle to deal making in particular cases. Yet, with some creativity, it is possible to structure a deal in such a way that the ideological principle is respected but business goes forward. For example, worker participation in management need not mean a seat on the company's board of directors, but simply an advisory committee that meets regularly with an officer of the company. And a petroleum development contract could be written in such a way that the ownership of oil is transferred not when the oil is in the ground but at the point that it leaves the flange of the well.

8. Maintain confidentiality. The more public the negotiations, the more likely that ideological differences will surface. In the glare of publicity, local executives and officials feel a strong need to show to the government, the public, and their colleagues that they are adhering to appropriate ideological positions. For example, in a highly publicized mineral negotiation, officials representing the government may feel obliged to show that they are not selling out to foreigners. As a result, their positions may harden, and they may prove to be inflexible at the table.

Executives should therefore seek to establish and maintain confidentiality in negotiations as one way to soften the influence of ideology. To create a confidential atmosphere, negotiators should be careful in what they say to others outside the negotiating room. They should naturally avoid comments to the press and, indeed, should specifically agree that the host country's negotiating team will be the principal source of public commentary on the negotiations. Another way to foster confidentiality, as chapter 6 pointed out, is to hold discussions in another country or at some out-of-the-way site.

9

SPECIAL BARRIER NO. 4:
FOREIGN ORGANIZATIONS
AND BUREAUCRACIES

Deals link organizations. Behind any international business negotiation are the companies, partnerships, government agencies, and state corporations whose interests are being discussed at the table. In virtually all cases, global negotiators are agents. They are agents in the sense that they are negotiating on behalf of their organizations, not themselves. Their job is to find a way to get their respective organizations to agree on an advantageous business relationship. Although deal making is an intensely personal activity driven by the personalities, skills, and experience of the individual negotiators, it is also a bureaucratic activity strongly influenced by the nature of the organizations involved.

As a result, a negotiator not only has to be concerned about the person sitting across the table but must also constantly think about the organizations and bureaucracies that they both represent. When you negotiate any deal, remember that internal negotiations are taking place in your counterpart's organization about the proposed deal just as similar internal negotiations are occurring in your own organization. As the diagram on page 128 indicates, deal making always involves at least three separate but linked negotiations: the external discussions with your counterpart and the internal discussions within each of the two organizations. What happens in each of the three negotiations can profoundly influence the deal-making process and ultimately the shape of the deal itself; consequently, deal makers should take account of all three negotiations in planning and executing their negotiation strategies.

Figure 9.1

Deal Making's Three Sets of Negotiations

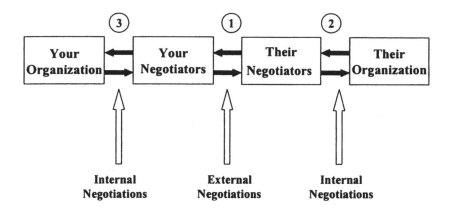

THE IMPORTANCE OF THE RIGHT APPROACH

The variety of bureaucracies engaged in global business is endless: Dutch multinational corporations, Korean *chaibols*, Arab bank consortia, Indian software companies, Chinese state corporations, German family-owned enterprises, and governmental agencies of every shape and size, to mention just a few. Each has it own particular bureaucratic culture, its own methods of making decisions, its own special interests and goals. Before plunging into a negotiation with any foreign organization, you therefore need to try to understand the bureaucracy with which you are dealing, to learn how it makes decisions, to determine if other organizations should be involved in the discussions, and to decide the most effective way to approach and penetrate the organizations with which you hope to make a deal. That all begins with deciding on the right approach.

For a tennis player, the right approach to the ball is essential to making the shot. For a diver, the right approach on the board can mean a graceful entry into the water as opposed to an embarrassing splash. So, too, the right approach to a foreign organization can mean the difference between making a deal or walking away with empty hands. Instead of merely plunging into deal making like an enthusiastic but uncoordinated ten-year-old leaping into a swimming pool, the wise negotiator seeks to answer a variety of questions and to consider a variety of options *before* actually moving to engage a foreign organization in negotiations.

Do You Have the Right One?

In even the smallest country, a deal maker confronts many organizations. In virtually all countries, government departments and agencies, even in the current era of privatization and deregulation, will in some way be involved in the negotiation if the deal is ever to become a reality. Global negotiators must therefore answer a fundamental question: With whom do I have to negotiate in order to make the deal? Is the company I have chosen the one that can deliver what I want?

The questions may appear elementary, even simplistic. But more than one executive has entered negotiations with a foreign company on the untested assumption that the foreign firm could deliver the goods when, in fact, it could not. For example, a few years ago representatives of a U.S. corporation spent several weeks discussing an agreement with a Korean firm to obtain the rights to manufacture a novelty electronic calculator made by that firm, only to discover that the firm had no authority to license that technology outside Asia. Another Korean firm held those rights.

In countries where bureaucratic dividing lines may be unclear, a foreign firm seeking to make a business transaction may have to conduct multiple negotiations in order to identify the organization or agency with which it should deal. During the early days of privatization in some countries, it was not clear to foreign investors whether they should negotiate directly with the state corporation to be privatized or with the ministry responsible for privatization. In order to hedge their bets and improve their chances of success, investors often engaged in dual-track negotiations, one with the firm to be privatized and the other with the privatization ministry.

Is One Enough?

Even if the company you choose to deal with can deliver what you want, you may have to negotiate with other organizations to make the deal effective. Sometimes you have to bring them to the table and make them part of the agreement. At other times, you are better off dealing with them separately, as American executives did when negotiating a long-term purchase of natural gas from Algeria. They had to be careful in choosing which Algerian ministries to talk with and had to avoid being caught in fights between the Ministry of Energy and the Ministry of Foreign Affairs. In the same vein, when the author was living in the Sudan in the 1970s, he observed that potential foreign investors seeking to develop agro-industrial projects, such as a sugar plantation and refinery, sometimes found themselves in the middle of a conflict between the Ministry of Agriculture and the Ministry of Industry as to which had control over the undertaking. Because of intense jealousy between the two ministries, investors preferred to deal with each one separately since that approach made each ministry feel that it had primary authority over agro-industrial projects.

The potential for bureaucratic conflict is almost always present, and the global negotiator should watch for it constantly. The risk is particularly high when one of the parties on the other side is a government agency or department. If you leave an important agency out of the negotiations, the omission may kill or at least delay a deal. Much time has to be spent in soothing hurt feelings, and the neglected organization invariably feels the need to be difficult to demonstrate its importance. It is not likely to come running to the negotiation table just because you belatedly extend an invitation.

Have You Found the Right Branch?

Often it is not enough to negotiate with the right organization; you must be sure that you are dealing with the right branch of that organization. If you are seeking an alliance with a subsidiary of a decentralized conglomerate, it may be pointless to try negotiations with group headquarters rather than with the subsidiary itself. On the other hand, in a highly centralized corporate structure, it may be essential to negotiate certain deals with the parent company.

In one Soviet-era case in which the author was involved, high-level officials from a ministry in the Soviet Union on a visit to the United States met with executives of an American organization and strongly urged them to begin negotiating a deal with two institutions under the ministry's control. Shortly after, the ministry sent a formal invitation to the Americans to visit Moscow, and the Soviet embassy in Washington also made encouraging noises. Convinced of the Soviet's readiness to deal, the Americans sent a team of executives to Moscow.

Ministry officials hosted a first meeting between the Americans and the heads of the two organizations under the ministry's control. The two organization heads were polite but cool. They found a "problem" or a "difficulty" for each proposal put forward by the Americans. At the end of the day, nothing had been accomplished. That evening, at a reception, one of the American executives and a Soviet organization head, discovering that they had both spent considerable time in France, dismissed their translator and spoke directly to each other in French. As the two warmed up to each other, the American asked why the negotiations were going nowhere. The Soviet negotiator responded that the proposed deal had been dreamed up by the ministry, that he had not been consulted until two days earlier, and that the ministry expected his already constrained budget to finance the deal—something he refused to do. When the American asked about the high-level ministry officials who had been so encouraging, the negotiator dismissed them with a wave of his hand. "Them? They are generals without armies. We've got the equipment and the people. It's our budget, not theirs. If you want to do business, you've got to deal directly with us." So much for the legendary monolithic bureaucracy of the Soviet Union!

LEARNING BUREAUCRACY

Only with careful study can you tell whether you have identified (1) the right organization, (2) the right branch of the organization, and (3) all the organizations necessary to make the deal. Rather than plunge into negotiations with the hope of learning as you go, invest time and resources on getting to know the organizations with which you hope to make a deal *before you go to the negotiating table.*

In addition to understanding its finances and technology, you should also seek to learn its organizational and bureaucratic nature. That investigation should analyze its structure to discover where various functions and tasks are performed in the hierarchy. It should also examine the nature of the organization's leadership, the way decisions are implemented internally, the background of its senior management, and its relationships with clients and supporting organizations.

Where will you find this information? Not all the information that you will need will be found in published documents. Few countries publish as much data about their companies as does the United States. Nonetheless, useful information can be obtained from local and regional publications, as well as from the company's own website and publications. To a large extent, you will find your most valuable source of information in persons who have dealt with the organization. Companies that have already negotiated deals with organizations can be extremely helpful. Multinational banks, the local U.S. embassy, resident representatives of international organizations, business consultants, lawyers, and local companies can give you varying but important perspectives on the bureaucratic culture of the organization you are planning to approach. Once you gather that information, try to answer some basic questions that will help you decide on making your approach.

- Will you be talking to the organization that will actually produce or deliver what you want?
- If not, what assurances do you need that this organization can get it for you?
- Within the country, what organizations and agencies will need to cooperate with the target organization to make the deal a success?
- What is the nature of current relationships between the target organization and those other organizations and agencies?
- If those relationships appear strong, what external factors might weaken them during the course of the deal you hope to negotiate?
- How does the target organization make decisions?

The answers to these questions are not only necessary to determine your approach to the target company or agency but will also help you in actually conducting negotiations. Few organizations are monolithic structures in which orders are given at the top and all units instantly obey. Within an organization, whether public or private, some branches have more independence than others and some executives have more power and influence than others. What this means, of course, is that within virtually all organizations, bureaucratic decisions and their implementation require internal negotiations.

Experienced deal makers seek to learn about the other side's internal negotiations and, to the extent possible, influence them in order to reach an agreement. For example, in shaping your proposals, you must not only try to estimate their impact on your counterparts across the table but on their internal organization as well. In many cases, the arguments and reasons you advance in the negotiation will be precisely the same arguments and reasons that your counterparts will advance to secure the approval of their bureaucracies to any tentative agreement they make with you. In a sense then, you should see one of your roles as helping your counterparts to sell the agreements they make with you.

To deal effectively with bureaucratic obstacles to negotiation, you must therefore not only understand the team across the table but must also get to know something about the other side's organization and how its bureaucracy operates. For instance, should you learn that the other side's organization is badly divided over what it wants out of the deal under consideration, that information may lead you to restructure your proposal or drop out of negotiations entirely in preference to wasting time and money in a fruitless attempt to persuade what you had assumed was a united organization.

The nature of the other side's bureaucracy may not only influence the negotiating process but the operation of the deal itself. For example, if you enter into a joint venture with a public sector partner in some countries, the bureaucrats representing your partner may be more interested in their power and prestige than in the profits to be made from the venture. In China, it is said that in a 50–50 joint venture the Chinese are always highly concerned to be treated and seen as equals with their foreign partners, but in 60–40 ventures, in which it is obvious they are minority partners, they are less concerned about visibly exercising control.

THE OTHER TEAM

In negotiating a deal, you initially do not engage the other side's entire organization, only its negotiating team. The members of that team are usually your primary link to the other organization until the deal is made. Similarly, the other organization's primary link to your company is its negotiating team. It is through its team that the other organization will gain information and form judgments about your company. Consequently, the negotiators on the other team control the information about the proposed deal that flows to their bureaucracy. This control over information can give the negotiators power to influence their bureaucracy's decisions.

Members of the other side's bureaucracy may have different views about you and the deal you are trying to put together. Some may favor it; others may be opposed. Without adequate information, neither potential supporters nor potential opponents can act effectively to influence their bureaucracy's decision-making process. Negotiators who want to make a deal often try to deny information about the negotiations to potential opponents within their own company. If you feel that negotiations are going well, it may therefore be a good idea to allow the other team to be the only conduit of information to its bureaucracy. Providing additional information to the wrong quarters may cause problems for both you and the other negotiating team. In social or other events that bring you into contact with members of the other side's bureaucracy, you should keep your comments to small talk and not inadvertently become another conduit for information, a conduit that undermines the position of the other company's negotiators. Even something like telling one of the other organization's bureaucrats that its negotiating team was being extremely cooperative might cause opponents of the deal to criticize its representatives for not being tough enough and for caving in to foreigners.

On the other hand, if negotiations are not going well because of the other team's intransigence or pursuit of its own interests, it may be useful to find a way to open another channel of communication to its bureaucracy. How and where you open that channel will depend on the nature of the deal, the two organizations involved, and the existing relationships between executives on both sides.

Sometimes negotiators try to build a second channel at the top; sometimes they do it at the bottom. In one joint venture negotiation between a French and an American company, the Americans believed that the French team was not accurately conveying the American proposals to its headquarters. While negotiations ground on unproductively, the chairman of the American company scheduled a vacation in Cannes, where the French company president had a summer home, and he asked a mutual friend to invite them to the same reception. The two men met and had a quiet chat about their business plans. Soon both companies changed the heads of their negotiating teams, and the two companies eventually struck a deal.

In another negotiation of a joint venture between an American company and a Japanese corporation to manufacture gauges and instrumentation equipment, the American company's bureaucracy was of two minds about the deal: The engineering people wanted it because it gave them excellent access to new technology, but the financial people were concerned about the deal's costs. Financial managers controlled the American negotiating team. Sensing that the financial managers were not giving the U.S. company a complete picture of the technological potential of the deal, the Japanese company, through one of its engineers who had worked for several years in the United States, began to provide that information to a former colleague who now worked as an engineer for the American company. The American engineer, in turn, passed the information along to his engineering colleagues. The American company president, who was himself an engineer, took over the negotiations and signed a contract with the Japanese firm.

The nature and size of the negotiating team may reflect something about the bureaucracy it represents. A large team across the table from you may indicate that the other side has a large number of organizational units that feel they need to be represented at the negotiation in order to have their own bureaucratic interests protected. A small team, on the other hand, may indicate a centralized bureaucratic structure in which individual units have relatively little autonomy.

What is the Composition of the Other Team?

The kind of team you face will vary from country to country, from company to company, and from deal to deal. Negotiating a joint venture in China will probably bring you into contact with a team of ten or more officials whose individual responsibilities are vague and whose leader is difficult to identify. In a poor African country, for the same type of transaction, the opposing team may consist of one or two government bureaucrats who have had no experience in global deal making, but whose leader is a deputy minister with considerable power within the bureaucracy.

The precise team that you meet deserves considerable study. In the very early stages of negotiation, you should try to obtain answers to some important questions about the other team. The following is one of the most basic.

How Much Clout Does the Team Have?

We often judge the effectiveness of negotiating agents in terms of their authority, their power to make legal commitments for the principals they represent. But of equal if not greater importance is the negotiators' *clout*—their power to persuade their organizations to accept the deals they have negotiated.

Are the persons on the other side of the table decision makers or merely mouthpieces for faceless managers somewhere in the company's bureaucracy? You may find it more advantageous to negotiate with an agent who has no authority but significant clout than with a negotiator who has specific moderate authority and no clout. In the former case, you have greater assurance that the other company will approve deals negotiated at the table. Moreover, negotiators with clout may be more open to exploring creative solutions to problems than negotiators without clout who feel they must hold to their instructions and refer back to the bureaucracy constantly to seek approval for the smallest changes.

Determining whether the other side has clout is not always easy. One must look to a variety of sources. First, try to gather information about the experience of other companies in negotiating with this particular organization. The seniority of the negotiators may also reveal their influence within their own bureaucracies, as does the degree of respect that their colleagues show them. Titles and positions in the organization may also give a clue to the clout they wield.

Even before negotiations start, you can begin learning these facts by asking in your preparatory communications with the other company the identity of the members of their negotiating team, their titles, and the units they serve within the organization. At the beginning of the negotiating session, when introductions are made, give each member of the other side your business card and indicate that you would like to have each of theirs. While this formality may seem elementary, negotiators sometimes fail to do it and thereby lose an excellent opportunity to identify all the members of the other team. As a way of securing additional information about the other team's members, you might begin the first negotiating session by briefly describing the background of each of your team's members. When you have finished, turn to the leader or spokesperson of the other team with an indication, subtle or otherwise, that you expect the same from them.

If the other team has clout, negotiations are likely to go more quickly than if it does not. Also, you need to be very careful about making concessions to a mere mouthpiece because of the risk that the negotiator's home office will decide that your concessions are not sufficient. In this case, your concessions have gained you nothing. Having revealed your position, you will be led to make more concessions. On the other hand, when you make reciprocal concessions to a person with clout, you have some confidence that the other side's headquarters will accept the deal you make.

Who Is in Charge?

A second important matter is to determine who is in charge of the other side's negotiating team. In many countries, knowing the leader is to know the person you have to persuade to make the deal. Knowing the leader also tells you whom to watch to gauge reactions to your proposals.

Team leadership may or may not be evident from the title and behavior of the negotiators. While the spokesperson for an American team is invariably its leader, the spokesperson for a Chinese team may have relatively little authority. The real leader of the team may merely sit quietly in the negotiating session and let others do the talking. In this type of situation, you need to look for clues. As an example, one experienced negotiator in China has his own rule of thumb that the person who pours the tea for others is the leader of the Chinese team. Often, if you get to know a junior member of the other team, that individual can give you an idea of the identity of the leader and the relative importance of the other members. In other countries, perquisites such as a car and driver, office furnishings, or a personal assistant to carry papers and run errands may signal leadership status.

Just as it is important to know the leader, it is also useful to understand what enabled that person to become head of the negotiating team. Leadership qualities vary from country to country. The appointment as leader of a negotiating team may have been influenced by numerous factors, some of which to outsiders may seem unrelated to a person's technical competence in the matter under discussion. State enterprises in countries with an autocratic political system sometimes choose team leaders because of their political ties and loyalty to the regime in power. In certain parts of Latin America, social connections count a great deal in achieving business leadership positions. Coming from a "good family" may be more important than having an MBA.

Other countries, Japan for one, may place greater emphasis on broad administrative experience in many departments of a company than on in-depth background in a single area such as finance or sales. Moreover, unlike most American business negotiators, the other team's leader, despite the appearance of age, may have had relatively few years of experience in business. In

France, for example, one sometimes finds high corporate executives who have joined a company after distinguished careers in government. As a result, they bring to business negotiations the attitudes, habits, and practices common to civil servants, in contrast to those of managers in the private sector.

These different bureaucratic backgrounds of negotiators from different countries can create obstacles in making deals. In one negotiation between an American company and a Japanese firm, an executive vice president for manufacturing, who had begun his career many years earlier as an engineer with the company, led the U.S. team. An experienced manager and a law graduate of the University of Tokyo, who had held a wide variety of positions with his firm, led the Japanese negotiators. The American, who insisted on directing all technical questions to the leader of the Japanese team, was dismayed when he did not receive detailed responses. He might more appropriately have addressed his comments to the Japanese team as a whole, which included two highly competent engineers. In another case, a U.S. team became frustrated with the leader of a French team, a graduate of France's prestigious National School of Administration and a former inspector in the Ministry of Finance, who conducted business dealings as though they were diplomatic negotiations. The Americans might have been more tolerant of the approach had they been aware of the French executive's background.

Will the Other Team Remain Stable?

Making a deal may stretch over months or even years and may require many meetings between the two teams. During that time, the negotiators become educated about their transaction, their companies, and one another. Their shared knowledge and personal ties can help the two sides reach an agreement. Continuity of negotiating team members is therefore important and desirable.

Too often, however, negotiators are faced with a problem when the members of the other team keep changing. They start discussions on a deal with one manager, set a date for a subsequent session, and return at the scheduled time only to find that another person has replaced the manager with whom they had made a promising start and that person knows virtually nothing about the proposed deal. This happened to a British multinational corporation that wanted to build a sugar refinery in the Sudan; it had to go through negotiations with five different Sudanese team leaders before it was able to sign a contract.

In most cases, the other team's instability is not a deliberate tactic to disconcert you but a response to the demands of its own bureaucracy. Many small countries have extremely limited numbers of trained managers and officials. Those who gain some experience or prove their ability are promoted rapidly and transferred to more pressing duties. Political shifts can also have a significant impact on both state corporations and private companies in many countries, with the result that experienced managers are fired, transferred, or led to seek better jobs elsewhere. For example, the lure of high paying jobs in Saudi Arabia and the Persian Gulf during the oil boom of the 1970s caused hundreds, perhaps thousands, of skilled negotiators throughout the Arab world to leave influential positions to work in the Arabian peninsula. Government policies to privatize state enterprises and encourage the private sector have also produced bureaucratic instability in many countries as talented, experienced officials in government and state organizations left their jobs, often in the middle of negotiating a deal, to earn a larger salary someplace else.

The result of these trends is that in negotiating a major deal over a significant period of time, you are liable to face a different set of representatives on the other side of the table each time you return for a session. This instability has various effects on deal making. On the one hand, it may give you an advantage because you have superior knowledge about the emerging transaction. That knowledge may allow you to dominate discussions when you are faced with a new team that understands little about the deal except what it has gleaned from the file. It may also allow you to reintroduce to the negotiations issues that you lost in earlier meetings.

On the other hand, a change in membership of the other team can slow the process as they spend time learning from you and others about the deal and your company, an exercise that you have already gone through at length with their predecessors. And, a new team may reopen issues that had been settled in your favor at earlier negotiating sessions.

How do you handle the problem of the other negotiating team's instability? Here are a few simple suggestions.

1. Recognize the possibility of instability at the outset. Try to estimate the likelihood of changes occurring and their possible impact on the progress of your deal. A change of a junior official in a ten-person Chinese negotiating team is not too significant. A change in a deputy minister leading a two-person team in Kenya may mean that negotiations have to start again from scratch.

2. Make a paper trail. Thoroughly document what happens at each negotiating session and send copies to the other side.

3. Make it a point to get to know every member, no matter how junior, of the other side's team. A junior member may later become a senior member. A junior member who continues on an otherwise unstable team may eventually become its official memory. If that person has confidence in you and your company, that member will communicate that fact to other persons who later join the team.

4. Always bring extra copies of all previous letters, memorandums, and drafts to every meeting. The former members of the other team may have taken their copies with them and the new members may be unfamiliar with or unable to find the file.

5. Have patience. Showing annoyance at the other team's instability yields nothing productive. It is not the fault of the new members, who are doing their best to cope. Your expression of irritation only makes you appear unreasonable and serves to undermine your credibility.

What Is Their Agenda?

Negotiators are supposed to act only in the best interests of their company; their sole agenda should be their company's agenda. Of course, executives at the table are also influenced by their personal goals and needs. As a result, negotiators invariably have two agendas, one organizational and the other personal. Unyielding rejection of your proposals may be the result of your counterparts' objective judgment that they are not in the best interests of their company. Or it may be prompted by a fear that opponents within their organizations will accuse them of caving in to foreigners. Or your counterparts may be afraid that the deal, while good for the company as a whole, will be bad for their department or for them personally. As a result, as you evaluate the other side's team, try to determine the personal agendas of each member, particularly of that of its leader.

This knowledge may help you make a deal, or it may tell you that further discussions are pointless. For instance, if you realize that members of the other team are concerned that the proposed deal may hurt their department or lower their status in the company, this knowledge may prompt you to re-structure the deal to reassure them. And should you learn, as one U.S. company did, that the negotiator on the other side had been through a series of failed negotiations and that another failure would cause him to lose face at home, this information may give you the confidence to stand firm behind your proposal and not offer concessions.

The extreme pursuit of a private agenda at the negotiating table can lead to bribery and corruption. The official or executive who wants a personal payment to make a deal with your company is, unfortunately, often found in many parts of the world. If you are confronted with such a demand, you must refuse. The U.S. Foreign Corrupt Practices Acts imposes severe penalties on U.S. companies and persons who pay bribes to foreign officials. Moreover, indulging in bribery has a corrosive effect on your own company and employees.

Precisely *how* you handle a demand for a bribe can be the difference between making a deal and watching the negotiations collapse. While the subject of bribery is complex and a full treatment is beyond the scope of this book, the following suggestions may be helpful.

1. Recognize that in many cultures gifts are an essential part of building relationships between persons and groups. Not all such gifts are necessarily corrupt or equivalent to bribes. To reject abruptly and moralistically any suggested request for a gift may be interpreted as a rejection of the relationship that the other side considers necessary for doing business with you. Try to set a policy as to the kind of gifts you are prepared to give that are consistent with the law and with your own company's business ethics.

2. If your company has prepared a code of business ethics or similar document, provide it to the other side as part of the introductory material you ordinarily furnish before or at the beginning of negotiations. When introducing your company to the other side, you might review that statement in some detail.

3. Explain that while you have great respect for your counterpart, you risk prosecution under the Foreign Corrupt Practices Act if you make corrupt payments. When a West African minister during a break in a negotiating session poetically told an American executive that the minister was "the first tree in the forest and needed water," the American replied in friendly but blunt terms: "If I pay you, I'll go to jail. And since you are my friend, I know you don't want that to happen."

4. You might deflect a demand for a bribe by making a donation or providing a service that benefits the country or the local community. Your company might build a playground for a school or a dispensary for a village, allowing the officials with whom you have been negotiating to take full credit for persuading you to make this gift. Your company might also sponsor free cultural events such as an art exhibit, a play, or a rock concert. If you choose to go this route, you must be absolutely sure that the payments you make do indeed go to finance these charitable and social activities, not to line the pockets of local officials.

5. If corruption is pervasive within an organization with which you are negotiating, you may have no other option than to walk away from the deal. If corruption is not pervasive, you might attempt to involve in the negotiation process persons or departments that are not corrupt with the hope that their presence will serve to control the behavior of negotiators seeking a bribe. In negotiating a long-term sales contract with a manufacturer's representative who is signaling the need for a payoff, you might stress your concerns over technology or quality control and ask that appropriate members of the company's engineering division participate in the discussions. Another approach is to build a channel of communication at another, you might hope, higher level, then use that channel to persuade the company of the benefits of dealing with you.

NEGOTIATING WITH YOURSELF

To close any deal, you not only have to persuade your counterparts across the table who in turn will have to sell the agreement to their organization, you also have to convince your own bureaucracy that the deal is in your company's best interests. So, in a real sense, successful global deal making requires you to negotiate with yourself. Indeed, you may find that you are conducting *several* negotiations within your own organization as you try to convince its various departments—for example, the general counsel's office, the finance division, and the product development unit—that they should sign off on the deal that you have been working hard on over the last six months. To conduct those negotiations effectively, you will need to employ some of the same strategies and tactics discussed earlier in this book. You will need to understand their individual bureaucratic interests. You will need to base your proposals on objective criteria that are understood and accepted by the various departments within your organization.

A particular problem is to make them understand the special context and challenges of operating globally. Because you have been conducting negotiations in Cairo or Kuala Lumpur or Lima, you have gained a special understanding of the culture, governmental policies, and bureaucratic traditions of those places and have shaped your deals accordingly. Those same cultures, policies, and traditions may seem a mystery at best or totally unreasonable at worst to your colleagues at home. They may therefore resist or oppose the deals you have made, and perhaps even accuse you of "going native." As a global negotiator, it is important to see one of your permanent functions as continually educating key individuals in your organization about the special needs and challenges of the countries in which you are negotiating. You may wage your educational campaign in a variety of ways. You might provide key individuals with regular reports on local conditions. You might keep them informed of similar deals being made in those countries by your competitors. You might arrange visits to your home offices for key counterparts from the field. And finally, you might seek to persuade your superiors to travel with you periodically to the countries in which you are working so that they might learn firsthand the nature of local conditions and meet face-to-face the local persons who are important to your company's business.

10

SPECIAL BARRIER NO. 5:
FOREIGN GOVERNMENTS AND LAWS

In this age of globalization, borders still count. Despite the growth of global markets and international communications, the world is still made up of sovereign, independent countries, each with its own legal and political system. At last count, there were over 200 of those systems, not to mention many national subdivisions—like states, provinces, or autonomous regions—with their own sets of laws and government agencies. What this means, of course, is that executives negotiating international business transactions must be prepared to confront and deal with a bewildering array of foreign governments and laws.

Companies have to cope with law and government all the time in their home markets. They structure mergers in intricate ways to take advantage of their country's tax codes. They hire lobbyists to convince legislators to vote for laws favoring their industries. They entertain politicians and officials in hopes of landing government contracts. So what is really different about international business?

The difference is that negotiating deals around the world forces executives and their companies to cope with *foreign* governments and *foreign* laws. The fact that these systems are foreign creates three major challenges that the global deal maker does not face at home. First, foreign political and legal systems are not only different, they are largely unknown to the company seeking to do business abroad. For the inexperienced business executive, foreign laws and politics are a mysterious black box whose inner workings are incomprehensible and often produce unpredictable results. Second, because the laws and government decisions of one country are equal to those of other

countries, a company in the international arena must deal with many different such systems, each equally authoritative. As a result, a company doing
business abroad always runs the risk that it may be squeezed between the law
of the country in which it is trying to make a deal and that of its home country, or of any other country in which it has interests. Finally, foreigners in any
legal and political system must always be concerned about unfair discrimination. Will they be subject to unfavorable decisions merely because they are
foreigners? Will the courts treat them impartially in cases involving nationals
of that country? Will they be able to compete on equal footing with local
businesses? Or will they be subject to the vagaries of "hometown justice"? To
cope with foreign laws and government effectively, global negotiators must
learn to deal with each of these problems.

THE BLACK BOX OF POLITICAL SYSTEMS

Like cultures, each of the world's legal and political systems is distinct and
different. The French government does not make policy the way the German
government does. The laws and court procedures of India are distinct from
those of England, even though India was part of the British Empire for many
years and today retains the English common law tradition. And an American
executive cannot assume that governments abroad work the way the U.S.
government does at home.

Raytheon, a major U.S. defense contractor, learned this lesson several
years ago when it tried to put together a consortium of European companies
to produce for NATO a weapons system that it had already built successfully
for the U.S. military. Knowing the capabilities of various European firms, it
selected those it thought would do the best job and began negotiating with
them. These conversations were abruptly cut short when individual NATO
governments told Raytheon that they, not the American manufacturer, would
choose the European participants in the consortium. Recognizing political
realities, Raytheon ended discussions with the firms it had selected, began
negotiations with those chosen by individual governments, and ultimately
put together a consortium that successfully produced the weapons system for
NATO.

A few years later, at the urging of the American government, Raytheon
sought to produce a version of the same weapons system for Japan. Having
learned what it thought was a useful lesson from its earlier experience in Eu-

rope, it opened talks directly with the Japanese government, expecting the government to indicate with which Japanese companies the U.S. manufacturer was to work. No such indication was forthcoming. Japanese officials studiously avoided suggesting appropriate Japanese partners. Finally, in a private conversation with a Raytheon senior executive, the Japanese deputy minister of defense made it clear that the U.S. manufacturer, not the Japanese government, should decide on the Japanese company to participate in producing the weapons system. The reason was that two very powerful Japanese electronics firms were the primary contenders for participation, and the Japanese government did not want to incur the wrath and political antagonism of either one by choosing the other.[1]

In both the European and Japanese cases, the black box of government processed a political decision, but each came out with a different result. In Europe, in matters of national defense and the allocation of contracts among companies in different countries, government was dominant over industry. In Japan, a single government, when faced with two competing electronics giants of its own, clearly chose not to dominate. With knowledge of the workings of their governments, local experts in both Europe and Japan probably could have predicted these results. Without that knowledge of the black box of government, an outsider, such as Raytheon, could not.

Government Interest

It is important in negotiating any deal to understand the positions of the governments of the countries concerned toward the deal. Although markets have replaced government plans in much of the world and pervasive government regulation has yielded to deregulation, few countries, even the most stoutly capitalist, are willing to let foreigners make any kind of business deal they wish. For example, in 2001, although the U.S. government had approved General Electric's acquisition of Honeywell, the European Union competition authorities rejected it and thereby scuttled the entire deal. Earlier, the same authorities responsible for competition in Europe had approved the AOL–Time Warner merger only on the condition that AOL–Time Warner agree to drop Time Warner's proposed acquisition of EMI, a large British music company, to prove to the European commission that it had no intention of dominating online music distribution. And of course, the U.S. itself has numerous special laws and regulations that foreign businesses must comply with if they want to do business in the country. So in making any deal, it is wise to make clear to your counterparts during negotiations and to include specifically in any contemplated contract that the agreement is conditioned on securing all appropriate governmental approvals.

If a government senses that a proposed deal is not in its interest, it will intervene in the negotiation process or, if a contract has already been signed, take action, as the European competition authorities did, to make its execution difficult if not impossible. Thus, the first and most basic question for a global deal maker is whether the governments of the countries concerned have an interest in the transaction and will permit it to happen.

A careful reading of economic policy statements, related legislation, and national development plans can reveal national priorities and how they may affect private business transactions. Conversations with government officials will indicate how legislation and policy are applied in practice, particularly to the transaction that you are contemplating. Sometimes a country does not seem to have well-defined priorities. Initially, a foreign executive may interpret the lack of stated priorities as a favorable openness by that country to all sorts of business deals and investment by foreign companies. That initial reading often proves wrong. In the economies of scarcity that exist in many countries, unstated priorities in relatively good times inevitably emerge in tough times when governments have to make hard decisions about allocating foreign exchange, energy, raw materials, or even space for freight in an antiquated railroad or port. The discovery of these priorities *after* a foreign company has invested time and money in a transaction can prove costly if a government eventually decides that the deal is not important. In planning any international deal, do not take the government's general statements of economic openness at face value. You need to make your own hard-headed analysis of how the government will react toward your deal in both good times and bad. One important way of getting this information is by talking to local business people with firsthand knowledge of how the government has reacted to economic hard times in the past.

Government at the Table

Once you have determined the nature of government interest in a transaction, you need to consider whether the government should be part of the deal. Should the government be at the negotiating table? The answer to this question depends on the kind of deal you are trying to make, the kind of economy you will have to operate in, and the kind of political system you will have to cope with.

A U.S. auto company faced this problem when it negotiated one of the first joint ventures to produce motor vehicles in China. To operate effectively, the new factory would need a supply of parts, but China at that time had no plants to manufacture them. After the deal was signed and the factory constructed, the U.S. company applied to the Chinese government for foreign exchange to import the parts. The government, which had not signed the joint-venture agreement, felt under no obligation to provide foreign exchange for this purpose. As a result, a period of intense conflict between the government and the U.S. automaker followed. Clearly this was a case in which the government should have been brought to the table at the time the joint venture was being arranged so that the partners could obtain a commitment from the government to provide foreign exchange for the parts.

Does the presence of a government at the table make a difference in negotiating a deal? As one experienced international lawyer told the author, "Negotiating with governments feels different." For one thing, deal making with state corporations and agencies involves a host of special considerations that do not usually arise in negotiations between purely private firms. Laws or regulations may limit the freedom of contract of governmental departments and state corporations. They may be required to use standard form contracts that include mandatory clauses on payment terms, insurance, and guarantees, to mention just a few. They may also be tied by rigid rules and regulations limiting the kind of transactions they may make. It is therefore important to understand the laws and regulations affecting the governmental department or state-owned corporation whose representatives are sitting on the other side of the table.

It is also important to understand how the state-owned corporation or agency relates to the government itself. For example, most state corporations are supervised by a particular government ministry. A national hotel corporation may be supervised by a ministry of tourism and the national airline may be controlled by a ministry of transport. Are the individual corporations free to contract on their own or must their agreements be approved by the relevant ministry to become effective? On the other hand, if the credit worthiness or reliability of a state corporation is uncertain, you may wish to make a government ministry a party to the deal or to secure its guarantee.

If you want the government to be a party to a deal, be sure that its representatives thoroughly understand your intent and that the contract clearly reflects that fact. In one case that became the subject of much litigation, an investment contract for the development of a resort near the Giza pyramids in Egypt stated that the parties to the deal were the state-owned General Organization for Tourism and Hotels and a foreign company. At the closing, the negotiators for the foreign company insisted that the Egyptian minister of tourism also sign the agreement on behalf of the Egyptian government. Eventually the minister did sign, adding the words "approved, agreed, and ratified." Three years later the Egyptian government summarily canceled the contract in the face of a public outcry against building a "Disneyland" so close to one of the world's most revered archeological sites. The foreign investor sued both the Egyptian government and the government hotel organization in arbitration. Throughout the litigation, which languished for fifteen years in various tribunals and courts, the Egyptian government argued that the minister had not signed as a party to the contract but only as the supervising authority over the hotel corporation: he was merely approving the hotel organization's participation in the deal. Eventually, the Egyptian government settled with the investors for $17.5 million. Had the original contract made it clear that the Egyptian government was a party to the contract, the government would not have had a basis for resisting the claim, and a settlement would probably have been reached much sooner.

Governments not only feel different from private parties in a negotiation, they *are* different. For one thing, governments enjoy sovereign immunity, which means that they cannot be sued in a court without their permission. In commercial deals, government departments or state corporations may also claim immunity from lawsuits, but the laws of many countries take the position that a foreign government may not claim immunity for "commercial acts." So, if an Indonesian government corporation refused to honor its contract to purchase rice, it could not avoid a lawsuit in the United States or in many other countries by claiming sovereign immunity since the purchase of rice is a commercial act. Some countries, however, do not recognize the commercial-act exception to the doctrine of sovereign immunity. To avoid any doubt on this question in negotiating a deal, a government or state agency should specifically agree in the contract to waive or give up its sovereign immunity should a dispute arise in connection with the transaction. Courts throughout the world recognize and enforce these explicit waivers.

Since government entities in business are usually subsidized by the state treasury and are controlled by government officials, their principal goal may not be the maximization of profit, as is the case with private firms, but the advancement of social and political ends. For example, if a manufacturing joint venture between a U.S. company and a foreign state-owned corporation were to be faced with a decline in demand for its products, the reaction of the U.S. partner might be to lay off workers. However, the state corporation, despite reduced profitability, might reject that solution to prevent an increase in unemployment in the country. In negotiating a transaction, it is important to recognize and discuss at the table divergences in goals, rather than be surprised by them later on.

By virtue of their governmental status, ministries and state corporations often behave differently in negotiations than private companies would. Officials of government agencies and corporations frequently bring to the negotiating table bureaucratic attitudes and approaches that introduce rigidity into the deal-making process. For one thing, they resist being considered as equals to the private business persons on the other side of the table. Indeed, any suggestion that the two sides are equals may be considered an insult. Government officials represent their country, and a sovereign country is not the equal of a private business firm, no matter how large. Any slight to a government official may be considered an affront to the dignity of the nation.

In one instance, an African minister asked for a meeting with the head of a foreign mining company that had operations in his country. The meeting took place in the office of the minister of mines and was attended by nine other government ministers. The minister of mines said that the government wanted to renegotiate its concession agreement with the company to obtain a greater share of mineral revenues, and he listed the points that needed to be discussed. In response, the chairman of the mining company reviewed each item, but at one point he flatly said, "We cannot entertain that." To emphasize his position, he struck the table with his hand. The minister immediately adjourned the meeting and refused to continue the discussions. While the response of the mining company chairman might have been acceptable in a negotiation between two private companies, it was inappropriate in a discussion with what amounted to nearly the entire government of a sovereign state. Instead of an outright rebuff, the chairman should have shown a willingness to listen and to discuss all of the government's concerns. Such flexibility, of course, does not mean that a company has to give in on every point. In this case, it took nearly nine months to get the negotiations going again, and during that time the government made operations difficult for the company. Ultimately, the two sides did renegotiate the mining concession.

The failure to give governmental negotiators proper respect and dignity may also have contributed to General Electric's inability to secure approval of its acquisition of Honeywell from the European competition authorities in 2001. According to some observers, GE executives approached their discussions with the Europeans arrogantly and showed little deference to European officials. In essence, they considered the approval a "done deal." At one point early in their discussions, Jack Welch, GE's legendary CEO, said to Mario Monti, the European commissioner for competition, as if he were conducting a private business negotiation, "Please call me Jack." Monti, a rather formal individual who was keenly aware that he was representing important public interests, replied: "I'll only call you Jack when this deal is over."[2]

If governments have special powers and privileges in business negotiations that private companies do not, they are also at times vulnerable to pressures that companies usually do not face. For one thing, governments depend on a wide variety of supporters—political parties, labor unions, military officers, the media, and civic organizations. Business negotiators may use these various pressure groups to influence a government's position in negotiations. When Chrysler negotiated to sell its money-losing operations in the United Kingdom to the British government, it reacted to the government's low initial offer by threatening to liquidate its factories one by one, beginning with a plant located in an important electoral district in Scotland. The British Labour government at the time had a very slim majority and depended on Scotland for support. In response to Chrysler's threat, Labour leaders in Scotland put strong pressure on the government to keep the plant open. In the end, the government increased its offer significantly and made a deal with Chrysler.[3]

LAW IN THE BLACK BOX

If a country's political system is a black box for a foreign negotiator, so is its legal system. One must be concerned about the impact of local law on the negotiating process as well as on the final deal that may emerge. The law in the

United States and other common-law countries has traditionally recognized a broad, unrestrained freedom of negotiation that permits a party to begin or end a negotiation at any time for any reason.[4] The reason for this rule is that limitations on the freedom to negotiate might discourage persons from making transactions in the first place. Other countries take a less liberal approach to permissible behavior in business negotiations. In those countries, once a party has begun negotiations, it has an obligation to negotiate in good faith. For example, under French law, beginning negotiations for a purpose other than trying to make a contract may be a civil wrong resulting in liability to pay compensation for any injury caused to the other side by this action. The precise content of the duty to negotiate in good faith varies from country to country. Generally, it includes obligations of good faith and honesty. In its specific application in a given country, the duty to negotiate in good faith may require the disclosure of pertinent information, an obligation not to negotiate with a third person until the negotiations in question have failed, and not to terminate negotiations without reasonable cause and without having persevered for a reasonable length of time.

The process of negotiation involves making proposals and counterproposals. It requires putting options on the table and then considering alternatives. The parties may agree on individual points on the often-unstated condition that other issues are settled. In this situation of flux, there is sometimes a danger that local law will find that the parties made a contract as to certain points before actually signing a formal document.

Suppose that a U.S. manufacturer, seeking to sell aircraft to a foreign government, is met with a demand that the company also buy a large quantity of canned hams, one of the country's important products. If the two sides work out satisfactory terms for the canned hams but cannot agree on a deal for the aircraft, the U. S. manufacturer does not want to find itself obligated to buy the hams because it clearly intended that the two contracts were to be linked. To prevent such a result, a negotiator at the outset should make it clear to the other side, preferably in writing, that no contract will come into existence unless and until the parties sign a formal document embodying their entire agreement. The letter of intent that normally sets the stage for detailed negotiations should include such a clause. This stipulation has the added benefit of facilitating a negotiating atmosphere in which the parties feel free to propose creative options without fear of being prematurely trapped into a contract. In a few cases when a party did not make this condition clear, the other side was able to argue that it had arrived at an oral contract in the negotiations and that the written contract was simply a formality, a memorandum for the record, not the essence of the contract itself.

Foreign law also directly affects the negotiation process when, in response to a proposal or request, the other side responds flatly, "Our law doesn't permit that." In a negotiation between two persons from the same country, that response would not go unquestioned or unchallenged. One side would at least ask the other for a citation of the chapter and article of the law in question. When a local manager or official makes that statement in a negotiation with a foreign executive, the foreigner often accepts this pronouncement without serious question. After all, the local official or manager must know what he is talking about—it's his law, isn't it? Then too, the foreign negotiator usually has no basis to challenge his counterpart on this point: He simply does not know the local law.

Unquestioning acceptance of the other side's pronouncements on its law is a mistake. The local official or manager is as likely to be wrong about a point of local law as a U.S. executive is about American law. The law in question may be capable of more than one interpretation, and a skilled lawyer may be able to develop an interpretation favoring your position. If the other side does raise a legal objection to a proposal, you should ask politely for a full explanation of the point and, if possible, a copy of the law or regulation it is relying on. Once you fully understand its legal position, seek independent legal advice to verify it.

Law Talk at the Table

Much of the talk at a negotiating table involves legal words, even if no lawyers are present. Words such as "property," "company," "contract," and "debt," to name just a few, are basic to a deal maker's vocabulary. They are legal concepts that have meaning for a business executive by reference to a particular legal system. Different legal systems may define these words in different ways.

An American executive encountering a foreign legal system for the first time should be aware that the differences between U.S. laws and foreign laws are often much more fundamental than the variations among state laws within the United States. The two sides in an international negotiation often come from two different legal traditions, so the legal concepts, categories, and techniques each uses in thinking about a business problem are totally dissimilar. For example, many countries in Europe influenced by the civil law tradition have a separate system of administrative courts with exclusive jurisdiction over suits brought by individuals against governmental departments and agencies. Over the years, these courts have developed a separate body of administrative law, which includes detailed rules governing administrative contracts. Legal systems influenced by the English common-law tradition have no real equivalent to these European institutions and concepts.

Persons coming from different legal traditions may approach the task of making contracts differently. For example, executives from certain European and Asian countries prefer a contract to be a statement of general principles to guide the parties' relationship. But American and English executives believe that an appropriate contract is a detailed set of rules drawn up to govern all future contingencies. Insistence on adhering to one approach over the other can sometimes create friction. The American or English executive considers the European or Asian generalist approach as creating future uncertainties and opportunities for the other side to wiggle out of the deal. Europeans may view the American or English detailed approach as evidence of mistrust and a fruitless attempt to control future events.

Beyond questions of vocabulary and technique, the very notion of law may have different meanings in different countries. In many parts of the world, unwritten tribal, religious, or ethnic customs have the force of law and are recognized and applied by governments and the courts. They therefore can have a direct impact on the deal you are trying to make.

In Africa, customary tribal law affects rights to land. Although the government may grant you a piece of land on which to build your factory, you may find that local groups hold grazing or agricultural rights that will interfere with your use. What should you do in this situation? You might ask the government to send in the military or the police to get rid of what you consider to be illegal squatters. If the government does send the troops, you will be faced with trying to run your operation while engaging in a continuing conflict with the local people. Their position will undoubtedly be that their rights to the land predate the very existence of the government and that the government had no right to give you something it does not own. In their eyes, the government acted illegally. The other option, probably the far wiser alternative, is to negotiate a settlement with the local tribe or group.

The best solution of all, of course, is to identify and solve the problem *before* you sign any deal. A multinational corporation negotiated to build an agro-industrial complex in the Sudan on 100,000 acres to be granted to it by the government. Before making the contract, it hired an anthropologist to determine precisely the rights that local tribes had in that land. As a result, the corporation identified specific groups and customary rights that might affect its future use of land, and it proceeded, with the government's help, to work out arrangements with the tribes so that traditional cattle-grazing rights would not interfere with the crops that the corporation intended to grow.

In order to penetrate the black box of foreign law and government, a foreign executive should follow a few basic rules:

1. Never assume that the other side's system works exactly the way yours does.
2. Do not take for granted that the words and concepts you use have exact equivalents for the other side in a negotiation, and do not assume that the words and concepts used by the other side fit precisely with yours.
3. To clarify legal meanings during discussions, seek to define terms and, above all, give examples of how they apply in practice.
4. For any sizable deal, obtain the help of an expert on local law.

Foreign Legal Advice

In most cases, you will need help to penetrate the black box of foreign law. That help will ordinarily take the form of a lawyer or legal adviser in the country where you are trying to do business. An initial task is for you or your lawyer to choose the right person.

The selection of a local lawyer is complicated by several factors. First, the organization and operation of the legal profession in a foreign country may be quite different from what exists at home. For example, in Indonesia, you would not approach a lawyer to organize a corporation, but would seek out a notary, a legally trained professional who bears no resemblance at all to the American notary public. In many countries, lawyers do not specialize in taxation. If you want tax advice, you consult an accountant. Generally, when you are looking for a local lawyer, you should specify the kinds of tasks you want to accomplish. It sometimes happens that the best person to accomplish that task in a given country is not a lawyer at all. For instance, the agro-industrial company mentioned above turned to an anthropologist, not a lawyer, to gain an understanding of the customary law affecting its proposed land grant in the Sudan.

A global negotiator's second problem in obtaining good legal advice in a foreign country is that while that country may have many lawyers, few of them may have the requisite skills to work on a big international deal. Most probably are not fluent in written and spoken English. More often than not, they have been trained for the courtroom, so they have little knowledge of and experience with financial, corporate, and business matters essential to an international transaction. As a result, except in large industrialized nations, only a handful of lawyers—perhaps as few as four or five in small developing nations—handle most foreign business in many countries.

Identifying candidates can be a time-consuming process. Directories of lawyers may help in this respect, but these publications are merely starting points since they do not provide qualitative evaluations of the lawyers listed. The best source of guidance is a person who knows a local lawyer and has had an opportunity to observe that lawyer's work. Foreign companies already doing business in a country can be of great help, and the consular section of your embassy in the country may keep a list of local lawyers who serve major foreign clients. Local business persons, banks, foreign lawyers in neighboring countries and international law firms with foreign offices may also provide you with useful information.

Do not select a local legal adviser without a personal interview. It is best to interview three or four candidates before making a final decision. During the interview, you want not only to determine the candidate's training, experience, English language ability, and scale of fees but also to learn about the candidate's relationships with the host government, knowledge of the bureaucracy, and any possible conflicts of interest. In countries where a relatively few lawyers handle virtually all foreign business, possibilities for conflicts of interest are rife, and local lawyers sometimes are not sufficiently sensitive to that issue.

You should ordinarily interview a candidate in his or her office during business hours rather than at a hotel or restaurant, as is sometimes done. In this way, you can come to know the candidate's organization, support services, and facilities. It often happens that a brilliant and polished foreign lawyer does not have the secretarial support, library, or legal associates necessary to meet the needs of a large foreign company. Because foreign clients tend to give their business to a few local lawyers, the lawyers may take on a work load that they cannot handle expeditiously, especially in countries in which lawyers usually practice individually rather than in firms.

THE SQUEEZE

The challenge posed by foreign laws and governments to an international company is not only to understand them but also to operate simultaneously within two or more legal and political systems at the same time. By engaging in global business, a company enters into an arena of intense legal and political pluralism. An export sale, a direct foreign investment, or a technology transfer brings you into contact with the laws and political authority of another country, but at the same time you remain subject to the laws and governmental authority of your own country. Legal and political pluralism means that a transaction may be taxed by two or more governments, a contract may be subject to two or more legal systems, and a dispute may be decided by courts in two different countries.

An extreme example of the kind of legal and political pluralism that a business deal may face was the construction of the Soviet trans-Siberian pipeline in the early 1980s. American companies and their European subsidiaries were squeezed between the law and political power of the United States and the law and political power of our European allies. In that case, European subsidiaries of U S. corporations arranged contracts to supply equipment and technology to a pipeline that the Soviets were building to carry natural gas from Siberia to Europe. The U.S. government at the time considered the pipeline a security threat, so it ordered the European subsidiaries of American companies not to participate. Attracted by the economic benefits of the project, the European governments demanded that those subsidiaries respect their supply contracts. Only diplomacy at the highest level between the United States and European countries finally solved the problem.[5]

Although the Soviet pipeline case attracted considerable attention, it is certainly not a unique example of legal and political pluralism in international business. As businesses develop a global reach and pursue global strategies, they encounter and must deal with legal and political pluralism constantly. For example, as the case mentioned earlier of General Electric's failed acquisition of Honeywell illustrates, American companies acquiring European firms and European firms acquiring American companies sometimes find themselves squeezed between the differing policies of U.S. and European Union competition authorities, a squeeze that may lead to abandoning the proposed merger.

Different laws give the parties different expectations. Under U.S. law, a failing corporation can seek the protection of a bankruptcy court. Instead of being liquidated, it is given an opportunity to reorganize and continue doing business. In other countries, corporate reorganization in bankruptcy does not exist. A failing company either makes a deal with its creditors or it liquidates. Therefore, creditors in the United States and those in other countries where corporate reorganization does not exist have two different sets of expectations. If they want to do business in each other's country, they must adjust those expectations to the prevailing laws.

The practice of global deal making is always a matter of complying with or avoiding a multiplicity of different countries' laws, regulations, and policies, of weaving between overlapping legislation and political decisions made by several governments. The problem of the legal and political squeeze is always on the minds of international negotiators.

Approaches to Pluralism

Deal makers use a variety of techniques to cope with legal pluralism. One approach is to specify in detail the rules that are to govern their agreement in every possible situation imaginable by the negotiators. Transaction costs and the inherent inability of negotiators to foretell the future place obvious limits on the utility of this approach.

A second method, often used in combination with the first, is for the negotiators to agree on one set of laws to govern the transaction. In practice, virtually all international transactions of any significance contain a clause stating that the law of a particular country, to the exclusion of all other laws, will apply to the transaction and to any disputes that may arise between the parties. The negotiators' purpose here is to assure that their agreement will be applied and interpreted in a predictable manner consistent with their original intent. Making no choice of a governing law increases uncertainty. Without any specific choice of law to govern the contract, a court will usually apply the law of the country judged to have the "most significant relation-ship" to the deal, a concept that may lead to a variety of results. A choice of law clause affects only the application and interpretation of the contract. It has no effect against regulations by governments, as in the Soviet pipeline case, made in the public interest, nor does it have effect against persons or companies who are not parties to the contract.

Beyond mere predictability, a particular law may be chosen because it is favorable to one of the parties or is highly developed in the matter concerned by the transaction. Or the choice may be motivated by a desire to avoid a country whose law is unclear or undeveloped. It is for these reasons that vir-tually all international loans to developing countries by commercial banks opt for the application of the law of the bank's home country rather than the law of the borrower.

The selection of a particular law to govern a contract may occasionally lead to conflict in certain negotiations. For example, a government, for rea-sons of sovereignty and national pride, is often reluctant to accept a law other than its own to govern a transaction in which it is a party. On the other hand, foreign corporations are often unwilling to accept that government's law to govern the contract because the government has the power to change the law later on and therefore change the contract unilaterally. In such cases, the par-ties may agree to accept "general principles of law common to international business" or "general principles of international law" as the basic rules to govern the contract in any future disputes. The parties usually couple this ap-proach with the technique of writing as detailed and comprehensive a con-tract as possible in hopes of minimizing the need to refer to any law to interpret the contract during the life of the deal.

Yet another method of coping with legal pluralism is for the parties to agree on a particular court, to the exclusion of any other court, to judge any disputes that may arise between them in the future. Sometimes, as in the case of international loan agreements, they may agree on the court of a particular place, such as the state of New York. In most international transactions, the parties agree to submit future disputes to international commercial arbitra-tion, discussed in chapter 4.

A final technique for avoiding the squeeze is to organize and manage the transaction so that certain parts of it have contact with countries whose laws and policies are favorable, while scrupulously avoiding countries whose laws and policies are unfavorable. To illustrate, some territories, like Bermuda and the Channel Islands, impose tax only on income earned within their borders while others, like the United States, tax the income of their companies on a worldwide basis. The first type may be a good place to establish a corporation that will receive income from foreign investments or licensing arrangements. Some U.S. companies, for example, have created special entities in Bermuda through which they make investments in order to protect income from those investments from both U.S. and Bermuda taxation.

HOMETOWN JUSTICE

For global negotiators, the final and perhaps ultimate challenge posed by the law and politics of another country is that, at some point, their company may be unfairly treated because it is foreign. This is the problem of hometown justice that negotiators may face either before or after the deal is made. The defensive tactics that the deal maker may use differ in each case.

Government as Ghost Negotiator

Before a deal is made, discriminatory government action may take many forms. Whatever form it takes, its ultimate purpose is to prevent the making of a contract or to extract a better deal than usual for the government itself or for local companies. A government may order state-owned corporations, or even local private companies, not to negotiate with you. It may have laws and regulations requiring governmental review of all contracts with foreigners or even specifying terms to be included in those contracts. For example, rather than allow companies to work out foreign investment through the give-and-take of negotiations and market forces, local law may specify performance requirements for a project, such as stipulating a proportion of local materials to be used in manufacturing or a minimum amount of products to be exported. Government regulations may also fix a ceiling on the amount of royalty payments or licensing fees. Thus, the government, through the legal and regulatory system it controls, may be an unseen ghost negotiator at the table. For executives accustomed to a free-market economy, this kind of system tilts unfairly in favor of local companies. But for the government, the system is merely a way to strengthen the inferior bargaining power of local business interests.

Faced with these challenges before a deal has even been set, what should a foreign executive do? The first task is to learn the facts. If discriminatory action has been taken because of a law or regulation, obtain a copy of that legislation and analyze it carefully. If a government has directed a local firm not to do business with you, that direction is not likely to be a matter of public record. You will have to use indirect methods to learn of the order and why it was given. The government may have taken that action because of its relations with your home country, its relations with the country of one of your competitors, or for many other reasons. Once you understand the reason, you may be able to devise a deal that meets the government's interests and at the same time accomplishes what you want.

If you are able to establish that a foreign government is discriminating against you, one course of action is to seek the help of your home government. The country concerned may have made treaties and agreements with your home country to protect its companies against discrimination and to guarantee them "most favored nation treatment," which means that the host country may not treat companies from your home country any worse than it treats companies from other countries. Treaties may also guarantee companies "national treatment," which means that the host government is to give companies from your home country the same level of treatment that it grants its local companies. These treaties and agreements will give your government a strong basis to press the host government to grant you the same freedom to negotiate deals as other companies. Thus, faced with an obstructionist foreign government behind the scenes, you might adopt a strategy of bringing your government into your negotiations.

Whether your government will work actively on your behalf depends on a variety of factors, including the state of its relations with the host country, the existence of similar cases, and the views and background of the ambassador. Your government will look at your problem not as a separate and distinct concern but as one element in the entire fabric of its relations with the host country. If it is in the process of seeking major concessions, such as the right to build a naval base in the country, it may not press your concerns actively with the local government. If, on the other hand, several other companies from your home country have complained of discriminatory treatment, your embassy will probably take more vigorous action.

When the Party Is Over

Deals are done with high hopes and champagne toasts. Having signed a contract, the parties to the transaction look to the future with great expectations.

Yet, there is always the risk that some time after you sign the documents and begin the project the local government will intervene to change the deal, usually in its favor. The plant you have built is nationalized. The long-term supply contract you are relying on is canceled. The profits you have made in local currency are no longer convertible into dollars. Your managers and technicians are thrown out of the country. And, for some strange reason, you can't get a visa to visit the country to inspect operations. These are the political risks of a global deal.

In making any deal, a negotiator must identify the political risks and then structure the transaction to minimize them. As part of a foreign investment project, an investor might obtain political risk insurance against expropriation, inconvertibility of local currency, or physical damage due to war, revolution, or civil disturbance. It might also obtain guarantees from the country's central bank to convert sufficient local currency into dollars to allow the project to pay its debts and distribute profits to its owners. In certain cases, the local government may be willing to enter into a "stabilization agreement," by which it agrees that future laws and regulations will not have the effect of placing a more onerous burden on the investor than they do at the time the agreement is signed. An investor might also organize its operation so that its foreign subsidiary in the host country is dependent on the parent for components, technology, and other production needs. The host government might then hesitate to expropriate or intervene lest the parent company stop supplying these essentials and thereby make the subsidiary valueless.

Once the deal is signed, a foreign company should also take care to maintain good relations with the host government and to foster a positive public image in the country. One useful approach is to give the project as much of a local identity as possible through the use of local managers and partners and the training of host country nationals to assume skilled positions. As one experienced international executive advised the author, "Nationalize yourself before they nationalize you." In a real sense, protection of a signed deal from political risks is a continuing process of negotiation between you and the host government. The aim of that negotiation is to convince the government that its goals and yours remain compatible. Troubles develop when the government comes to believe that your goals and theirs have diverged.

These and other techniques help to lower the political risks of international deals, but they are not foolproof. In the end, a sovereign state has the power to take property, cancel contracts, and stop business activity. If these actions cost you money, the real issue is whether you simply have to bear the cost or whether the host government will be forced to compensate you. A question of equal importance is who will make that decision. To leave the matter to the courts of the country concerned is to raise the specter of home-town justice, of biased decisions that are made to protect national interests rather than to arrive at a fair and legal result. What is needed is a neutral decision maker outside the control or influence of the local government or business interests. As we saw in chapter 4, one way to achieve a satisfactory result is for the parties to a deal to agree to submit any future disputes between them to a neutral decision maker. This, in fact, is what is done in the vast majority of international transactions that provide for international arbitration to settle disputes that may arise.

11

SPECIAL BARRIER NO. 6: MOVING MONEY

When you make a business deal in the United States, you expect to pay or to be paid in dollars. So in a negotiation for the long-term supply contract between Houston Glue and Dallas Adhesive, both sides will want the medium of payment to be U.S. dollars. When you make a deal outside the United States, you have many more payment options. You can make a deal in Japanese yen, British pounds, Argentinean pesos, Saudi riyals, European euros, U.S. dollars, or any of the globe's many other currencies. In negotiating the deal between Houston Glue and Budapest Adhesive, the two sides may have to bargain over the issue of whether payment will be made in Hungarian forints, U.S. dollars, or some other currency, since the choice of a particular currency may have distinct advantages for one party and definite risks for the other.

Unlike purely domestic deals, international transactions take place in an arena of many different monetary systems and currencies. There is no single global money for making payment. The existence of so many currencies creates another potential barrier in international business negotiations. In making any deal, the parties at the table not only have to decide the price and the payment date, but they also must agree on which currency to make payment in. The decision on a specific currency can have far-reaching implications for the management and profitability of the deal that they are negotiating.

For the global dealmaker, so many different monetary systems create the problem of *moving money*, a problem that has two dimensions. First, the relative values of the world's currencies are constantly changing—fluctuating in relation to one another. That problem creates special risks and challenges in structuring an international business deal. Second, many countries' currencies are not freely convertible into other currencies; consequently, the deal maker who is to be paid in currencies of limited convertibility must constantly be concerned about ways to move the value stored in them into more usable funds. This chapter considers both of these problems of moving money. It will determine how they affect negotiations and what solutions are available to handle them.

MOVABLE MONEY

The value of money, like any other commodity, responds to the forces of supply and demand. Supply and demand for a country's currency depend on many factors, including that country's inflation rate, prevailing interest rates, economic growth, political stability, and the actions of its monetary authorities. Most emerging-market countries seek to manage their foreign exchange rates so that the value of their currency is not strictly tied to the forces of supply and demand. The central banks in such countries allow their currencies' values to fluctuate within a narrow band of value linked or "pegged" to a leading international currency like the U. S. dollar. If the value of the local currency in relation to that international currency falls below the designated band, the central bank buys its currency using foreign exchange, thereby increasing the value of its local currency. If the value moves above the band, the central bank sells its currency, thereby lowering its value. If a country encounters significant economic difficulties and the central bank depletes its store of foreign exchange needed to support the local currency, it will allow the local currency to find a new level, thus effecting a currency devaluation.

The Foreign Exchange Risk

For a negotiator, the inclusion of a foreign currency in a deal creates a risk. In particular, it creates a risk for the company that has to pay or be paid in a currency other than the one in which it keeps its books. Between the time the agreement is signed and the time payment is received, the value of the foreign currency in relation to that company's national or desired currency may decrease so that the company ultimately receives, after conversion, less of its own currency than it expected. Similarly, if a company has to pay in foreign currency, the value of that currency may increase so that the paying company has to spend more of its own money than it intended in order to buy the foreign currency necessary to make payment under its contract.

A foreign exchange risk is always present for one of the parties in an international business transaction. The longer the period of the deal, the greater the risk. In 1980, a small U.S. company found a Japanese manufacturer whose price for an important type of adhesive was far cheaper than that of any manufacturer in the United States. To lock in this low-cost supply, the U.S. company signed a long-term purchase agreement with the Japanese company. In the negotiations, the Japanese company insisted on payment in Japanese yen since all its manufacturing costs were payable in yen. The American company agreed and therefore assumed the risks of future foreign exchange fluctuations.

Having reduced its raw material costs significantly, the U.S. company began making substantial profits with its line of adhesives. At the time the deal was signed, the exchange rate between the Japanese yen and the U.S. dollar was 185 yen to $1. Later, the U.S. company made even more money as the exchange rate fell to over 250 yen to $1, thus reducing its cost of raw materials even further. In 1985, however, the relation between the yen and the dollar began to change dramatically, and by 1988 the value of the yen had increased to 140 to $1. The result was that the U.S. manufacturer began to lose money. Although the price in yen remained constant during this contract period, the total dollars that the U.S. company needed to buy those yen increased greatly. Facing competition from other American companies, it could not raise the selling price of its products to offset the rising yen costs of adhesives. As a result, a deal that was good in 1980 turned out to be a loser by 1988.

Had the two companies struck a deal for payment in dollars, the Japanese company would have been the one to assume the exchange risk, and the U S. company would have still made a profit. Under a dollar contract, the Japanese company would have received fewer yen for each dollar of payment it received. It would then have had the problem of figuring out how to meet the demands of its workers, suppliers, and bankers, all of whom expected to be paid in yen fixed by their own contracts with the Japanese manufacturer.

Because the foreign exchange risk is present in any international deal, the challenge for negotiators is to find a way to cope with it. Various techniques exist, but as a negotiator you have basically three choices: (1) give the risk to the other side; (2) accept the risk but protect yourself; or (3) share the risk.

Give the Risk to the Other Side.   To avoid the foreign exchange risk, a deal maker can simply insist on being paid or on making payment in the deal maker's home currency. This simple maneuver throws the foreign exchange risk to the other side. The American company mentioned above might have tried this approach in its negotiation with the Japanese adhesive manufacturer. In pursuing this strategy, you need to establish an objective principle that justifies allocating the foreign exchange risk to the other side. One useful principle is that the side that is better able to bear the foreign exchange risk should be the one to bear it. Thus, if you have substantial costs in a specific currency, you can argue that you should pay or be paid in that currency, and that the other side should bear the foreign exchange risk.

A variation on the technique of allocating the foreign exchange risk to the other side is to accept to pay or be paid in the other side's currency but stipulate that the amount of payment will be linked to the prevailing exchange rate between the two currencies. Enron used this approach in structuring the payments to its Indian subsidiary, the Dabhol Power Company, from the Maharashtra State Electricity Board, a public utility, for electricity that it bought from the subsidiary under a twenty-year power purchase agreement negotiated in the mid-1990s. At that time, 32 Indian rupees equaled one dollar on the foreign exchange markets.

The subsidiary had been financed by substantial loans in dollars from international financial institutions. It therefore had large, fixed dollar costs that it had to pay regularly so it needed to avoid the foreign exchange risks inherent in being paid in India rupees. At the same time, all of the revenue earned by the state of Maharashtra State Electricity Board from the resale of electricity purchased from the Dabhol Power Company was in Indian rupees, not dollars. The power purchase agreement negotiated by Enron with the utility provided that important components under a complex monthly pricing formula would be calculated in "real rupees," that is, the number of rupees required to purchase one thirty-second of a U.S. dollar at the prevailing market rate of exchange on the date when the pricing calculation was made. As a result, the price paid in rupees fluctuated with dollar-rupee exchange rate. As the rupee fell against the dollar, the price that the Maharashtra State Electricity Board paid in rupees for electricity rose. Through this device, although Enron was paid in rupees, the Board bore the foreign exchange risk.[1]

Many times, however, attempts to allocate the foreign exchange risk to the other side fail, either because that party to the transaction has the bargaining power to resist accepting it or because the transaction does not allow for it. Say an American and a Japanese company were negotiating a joint venture to establish a plant in Japan. The American company, by the very nature of the deal, assumes a foreign exchange risk since its assets in Japan will be valued in yen and any profits it makes will be earned in yen.

Accept the Risk, but Protect Yourself. A second technique of dealing with foreign exchange risk is to accept the risk, but take special measures to protect yourself against adverse fluctuations in exchange rates. One of the simplest applications of this approach is for the party bearing the risk to estimate the "cost" of foreign exchange fluctuation before completion of the payment and build that cost into the transaction. A seller of goods who agrees to be paid in a foreign currency might increase the price of the goods to take account of possible adverse changes in exchange rates between the time the contract is signed and the time payment is made. In effect, as a result of negotiations, the seller is being paid for bearing the exchange risk. This device does not eliminate the exchange risk because the actual change in the exchange rate may be greater than what the seller anticipated.

One of the most common approaches to protecting against the exchange risk in international trade transactions is to shift the risk to a third party or institution not directly involved in the deal that you are trying to put together. A variety of insurance-type techniques exist to achieve this goal. These devices are often referred to as "hedges."

One method of hedging is for the person bearing the exchange risk to make a contract to purchase the required amount of a specific foreign currency at a specific price and date in the "forward foreign exchange market." For example, suppose that on January 1, a U S. manufacturer has agreed to sell a shipment of computer printers to a London distributor for 100,000 pounds sterling to be paid on June 1. At the time it signed the contract, 100,000 pounds would yield the U.S. manufacturer $150,000. To protect itself against currency losses, the U.S. manufacturer, for a price, might enter into a contract in the forward foreign exchange market for the delivery of a specified dollar amount in exchange for 100,000 pounds sterling on June 1. This transaction enables the manufacturer to know exactly the number of dollars that it will receive on June 1, something which it cannot know without this hedging device. The transaction is self-liquidating. On June 1, when the manufacturer receives payment of 100,000 pounds, it will deliver them under its forward contract to receive the specified dollar amount for which it had contracted.

Another method to hedge against currency risks in trade transactions is to secure an option to buy or sell foreign currency for a fixed price in local currency during a specified period in the future. Businesses with significant international operations may use still other techniques such as establishing foreign currency accounts or purchasing foreign currency bonds. They may also use the money markets to hedge against foreign exchange risks. For example, a Japanese exporter who is to be paid in six months' time in euros might borrow the equivalent amount in euros from a French bank at the time of signing the contract, then immediately convert the loan proceeds into yen and invest them in a yen time deposit. When it receives payment in euros from its customers, it will use those funds to pay off its loan from the French bank. All of these techniques will protect you from adverse changes in currency rates, but they also have costs in the form of transaction fees and the diversion of working capital from more profitable uses.

A company with substantial international business can manage its foreign exchange risks by arranging offsetting transactions—sometimes called exposure netting—in which the risk of a loss in one transaction would be counterbalanced by the gain in another. In this way, an American company's risk stemming from an obligation to pay yen in the future might be offset by a debt in yen owed to that company by another firm and payable on the same future date.[2]

All hedging techniques have associated transaction costs. Sound financial advice by experts in the field is necessary to use them effectively. The purpose of this chapter is not to provide detailed instruction on their use, but merely to signal that a foreign exchange risk in global deals does exist and that the global negotiators should seek advice on protecting their companies against it.

Share the Risk.   It is also possible for the parties to agree on a formula that allows both of them to share the foreign exchange risk, although not necessarily equally. One technique is to negotiate an agreement that allows a portion of the payment to be made in one side's currency and another portion to be paid in the other side's currency. In a contract for the sale of Canadian iron ore with a domestic price of 110 Canadian dollars per metric ton by a Canadian mining company to a Japanese firm, the contract might provide that the price per metric ton will be 50 Canadian dollars plus 5,000 Japanese yen. Another method is to stipulate that the importer is to pay in the other side's currency as long as the exchange rate stays within a specified range. If it exceeds the specified range, the parties will share the change in costs according to an agreed-upon formula.

Parties to long-term transactions sometimes seek to deal with the foreign exchange risk by providing for payment in an artificial unit of account, such as the Special Drawing Right (SDR), made up of a basket of different currencies. The reason for using these units of account, rather than specific currencies, is that they are likely to maintain value and experience relatively little fluctuation since the constituent currencies are often inversely correlated. In case of a major fluctuation, the increases in the value of one currency are offset by corresponding decreases in the values of other currencies. However, the value of your company's desired single currency could still fluctuate unfavorably in relation to the SDR or other chosen unit of account.

These methods of sharing the exchange risks are complicated to negotiate and structure, involve transaction costs, and do not really eliminate foreign exchange risks. One final way to avoid seriously injuring one party in a long-term transaction is to provide that if the applicable exchange rate rises or falls by a certain percentage, the parties to the deal will renegotiate payment provisions. Chapter 16 discusses the challenges of renegotiation.

IMMOVABLE MONEY

So far we have been talking about freely convertible currencies, foreign exchange, in the language of international deal makers. However, many of the world's currencies are not freely convertible. These monies are in varying respects immovable.

For political and economic reasons, many governments use their powers to set exchange rates for their currencies and to restrict access to the foreign exchange market. Through a complex system of regulations known as exchange controls, governments regulate the entry to, possession in, and exit from their territories of both foreign and local currencies. Some countries have currencies that are partially convertible, that is they are convertible for certain types of transactions, such as trade, but not for others, such as investment.

A common feature of many exchange control systems is to make it a crime for any resident or company in the country to hold foreign exchange.

A subsidiary located in that country is therefore required to convert dollar or yen proceeds from its foreign sales immediately into local currency and deposit them with a bank in that country. In order to obtain dollars, euros, or yen to purchase foreign supplies, to pay foreign loans, or to repatriate dividends, the subsidiary has to apply to the country's central bank for a foreign exchange allotment. If the central bank decides that the request was justified, it will convert the local currency to dollars at a fixed rate of exchange. If not, the subsidiary will have to find another way to finance its external obligations.

As a result of exchange control and government regulations, a company's ability to make foreign payments depends in many cases on the host country's willingness to make foreign exchange available. In such countries a company's bank account may be stuffed with its profits in local currency, but the business may fail unless the government is willing to let the company move its money into another, more readily usable currency. The great challenge for the international deal maker working in exchange control countries is to find mechanisms to assure adequate freely convertible currency, more simply called "hard currency." If it is true, as former U. S. House of Representatives Speaker Thomas ("Tip") O'Neill remarked, that "money is the mother's milk of politics," it is equally true that foreign exchange is the mother's milk of global business.

Moving the Immovable

How should deal makers go about trying to move immovable money? First, you have to recognize the precise dimensions of the problem you are facing. This means that you have to understand the local exchange control system and how it applies to your deal. To do that, you must not only read the regulations, you must also talk to people who have had experience with them. At the same time, you must recognize that exchange control regulations are not static. A government can change them rapidly, sometimes retroactively. So a transaction that would get you a foreign exchange allotment from the central bank one day may be prohibited the next.

Second, the structure of a transaction may have an effect on your ability to secure foreign exchange. For example, royalty payments on technology agreements may have a higher priority at the central bank than dividend payments. It may therefore be prudent to structure your relationship with a company in that country as a technology transfer rather than an equity joint venture. If you have established an equity joint venture, it may be advantageous for your company to make a formal technology transfer agreement with substantial royalty payments with the venture. In this way, you will withdraw a portion of your profits from the venture as royalty payments rather than as dividends. Some parent companies inflate prices on the sale of raw materials and components to their foreign subsidiaries as a way to repatriate profits and evade exchange controls limiting the payment of dividends.

A third technique is to negotiate special exemptions and privileges with a country's monetary authorities. For example, you might secure a guarantee from the central bank that it will make hard currency available for certain types of payments to be made by the project. The willingness of the bank to make this kind of guarantee will depend on the project's importance to the local economy. If the project will have earnings in foreign currency—for example, from export sales—you might secure permission to hold these earnings offshore in a foreign exchange bank account rather than depositing them with a local bank in local currency.

A fourth approach is to seek a guarantee or assurance of hard currency from a sound financial institution outside the country in question. On a foreign investment project, you might obtain political risk insurance, from either public or private sources, against the inconvertibility of project revenues. And in connection with a long-term commodity purchase agreement, you might require the other side to obtain a letter of credit confirmed by a bank in New York, Paris, or London. A variation on this approach is to link transactions. For example, Mexicana de Cobre, S. A. (Mexcobre), a Mexican copper producer, negotiated to obtain a $210 million three-year loan from a syndicate of international banks led by Banque Paribas at an attractive interest rate. Although Mexcobre was a profitable company, the banks were concerned about the risk of governmental controls that might prevent payment of principal and interest, which amounted to $8 million a month for thirty-six months. To deal with this problem, Mexcobre entered into a long-term copper sales contract with SOGEM, a European copper buyer, whereby SOGEM would make its monthly payments for the copper into Mexcobre's escrow account with the Banque Paribas branch in New York. Banque Paribas would automatically deduct Mexcobre's payments on the loan each month from the account.[3]

Taking It Out In Trade

Finally, if all else fails in your efforts to avoid the risk of exchange controls, you might turn to an age-old practice that businesses have used when dealing with organizations that are strapped for cash: take it out in trade.

Countries with limited foreign exchange often seek to obtain the goods and services they need through bartering arrangements know as countertrade. Countertrade takes many forms and is called by many names. Each deal is tailored to particular circumstances. Nonetheless, one can group countertrade transactions into the following basic categories: barter, counterpurchase, offset, and compensation.

Barter.   Pure barter is the most ancient form of international trade. It is essentially an exchange of one type of goods for another type of goods—Chinese silk for Arabian dates. In the modern world, pure barter takes up a relatively small proportion of countertrade primarily because of the difficulty in matching precisely the available goods and desired needs of the two parties. A trading company is often brought into more complex barter arrangements to facilitate the sale of the goods, as when a small U.S. company wanted to sell enamel blackboards to the Russian Ministry of Education and was paid in bales of used paper from schools throughout Russia. The U.S. company turned to a European trading company to sell the paper to recycling firms in several countries.

Counterpurchase.   Counterpurchase, sometimes called parallel barter, is probably the most common form of countertrade. It consists of an arrangement whereby a company contracts to sell goods or technology to a foreign purchaser for hard currency, but at the same time makes a commitment to buy (also for hard currency) goods produced by the importing company. Structurally, the difference between barter and countertrade is that barter consists of a single contract, while counterpurchase consists of two contracts that are linked, usually through a protocol or master agreement.

Offset.   A variation of counterpurchase, offset is an arrangement through which a supplier of manufactured goods agrees to purchase certain components or services from an importing purchaser for use in making the final product to be imported. This type of countertrade has long been an element in the sale of defense systems and aircraft to foreign countries, as well as for large-scale government procurement projects. For example, New Zealand required that in any government tender for a construction project above a specified amount, at least 30 percent of the total person-hour value of the design and management of the project be supplied by New Zealand professional service organizations, such as architects and consulting engineers.[4]

Compensation.   Sometimes called buyback, compensation is often used to finance the sale of capital goods and equipment. A purchaser acquires machinery or a factory immediately and pays the seller of the machinery or factory in goods produced by that equipment over a period of years. The manufacturer of tire-making equipment would sell it to a foreign country and make a long-term contract to purchase a specific number of tires produced by the equipment during a fixed period of time.

Countertrade is costly and inefficient. Arranging a deal is time-consuming and the goods received may be difficult to sell except at a deep discount. Western companies usually translate these risks and costs into higher prices for the goods, services, and technology that they sell through countertrade arrangements. Nonetheless, they enter into countertrade deals in order to close sales that would otherwise be lost. Through their laws and policies, some governments require that a portion of major purchases be financed through countertrade. In a few cases, firms have used countertrade as a way to assure a continuing long-term supply of raw materials, components, or finished products, particularly if the arrangement is linked to a firm's investment in the country.

Negotiating a Countertrade Deal

Negotiating a countertrade deal is a complex process that involves many issues. The first and most basic problem is to determine whether the foreign government or country you are dealing with will try to make you accept a countertrade obligation. One tactic that they sometimes use is to negotiate a deal as if it were for cash and then announce in the final stages that they expect you to sign a countertrade contract as well. This maneuver places you in a difficult situation, since obviously your cash price and your countertrade price for goods will differ because of the added costs that a countertrade transaction involves. One way to avoid this tactic is to make sure before specifying the sale price that the other side will not require countertrade as part of the deal.

If a country requires countertrade, determine the precise nature and scope of that obligation. The countertrade obligation is usually stated in terms of a "compensation ratio," which is the percentage of the value of the export that will be subject to counterpurchase. Government directives on this point are often secret. Negotiators from some countries often begin by demanding a very high ratio—from 50 percent to 100 percent—but may ultimately settle for as little as 25 percent. Numerous factors may influence their final position on the ratio, including the state of the country's foreign currency reserves and the importance of the imported goods and technology to the country's development.

The nature of countertrade goods, their price, and their quality are also negotiated issues in putting together a countertrade deal. Sometimes the exact nature of the goods to be purchased is not specified at the time the contract is signed. Rather, the party with the countertrade obligation is to select them from lists to be supplied later by the country's foreign trade organization. Usually, the goods offered are exactly the ones that the country cannot sell for cash because of their poor quality or low market demand.

In planning its negotiation strategy, a company should decide precisely to what extent it is willing to make a countertrade commitment and specifically the kinds of products it is willing to accept. These goods fall into various categories:

1. products that can be used in the exporting company's own operations, such as components
2. raw materials, particularly if they are marketable at established world prices through known channels
3. goods that relate to the exporting company's own product lines and therefore can be sold through its own marketing organization
4. goods unrelated to the company's operations

Negotiators generally find this last group of goods to be the least desirable because they pose the greatest risks of unprofitable resale. They must either be assigned to a trading house for disposal or marketed at a discount to a third party with all the related costs. Obviously, within the category of manufactured goods, those that require no after-sale service are the most preferable.

Since countertrade goods are usually not determined at the time a contract is made, the specification of price for the goods can create problems. The seller may also be tempted to overreach. To deal with this problem in a buy-back arrangement involving agricultural goods or raw materials, the price may be set according to a recognized index or some other formula. In cases of finished or semifinished goods, the contract may call for periodic price adjustment. One formula often used provides that the price of the goods is to be the "acceptable international price at the time of purchase." Another protective mechanism is a most-favored customer clause, which provides that the price to be paid will not be more than the price charged to the customer who has obtained the most favorable price.

A company usually prefers as long a period as possible to make its countertrade purchases in order to have enough time to locate customers and reduce storage and other associated costs. The seller of countertrade goods usually insists on a penalty provision if the purchasing firm fails to fulfill its counterpurchase obligation. The penalty, most often stated as a percentage of the unfulfilled part of the obligation, may range from 10 percent to 15 percent. A guarantee or standby letter of credit may be required as security for this penalty.

Finally, a countertrade arrangement should allow a firm to assign its countertrade obligation to a trading company or other organization that will take over the goods and dispose of them through its own channels.

Although countertrade arrangements are complex, costly, and inefficient, they are a way for global negotiators to make deals that might otherwise never happen.

12

SPECIAL BARRIER NO. 7:
INSTABILITY AND SUDDEN CHANGE

Change, of course, is the one constant in life. Deal makers' predictions at a negotiating table inevitably confront the realities of change later on. Changes in circumstances may make the parties unable or unwilling to act as their contract had predicted they would.

Although changes in circumstances happen all the time in both domestic and international business, several factors heighten the risk of transactional instability in an international deal. First, because the international environment itself is so unstable, international business dealings seem particularly susceptible to sudden changes, such as unexpected currency devaluations, coups, wars, and radical shifts in governments and governmental policies. Specific examples in the last few decades include the disintegration of the Soviet bloc, Iraq's invasion of Kuwait, civil wars in the Balkans, Russia's default on its bonds, Argentina's financial collapse, and the U.S. war in Afghanistan. These events often drastically affect the calculations of costs and benefits made in uncounted deals. As a result, expected payments were not made, contracts cancelled, and markets closed. Even if such dramatic events do not affect a deal, other factors may lead one of the parties to conclude that performance of its contract is no longer in its interest. As Raymond Vernon argued over three decades ago with respect to foreign investment projects, a bargain once struck will inevitably become obsolete for one of the parties, and issues once agreed upon will be reopened at a later time. Long-term agreements, in Vernon's words, are "obsolescing bargains."[1]

Second, mechanisms for enforcing agreements are often less sure or more costly in the international arena than in the domestic setting. If a party faced with nonperformance by the other side does not have effective access to the courts to enforce the contract or to seize assets, the other side in a burdensome contract may feel it has little to lose by rejecting the contract or demanding renegotiation with an expressed or implied threat of outright repudiation. In short, lack of effective enforcement mechanisms reduces the costs of the other side's nonperformance.

Third, as shown in chapter 10, foreign governments and government corporations are important participants in international business dealings. They often reserve the right to repudiate burdensome contracts on the grounds of protecting national sovereignty and the public welfare. In addition, the costs of pursuing a government for nonperformance may be higher and the likelihood of winning lower than in a suit against a private company.

The fourth factor creating instability is the imperfect nature of all contracts. The goal of any written contract is to express the full meaning of the parties' agreement concerning their proposed transaction; however, the parties are inherently incapable of attaining this goal since, without perfect foresight, they cannot predict all the events that may affect their transaction in the future and, in any case, the transaction costs of making contracts limit the resources they are willing to devote to the contracting process. Even if the parties had perfect foresight and unlimited resources to draft a perfect contract, they have no assurance that a court will interpret their contract exactly as they intended.

In international transactions, the problem of accurately negotiating and articulating the parties' intent is particularly difficult because of their differing cultures, business practices, ideologies, political systems, and laws—factors that often impede a true common understanding and inhibit the development of a working relationship. The world's diverse cultures and legal systems attach different degrees of binding force to a signed contract and recognize varied causes to justify avoidance of onerous obligations. For example, an American company in a transaction with a Japanese firm may view their signed contract as the essence of the deal and the source of rules governing their relationship in its entirety. The Japanese, however, see the deal as a partnership that is subject to reasonable changes over time, a partnership in which one party ought not to take unfair advantage of purely fortuitous events like radical and unexpected movements in exchange rates or the price of raw materials.

THE COSTS AND BENEFITS OF CHANGE

In negotiating any deal, both parties are calculating the likelihood of each side's future performance under their agreement. That calculation will influence the kinds of deals they make and how they will make them. In general, both parties recognize that the ability and willingness of either side to perform its part of the bargain will depend to a great extent on that party's perception of the relative costs and benefits of performance at the time stipulated by their deal. To the extent that the net benefits of performance exceed the benefits of nonperformance, a rational party will perform its obligations according to the deal. But when for whatever reason a party to a deal judges the respective net benefits of nonperformance to exceed those of performance, the result will be a refusal to perform or, at the very least, a demand to renegotiate the original deal. For example, a developing country government, attracted by the prospect of high revenues from a French mining project, may quite eagerly enter into a mineral development contract with the French company. But if, after a few years, the revenues do not meet the government's expectations or if it believes that another mining company would bring higher revenues, it might cancel the contract if it concludes that the costs of doing so would not exceed the benefits to be derived from a new arrangement with either the French mining company or another firm. In making this calculation, the government would weigh the expected benefits from a new arrangement against such political and economic costs as defending against a lawsuit by the French mining company and the sanctions that the French government might impose.

The notion of costs and benefits is not limited to purely economic factors. One must also account for political and social costs and benefits. For example, in one case involving a foreign investment project to build a luxury resort near the Giza pyramids in Egypt, the Egyptian government originally signed the agreement because it believed the economic benefits of the project would exceed its potential costs. But when public and international opposition became strong and persistent, the government canceled the project because it judged that the political costs outweighed the economic benefits to be derived from its construction.[2]

In order to deal with the risk of nonperformance, each side in the deal-making process seeks to do one of two things or both: (1) structure the deal in such a way that the other side's calculations of its net costs and benefits at the time of its performance will always induce it to perform as required by the contract; and (2) shift some or all of the costs and risks of nonperformance to a reliable third party. The first approach might include provisions requiring international arbitration in a neutral country, nonrefundable advance payments or deposits, and collateral for loans. The second approach might involve letters of credit from an international bank to secure payment or the issuance of foreign investment insurance from a governmental program such as the United States Overseas Private Investment Corporation (OPIC).

Regardless of the structures devised by the parties, the risk of transactional instability is always present in any deal. Experienced deal makers know that the challenge of business negotiations is not just "getting to yes" but also staying there. Business agreements solemnly signed and sealed after hard bargaining often break down later on, causing the parties to walk away from each other for good, to begin a lawsuit, or to return to the negotiating table to renegotiate their deal. A traditional theme in international business circles is the lament over the "unstable contract," the profitable agreement that the other side refuses to respect.

COPING WITH THE RISK

If the risk of change is constant in international business, how should deal makers cope with it? Negotiators should ask themselves two basic questions:

1. At the time of making a deal, how can we reduce the likelihood that it will be repudiated or renegotiated in the future?
2. When changed circumstances actually do have an impact on a negotiated deal, how should the parties conduct themselves?

Here are a few principles that global negotiators should follow to help answer the first of these questions.

A Deal Is Not Forever

Most modern contracts deny the possibility of change, so they rarely provide for adjustments to meet changing circumstances. This assumption of contractual stability has proven false time and time again. For example, most mineral development contracts are designed to last from 15 to 99 years but they rarely remain unchanged for more than a few years.

While praising the principle of the sanctity of the contract, every experienced negotiator knows that no deal is forever. Accordingly, before you arrive at the negotiating table, calculate the risks of change in any eventual deal and take account of them in developing your plans and strategies. Throughout the negotiations, remember the principle stated earlier: When the costs to the other side of rejecting an agreed-upon deal are less than respecting it, the risk of repudiation is high. As a deal maker, your basic strategy to give stability to your deal is to ensure that the other side derives sufficient benefits from keeping the agreement and incurs unacceptable costs from breaking it.

Lock Them In

To apply this strategy, you first need a carefully written agreement with detailed provisions and guarantees to ensure respect for the contract to the maximum extent possible. This means anticipating possible changes in circumstances and providing for them in the contract. At the same time, it is necessary to calculate the realistic possibility of having to renegotiate the deal in the future and include that calculation in your plans. Consequently, prices, rates of return, and other essential items should reflect a hard-headed assessment of the actual duration of the initial agreement, rather than the duration stated in the contract document.

While the process of discussing these details may make the negotiation seem tedious, this type of negotiation serves the valuable function of educating both sides about each other and about the nature of their deal. That knowledge can help to create a genuine business relationship between the two sides.

The other side should fully understand the contract, particularly its inherent risks. If you try to hide those risks, you inevitably open yourself to charges of bad faith and demands for renegotiation later on. The agreement itself should identify those risks and allocate them to one of the sides or both. International contracts often include a force majeure clause, a provision that suspends or excuses performance of specified contractual obligations on the occurrence of stated events like war, strikes, or civil unrest.

The wise deal maker should also build into an agreement mechanisms to reduce the likelihood of rejection and renegotiation. Two common mechanisms are the performance bond and linkage.

Under a performance bond, the other side or some reliable third party puts up money, property, or an enforceable promise that one side may claim if the other fails to perform under the contract. In a large sale of a communications system that will require several years for installation, both the manufacturer and the buyer might be required to have their banks issue letters of credit. The purpose of the buyer's letter is to make payments to the manufacturer at specified times. The purpose of the manufacturer's letter of credit, sometimes called a "standby letter of credit," is to guarantee performance— or at least provide compensation for the failure to perform—if the manufacturer does not deliver the equipment as promised.

Linkage, a second technique that gives stability to a contract by increasing the costs of noncompliance, can take many forms. The approach here is to link any future failure to perform a contract to adverse consequences from other parties or other relationships. The basic idea behind linkage is that those adverse consequences increase the cost of rejection and therefore inhibit the other side from breaking its contract. For example, a foreign investor may involve corporations and banks from many countries in an investment project on the theory that the host country might risk a conflict with one foreign company, but it would not do so with several companies and countries.

Balance the Deal

Wise negotiators also know that the best deal is one that is good for both sides. An important step to a stable deal is to create a balanced agreement in the first place. If the agreement is mutually beneficial, both sides have an incentive to maintain it. Neither side will consider rejection or repudiation as an attractive alternative. A balanced agreement might be one that allocates specific risks in a venture to the party that is best able to bear that risk, rather than merely on the basis of raw bargaining power. It might also provide that unexpected windfalls or losses be shared by both parties, rather than accrue to one side or the other.

Create a Relationship

Recognize that a signed contract does not necessarily create a relationship. For a long-term transaction to be stable and productive for both sides, it must be founded on a relationship, a complex set of interactions characterized by cooperation and trust. The existence of a solid relationship between the parties to a transaction allows them to face unforeseen circumstances and hardships in a productive and creative manner. A contract, no matter how detailed and lengthy, does not create a business relationship. Just as a map is not a country but only an imperfect description of one, a contract is not a business relationship but only an imperfect sketch of what the relationship should be. While negotiators must be concerned about the adequacy of contractual provisions, they should also seek a solid foundation for a relationship. Accordingly, a negotiator should also ask a variety of noncontractual questions during the negotiating process: How well do the parties know one another? What mechanisms are in place to foster communications between the two sides after the contract is signed? To what extent are there genuine links and connections between the parties to the agreement? Is the deal balanced and advantageous for both sides?

Regardless of culture, in most countries whenever one party fails to respect its contractual obligations to another party, the existence of a valuable relationship between the parties is more likely to facilitate a negotiated resolution of their dispute than if no such relationship exists. The reason is that the aggrieved party views the relationship with the offending party as more valuable than the individual claim arising out of the failure to honor the contractual provision. For example, in dealing with a debtor who is in default on a loan, a bank is often willing to renegotiate a loan with the delinquent debtor company or country when the bank considers that the prospect of future business with that debtor is likely. Bondholders of the same debtor, on the other hand, will generally be more resistant to renegotiation than banks since bondholders generally do not have the same opportunity for a profitable business relationship in the future.

Chapter 2 outlined a variety of techniques that deal makers may use to lay the foundation for a relationship. You should review them as you contemplate ways to give stability to deals you are trying to make.

Provide for Renegotiation of Contractual Provisions

As suggested above, rather than to view a long-term transaction as frozen in the detailed provisions of a lengthy contract, it may be more realistic to think of the transaction as a *continuing negotiation* between the parties as they seek to adjust their relationship to the rapidly changing environment in which they must work together. Accordingly, the parties should consider providing in their contract that at specified times or specified events, they will renegotiate or at least review some of the contract's provisions. Since they cannot predict all possible future contingencies, some type of renegotiation clause can give needed flexibility to long-term agreements. As was discussed in chapter 4, western organizations and lawyers have traditionally been reluctant to use them.

TYPES OF RENEGOTIATION PROVISIONS

In recent years, the use of renegotiation clauses in long-term agreements has become somewhat more frequent.[3] A variety of intradeal renegotiation clauses exist to cope with the challenge of balancing contractual stability with adaptation to change. The following are some of the principal types.

Implicit Minor Renegotiation Clauses. Despite some lawyers' claims to the contrary, contracts with long-term arrangements, no matter how detailed, are not a comprehensive instruction booklet that the parties follow blindly. At best, such agreements are *frameworks* within which the participants constantly adjust their relationship.[4] One executive responsible for implementing long-term transactions put it this way: "Once the contract is signed, we put it in the drawer. After that what matters most is the relationship between us and our partner, and we are negotiating that relationship all the time." What this view means in practice is that certain matters in the agreement, usually but not always of a minor nature, are subject to renegotiation by the parties as part of their ongoing relationship, despite the fact that their contract contains no specific renegotiation clause. One can therefore argue that an implicit minor renegotiation clause is part of any transaction agreement.

Review Clauses. Long-term contracts, particularly in the oil and mineral industries, sometimes commit the parties to meet at specific times to "review" the operation of their agreement. For example, one mining agreement provided that the parties were to meet together every seven years "with a view to considering in good faith whether this Agreement is continuing to operate fairly to each of them and with a view further to discussing in good faith any problems arising from the practical operation of this agreement." Although the words "negotiation" or "renegotiation" appear nowhere in the clause, one reasonable interpretation of the provision is that it carries an implicit obligation for the parties to resolve problems through good-faith negotiation.

Automatic Adjustment Clauses.   Transaction agreements often contain certain terms, such as those concerning prices or interests rates, subject to automatic change by reference to specified indices, such as a cost of living index or the London Interbank Offered Rate (LIBOR). For example, an electricity supply contract might link the price to be paid for electricity by a public utility to variations in fuel costs or the local cost of living index. While the aim of such a provision is to provide for flexibility without the risks inherent in renegotiation, negotiation may still be necessary to apply the index in unanticipated situations or in the event that the index itself disappears or becomes inappropriate.

Open-term Provisions.   Because of the difficulties and risks inherent in trying to negotiate arrangements to take place far in the future, some transaction agreements specifically provide that certain matters will be negotiated at a later time, perhaps years after the contract has been signed and the transaction implemented. For example, a foreign investor undertaking a major infrastructure project, such as an electrical generating station, might agree to negotiate appropriate senior management training schemes after it has constructed the facility and begun to hire local managers. This type of provision might be called an "open-term clause" because the matter in question has been left open for negotiation.

In a strict sense, of course, the subsequent negotiation of an open term is not really a *renegotiation* of anything since the parties have not yet agreed on any elements of that provision. In a broader sense, however, the negotiation of an open term at a later time will have the effect of modifying the overall relationship between the parties. Moreover, it is not inconceivable that one or both of the parties could use the opportunity of negotiating the open term as an occasion to seek concessions or changes in other terms through the common negotiating device of linking issues. For example, the foreign investor might offer a particularly attractive management training program if the government would agree to certain desired regulatory changes.

Renegotiation Clauses.   In an effort to balance the imperatives of contractual stability with flexibility, long-term agreements sometimes contain a definite clause that obligates the parties to renegotiate specified terms affected by changes in circumstances or unforeseen developments, such as those concerning construction costs, governmental regulations, or commodity prices. For example, an oil exploration contract between the government of Qatar and an oil company provided that the two sides would negotiate future arrangements for the use of natural gas not associated with oil discoveries if commercial quantities of such "nonassociated" gas were later found in the contract area.[5] In addition, renegotiation clauses in investment contracts often accompany stabilization clauses by which a host country promises that any changes in laws or regulations will not adversely affect the foreign investment project. The effect of the two clauses is to obligate the host government and the project company to enter into negotiations to restore the financial equilibrium that such new laws and regulations might destroy.

A renegotiation clause obligates the parties only to negotiate, not to agree. If the two sides have negotiated in good faith but fail to agree, that failure cannot justify liability on one side. In order to bring finality to the process of renegotiation, long-term agreements sometimes include a "contract adaptation clause," which stipulates that on the occurrence of certain specified events, the parties will first seek to negotiate a solution and, failing that, refer their problem to a third party for either a recommendation or a binding decision, depending on the desire of the parties to the contract. Certain institutions, such as the International Chamber of Commerce, have developed rules and facilities to help carry out the contract adaptation process.

SEEING AROUND THE CORNER

Making global deals in this rapidly changing world requires executives to be able to see around the corner—to anticipate future trends that may have an impact on their deals. To a significant extent, those trends and forces are political in nature. They stem from the government decisions and policies that affect their own countries and their relations with other nations. Although the techniques suggested in this chapter may be useful in giving stability to international deals, they are no substitute for the global negotiator's own careful and constant study of international politics and the political dynamics at work in the countries in which they do business. In this connection, global negotiators would do well to remember the admonition of Ghana's first president, Kwame Nkrumah, which was engraved on his statue that once stood in Black Star Square in Accra: "Seek ye first the political kingdom." As a result of the coup that toppled Nkrumah, the statue is no longer there. But for global negotiators, the advice is still sound.

PART II

GLOBAL DEAL MANAGING

13

AFTER THE CONTRACT, WHAT?
THE CHALLENGES OF DEAL MANAGEMENT

The deal is done at last. After eighteen months of effort, nine trips across the Pacific, countless days and nights of discussions in China, Hong Kong, and at home, you have finally negotiated a signed contract establishing a joint venture between your firm and the Great Wall Company of Shenzhen to manufacture components for audio systems. The contract is clear and precise. It covers all the contingencies and has strong enforcement mechanisms. You look at the document with satisfaction. You have given your company a solid foundation on which to launch a profitable business abroad. As you return the contract to the file, a question occurs to you for the first time: What now?

THE FOREIGN PARTNERS CHALLENGE

Nearly all of the transactions discussed in this book have within them the potential for a long-term relationship between the parties. Rather than merely engaging in one-shot transactions or establishing foreign branches and wholly owned subsidiaries to pursue their objectives under their total control, companies are joining with businesses around the world in all sorts of long-term, ongoing relationships—joint ventures, strategic alliances, global franchising arrangements, fifty-year production-sharing agreements, construction consortia, and build-operate-transfer infrastructure deals, among others. Between 1995 and 1998, businesses created more than 32,000 alliances. Today, approximately 20 percent of the annual income of the United States' largest companies is derived from alliances.

An important result of this trend is that more companies are becoming enmeshed in relationships that often require them to work as partners in essence, if not in name, with foreign firms. Indeed, international business success today and for the foreseeable future in all countries is very much a matter of working effectively with foreign partners. Even when a company acquires a foreign firm, it will usually find that it faces the challenge of working with foreign partners—the personnel, management, and organizations that it has acquired. After the contract come the challenges of managing the deal, which in most cases means creating and managing a genuine working relationship with contractual partners.

As international transactions become bigger, longer, and more complex, the relational dimensions loom ever larger and overshadow the contractual dimensions. As working with foreign partners has become the essence of international business today, many executives find themselves unprepared for this challenge. Working with foreign partners in an international business relationship presents problems and obstacles that executives do not ordinarily encounter in purely domestic dealings. Although the parties to alliances, joint ventures, and mergers usually announce them with great fanfare at the start, they often become disappointed within a short time and in many cases terminate them earlier than expected. Various studies have found that between 33 percent and 70 percent of international alliances surveyed eventually broke up and that business executives generally consider joint ventures to be notoriously unstable.[1] One explanation for this instability is that after signing their contract, the parties were unable to create and manage profitable working relationships that are essential to the life of any business venture.[2]

The challenges of managing long-term deals and working effectively with foreign partners present themselves in many forms. Some are external to the partnership; some are internal to the relationship between the parties. Here are a few scenarios drawn from experience around the world:

- Your firm's foreign partner, a small emerging market company, feels that it is much weaker than your firm and constantly fears that you will take advantage of it. Consequently, in all dealings with your company, it is extremely guarded and slow to reach agreement, an attitude that is hampering the development of the venture.
- Your company has created a pharmaceutical joint venture in Russia and wants to confine it to narrow and specific areas, but your Russian

partner wants to expand into activities unrelated to your company's competence, such as the production of television programs. Disagreement over this question is causing tension in the relationship.

- A European company and a Chinese enterprise have established a joint venture that has clear mutual benefits, but both parties are very cautious about sharing information. The Chinese partner withholds information about customer problems with products and requests for new product features. In response, the Europeans have slowed the transfer of technology badly needed by the venture. The two sides are also in conflict over advertising expenses. The Europeans want to spend heavily on advertising while the Chinese oppose these expenditures as unnecessary.

- A U.S. pharmaceutical firm with a long tradition of strong presidents and top-down management has acquired a Swedish firm with a management style that entails getting the whole management group's approval before making big decisions, rather than handing down orders—"*alla aer I baten*" ("getting everybody in the boat")—according to the Swedes. The difference in style is causing severe internal conflict and the possible loss of talented managers and scientists.

Detailed contractual provisions, arbitration clauses, and threats of litigation alone can solve none of these problems. The true solution lies in the development of a healthy business relationship between the parties to the deal. The primary tool to create a healthy business relationship is negotiation, *deal-managing* negotiation.

A signed contract does not necessarily create an international business relationship. In the case of an isolated business transaction or short-term arrangement, such as a one-time export sale, signing a contract may be the only appropriate negotiation goal. However, to approach the negotiation of a long-term transaction with that perspective may result in failure to achieve the parties' objectives or to maximize their interests. Ultimately, a long-term alliance or transaction founded on a contract alone may collapse.

In long-term transactions, the parties are seeking to create a business relationship. That relationship, however, is not static. It is organic and evolves over time, regardless of what the legal contract says. Within the relationship lies the potential for business opportunities that the negotiators never foresaw, as well as the seeds for destructive conflict that they may have overlooked. The challenge for the business negotiator is to find ways to build and strengthen the connection between the two companies. Chapter 2 outlined measures that deal makers might take during their negotiations to lay the foundations for the development of a relationship once the contract is signed.

After the contract is signed, executives charged with managing the deal should think *relationally* about the transaction and should ask a variety of nonlegal and noncontractual questions as they plan their work:

- How well do the parties know one another?
- What is the nature of the personal chemistry between the two companies' leadership?
- To what extent do the two sides understand and respect each other's cultures, expectations, and goals?
- What mechanisms are in place to foster communications between the two sides after the contract is signed?
- To what extent is the proposed deal balanced and advantageous for both sides?
- Who are the potential spoilers of the deal and what external factors lie in wait to damage or destroy the relationship between the parties?

If the answers to these questions indicate that the deal makers have developed little basis for establishing an effective relationship between the companies concerned, wise deal managers should take measures to convert their signed contract into a working relationship.

CONVERTING THE CONTRACT
INTO A RELATIONSHIP

International business relationships have countless variations. Some will be close; others will be distant. Some will last for decades and lead to profitable business opportunities that neither party contemplated when they first began their negotiations. Others will collapse when they fail to attain their objectives or when one side feels that it has obtained everything it wanted.

In managing an international transaction, deal managers will need to apply all the techniques discussed earlier in this book with respect to deal making. They will also encounter the special barriers that global negotiators face in making deals. Thus, differences in culture between the parties will continue to be a potential obstacle to effective deal implementation long after the contract has been signed. Do not assume that a signed contract means that all barriers between the parties have permanently vanished.

To convert their contract into a relationship, deal managers should consider the following six measures:

1. Persons who negotiated the deal should be closely involved in its implementation, at least at the beginning stages.   As a result of negotiations, the deal makers have gained an enormous amount of information about each other and the deal. In the process, they have may well may formed a positive relationship with each other. All these factors are valuable assets in building a relationship between their two companies. The negotiators themselves can best bring these assets to bear and therefore should have some role in implementing the transaction, at least at the start.

Too often companies signing a long-term contract assume that a solid working relationship will automatically develop. For example, General Motors negotiated a series of international joint ventures that encountered difficulties once GM and its international partners began to work together. One reason for the problem was that the teams that negotiated the deal were not involved in actually implementing it. The negotiating teams at GM would put together a joint venture and then move on to negotiate another, leaving other executives the task of actually figuring out how to make things work. Within the company, this became known as "throwing it over the wall"—that is, negotiating a deal and then passing it along to someone else to implement.

2. Find ways to maintain leadership involvement and interest in the relationship.   Many deals are made through the active involvement of the companies' leaders. At the early stages of the relationship, it is important to find ways to maintain their visible interest. While company leaders are busy with a host of other matters, it may be wise to schedule periodic meetings for them to review progress on the evolution of the relationship between the companies after they have signed the contract.

3. Develop a plan of action to inform company personnel not involved in the negotiations of the nature of the deal and of its benefits to the organization.   Do not assume that other persons in the company will become as enthusiastic and knowledgeable about the deal as the negotiators. Indeed, they may see involvement with a foreign company, whose culture, business practices, and language they do not understand, as threatening. In order to overcome resistance within their own bureaucracies, the advocates of the deal should plan and be involved in educational efforts, including arranging meetings, retreats, seminars, or visits and circulating internal memoranda or newsletters. Remember: Organizational relationships begin with personal relationships. Consequently, the two companies should seek to foster good personal relationships between the employees who will work together on the venture. Inevitably, the implementation of any deal will encounter difficulties, such as delivery delays, miscommunications, and sudden changes in commodity prices or exchange rates. The two companies in the transaction will be better able to overcome these problems if their employees know and understand one another than if they view each other with suspicion and hostility.

4. Meticulously plan and oversee initial joint activities between the two sides.   Just as opening moves in a negotiation may either facilitate or hinder the progress of what follows, initial joint activities between the two companies in a deal can either ease or obstruct the creation of a productive working relationship. Consequently, the two sides should carefully define and supervise the initial activities in their relationship and not assume that everything will flow smoothly from the terms of their contract. In this respect, it may be better to start with small activities that are sure to succeed before moving the venture on to more ambitious projects.

5. At the outset, the two sides should agree upon a schedule of regular and frequent meetings to review the progress of the relationship.   Although a business relationship is organic and evolves over time, this fact does not mean that the two sides should not consciously shape it. In order to guide the evolution of a sound relationship, the two companies should set a regular schedule of meetings and adhere to it rigorously, rather than just meet "from time to time" or "when the need arises."

6. Each side should select with care the right persons to manage the relationship.   Launching an international business relationship requires diplomacy as well as technical expertise. Therefore each side should select persons to manage that relationship who have the appropriate skills, knowledge, and sensitivity to lay the foundation for a solid working relationship. Indeed, these qualities may be more important in the long run than the technical knowledge of engineering, marketing, or finance. In appointing persons to manage the relationship, each company should be certain that a candidate has the appropriate language expertise, cultural knowledge and sensitivity, flexibility, and interpersonal skills. Just as diplomats have to be approved or accredited by the receiving state, parties to major international alliances might agree that each company's executive appointed to manage the relationship should receive the approval of the other company.

FOUR BUILDING BLOCKS

Beyond these initial actions, the parties in implementing their deal should constantly bear in mind and work toward establishing the elements of a good working relationship between them. What are the characteristics of a good working relationship? The answer to this question is vital. Without a strong understanding of the important elements of a good working relationship, a global negotiator cannot manage a deal effectively.

A good working relationship rests on four building blocks:

- communication
- commitment
- reliability
- respect

Communication

A good working relationship between deal partners requires two-way communication, a relationship with information flowing easily in *both* directions. At the time executives negotiate a deal, they should address the modes of communication to be used after the contract has been signed. Too often negotiators overlook this issue and assume that communication between the two sides will happen naturally once they begin working together. Often the development of effective communication is anything but natural.

In one joint venture between an American company and a Japanese firm for the manufacture of equipment for sale in Asia, the American firm was to supply the technology and the Japanese partner the management, manufacturing, and marketing. Once a quarter, an American executive based in Hong Kong would visit the venture's operations to review strategies and major decisions. Between visits, the two sides communicated largely through correspondence and an occasional telephone call. As a result, the Japanese partner came to believe that the Americans were not strongly committed to the venture. Consequently, the Japanese firm's level of commitment declined as well. Over time, the American company's strategy changed to focus on a relatively small number of products, so the broad array of technology that the Japanese expected to be transferred began to decline. The Americans never communicated this change of strategy to their Japanese partner, who as a result became convinced that the Americans were acting in bad faith by denying the joint venture new technology that it needed to stay competitive. Eventually, the situation evolved into a bitter conflict that led to an arbitration proceeding and the liquidation of the joint venture. Had the two sides discussed and agreed upon a communication strategy during the negotiations for the joint venture, the conflict that led to its demise might never have taken place. The lesson is clear: During the negotiations, the parties should agree on a program of regular meetings and contacts after the deal is signed.

Communications in an international relationship encounter special problems because the two companies often speak different languages and come from different cultures. The two sides should recognize these problems at the outset and agree on ways to deal with them. In a strategic alliance between an American company and a European firm whose executives have strong English language competence, the two sides might agree that all communications relating to their alliance will be in English. On the other hand, if the staff of the European firm has little English language proficiency, the parties might agree to use another language, to work through interpreters and translators, or to hire executives with appropriate language skills. For example, in one joint venture between an American and a French company, the two sides agreed that they would use both languages and interpreters in their encounters. Meetings were twice as long as normal but the investment paid off in better communications between the two firms.

Means of communication between parties to a long-term transaction can be varied: personal visits, telephone calls, faxes, video teleconferences, and e-mail, among others. While each may be effective in communicating desired information, some are more useful than others in building and managing business relationships. The personal visit is usually the most powerful means of fostering relationships, because it allows the visitor not only to convey large amounts of information but also to learn much about its partner and to adjust the relationship to evolving and changing circumstances. Equally important, it demonstrates the visitor's commitment to the relationship. A visit to a joint venture partner in Japan is costly and time consuming. E-mail is quick and cheap. However, an e-mail message can sometimes injure a relationship. In choosing the proper means of communication, an executive should consider not only the effectiveness of that mode in conveying desired information but also its impact on building and maintaining relationships with its foreign partner. It is also well to remember that personal visits, unlike e-mail, telephone calls, and other forms of communication, may lead to brainstorming about new projects and business ideas that the two parties might profitably pursue.

Commitment

A good working relationship is one in which the two sides are committed to each other and to their relationship. Commitment, however, is more than just saying, "We are committed to the deal." Your partner will judge whether you have genuine commitment on the basis of your behavior over the course of the relationship. Often, parties to a deal will structure their transaction to involve increasing levels of effort, capital, and cooperation over time, in order to test the other side's degree of commitment to their relationship.

In one case, a Swiss diversified services company entered into a joint venture with a U.S. firm to undertake environmental clean-up operations in Eastern Europe, which had suffered serious pollution damage during the communist era. The Swiss firm had great hopes for the joint venture and believed that its American partner was firmly committed to the deal over the long-term. Within a year, it learned that the American company had only a modest commitment to the relationship when the Americans refused to provide new capital so that the venture could undertake a major project in Hungary. As it turned out, although the Swiss company had a long-term strategic interest in the joint venture, the U.S. company had joined because it believed the venture would yield quick profits. They dissolved their partnership shortly afterwards.[3]

Reliability

A third element in a good working relationship is reliability, the notion that each side can depend on the other to act in expected ways. In this respect, reliability becomes an important basis for trust. Reliability has at least two dimensions. It means that a business partner's conduct is predictable. It also means that one partner will honor its promises and commitments to the other. A business partner who consistently submits reports to the other side two months late, who persistently fails to show up for meetings on time, and who does not respond promptly to a partner's e-mails will soon be seen as unreliable. Once a partner feels that its counterpart is unreliable, that judgment will inevitably become an obstacle to developing a good working relationship and may eventually lead to abandonment of the deal.

The goal of reliability has several important implications for managing a business relationship. First, do not make commitments or set deadlines without a realistic expectation that you can meet them. Second, if you do find that you are unable to meet a promised deadline or commitment, contact your partner to explain your difficulty and try to renegotiate the time of the deadline or the nature of the commitment. Do not assume that your partner has forgotten or attaches little importance to them, or that you can ignore your promised deadline or commitment without damaging your relationship. Third, when trying to renegotiate a deadline or obligation with your partner, it is best to be frank about your difficulties rather than to offer false excuses that will only undermine your relationship even more.

Reliability implies honesty. A business partner expects and demands honesty from its counterpart. One of the quickest ways to erode a good working relationship is for a business partner to say or do something that seems dishonest. Once a partner suspects that its counterpart is dishonestly acting for its own ends and interests, rather than for those of the relationship, the relationship is at an end.

Respect

A final but no less important building block for a good working relationship is respect—respect by one partner for the other. Creating respect in a relationship begins with the principle of equality of the parties. This means that each side recognizes that the other brings something valuable to their common enterprise and that the view of each side deserves to be heard. Respect, like communication, is a two-way process. Too often a partner with superior technology or technical knowledge in a joint venture tries to dominate the relationship by lauding its superior knowledge and belittling the knowledge and experience of the partner. To say, as one U.S. executive did to a partner from a developing country, "Let me do the thinking for both of us" is hardly a statement of respect toward one's partner.

In many developing countries, face, status, and standing are extremely important for local companies. Recognizing their standing in appropriate ways is essential for a foreign partner in developing mutual respect with those companies and their executives. Consequently, it is vital for foreign firms entering into business deals with those companies to understand the symbols and formalities of status in that culture and to try to incorporate them into managing their relationship. For example, if it is common in business meetings in that country for the person running a meeting to be referred to as "Mr. Chairman" or "*Monsieur le président*," it would be wise for foreign joint venture partners to adopt the same formality in conducting quarterly board meetings in that country. Americans often view formalities as getting in the way of personal relationships, so they often seek to do away with them. In other cultures formalities are signs of respect. To disregard them in hopes of creating a relationship with a foreign counterpart may have the unintended result of harming the relationship through an act of disrespect.

The formalities of diplomacy are ways of acknowledging another country's status as a sovereign and equal member of the international community. Appropriate use of formalities can have the same effect in international business negotiations. For example, in the negotiation of an alliance between Northwest Airlines and KLM, the Dutch air carrier, Northwest knew that KLM, a much smaller airline, was very sensitive about its status as an equal in the negotiations and later in the alliance. To alleviate these fears, Northwest structured all aspects of the negotiation, from the shape of the negotiating table to the organization of social events, as a meeting between two sovereign states. As one Northwest executive told the author, "We used every symbol we could think of to recognize their sovereignty."

Respect for a business partner also entails respect for its culture. Stereotyping your partners to explain their behavior disrespects them as individuals and injects an irritant into the relationship that may eventually cause its demise. While culture certainly influences behavior, not all Japanese will evade giving a direct negative answer and not all Germans will tell you specifically what they think of a proposal. To say to a Japanese counterpart who is taking time to evaluate your suggested plans for a new product line, "You Japanese are all alike. You just can't give a straight answer," will not be taken as a sign of respect and a positive step in building a working relationship. Rather, it may be better to understand why your Japanese counterpart needs more time. Upon investigation you may discover that your Japanese partner's decision-making processes are time consuming because its organizational culture requires consultation with a far larger number of persons than your own internal decision making. Although you may be tempted to conclude that your organization is therefore more efficient than the Japanese, you may find that the Japanese are more efficient at implementing the decision since all the key participants have approved it, while your implementation may require you to educate a layer of personnel not involved in the original decision.

Working with a foreign partner may inevitably lead to situations where your culture and that of your counterpart come into conflict. Effective deal management requires you to perceive these cultural differences, understand their reasons, and find ways to resolve them without showing your partner disrespect. It is important therefore for executives managing an intercultural business relationship to understand the values inherent in the culture of their counterparts and not to characterize those values in a negative way. It is equally important to create mechanisms for the two sides to explore the ways cultural differences may be affecting the operation of their relationship and to find ways to bridge the cultural gaps that may arise.

THE LIMITS OF RELATIONSHIPS

Keep in mind that the purpose of any business relationship is to advance the goals of the parties. A business relationship is not valuable for itself alone. Once an international business relationship no longer serves a party's interests—for example, because of a change of company strategy—that party will need to take measures to renegotiate or to end it.

14

POWER TOOLS FOR GLOBAL DEALS

Power is a key element in making, managing, and mending deals. Effective negotiation requires the skillful application of power. Negotiators need to understand its uses and its limits, its sources, and its mechanisms. They need to know how to use the power tools of negotiation.

For some people, power has a bad name. They consider it a faintly disreputable subject that polite company ought to avoid. Just as sexuality was repressed in the nineteenth century, some quarters today deny or disparage preoccupations with power. Many books and articles on management, leadership, and negotiation either neglect the subject of power entirely or suggest that it does not matter, even though practitioners of those arts know full well that power is at the heart of what they do every day. Many commentators often approach the subject with an ideological predisposition to see virtue in weakness and evil in strength. Perhaps it is the fault of Lord Acton, whose famous statement "all power corrupts" is invariably quoted in any discussion of power.

Power is neither inherently good nor bad. Power in relationships at all levels is essential for accomplishing personal, company, or national goals, whether it is making a sale, completing a merger, or reorganizing a government department. However, international negotiators need to tend power constantly and use it properly to avoid losing control and causing damage.

THE NATURE OF POWER

So what is power, anyway? In essence, power is the means by which a state, company, or person attains a desired end in its relations with other states, companies, or persons.

Many people consider power to refer to the physical resources that a company, country, or individual has at its command. In a negotiation between General Motors and a small auto dealership in Fargo, North Dakota, General Motors is powerful because of its vast capital, wide political connections, and huge organization. However, this emphasis on physical resources distorts the nature of power in a negotiation. The goal of a negotiator in making, managing, or mending a deal is to convince the other side to agree to an action that is in the negotiator's interest. From this perspective, *"negotiating power" means the ability to influence or move the decisions of the other side at the bargaining table in a desired way.* In some situations, a party's physical resources, such as its capital, technology, or organization, may indeed influence the other side's decision. But in other cases, less tangible factors, such as an original idea, a strong relationship, or a reputation for honesty, may also be sources of influence and therefore of power at the negotiating table. These nonmaterial factors are important power tools for the global negotiator.

The use of the word "power" in the context of a negotiation nearly always implies a prediction and a comparison about one side's interactions with the other. It is a relative concept. The Fargo dealership may be weak in its relations with General Motors but strong in its negotiations with a local trucking company fallen on hard times. Moreover, power in relationships is constantly changing over time. Raymond Vernon, in his analysis of relationships between foreign investors and developing country governments, quite accurately pointed out that over time the power relationship between them shifts. Their original deal becomes an "obsolescing bargain" in favor of the host country once the investor actually makes an investment and places its assets under the physical control of the host state.[1]

If power in a negotiation or a relationship is defined as the ability to move the decisions of another party in a desired direction, then power also has a perceptual dimension. Since power for the negotiator is the ability to influence the other side's decisions in a desired way, it is important to understand how the other side perceives and evaluates both sides' resources, as well as the events and actions relating to the negotiation. Each party brings its own set of lenses—its prejudices, assumptions, and desires—to the negotiating table, and those lenses may prevent each one from objectively evaluating the nature and extent of its own and the other's power. For example, at the outset of the Korean War, the United States, and particularly General Douglas MacArthur, perceiving China through the lens of conventional military assessment, underestimated the power of that country, especially its will to defeat what it perceived as a threat to Chinese sovereignty.

Because culture always influences perceptions, differences in culture between the parties, a factor constantly present in international negotiations, can affect power. One culture may interpret certain symbols and phenomena as indications of power, but another may not. For example, youth in the United States is often a symbol of strength, but other cultures may view youth as immaturity and therefore a sign of weakness. So, Americans in 1961 saw John F. Kennedy as a youthful, vigorous president and therefore a powerful leader. On the other hand, Nikita Khrushchev, in his famous confrontation with Kennedy over Berlin in that same year, viewed the American president through a Ukrainian cultural lens: He saw Kennedy as a rich, spoiled, inexperienced young man; a weak leader, and he treated him accordingly. The same kind of miscalculations about power may happen in international business negotiations, for instance between a young American CEO and an elderly chairman of a Japanese company. To the American, the Japanese may seem tired and therefore weak; to the Japanese, the American may seem immature and therefore weak.

Scholars studying the role of power in relations among nations seem divided into two distinct schools of thought. For some, often called realists, power is the primary determinant that controls the nature and outcomes of negotiations between states. According to this view, the strong invariably prevail over the weak. A second school, more optimistic about interactions between the weak and the strong, holds that negotiation itself, if accomplished skillfully, can reduce initial disparities in power and establish increased equality in international relationships.

Most negotiation scholars tend to follow the second school. To do otherwise would be to admit that their primary field of professional interest has little significance in the real world. Some scholars even seem to approach the question of power with an ideological bias. They either ignore power completely or assume that, in the end, enlightened negotiation techniques will overcome power differentials. In support of this view, they readily cite cases where a "weak" party did surprisingly better than expected against a "stronger" adversary because of the weaker side's negotiating skills. The problem with this approach is that the surprising result can also be explained by the observer's overestimation of the power differential that existed between the parties at the start of their negotiation.

HOW SHOULD THE LAMB
NEGOTIATE WITH THE LION?

Several years ago, at an international conference of university presidents in Talloires, France, an American social psychologist argued that all universities should introduce the teaching of negotiation as an academic subject. The head of one of India's largest universities challenged the utility of teaching negotiation at all, particularly in developing countries where the need for other kinds of knowledge seemed much greater. Never one to duck an argument, the American psychologist replied that, on the contrary, the disparities in power between developing and developed nations made it particularly important for Third World officials and executives to master negotiating techniques to improve the results of their negotiations with industrialized countries and multinational corporations. The Indian dismissed this argument with a wave of his hand, saying, "A negotiation between the weak and the strong is a dialogue between the lamb and the lion: The lamb always gets eaten."

The exchange between the American professor and the Indian university head, while unique in its setting and participants, was like most discussions about negotiation, wherever they take place, in at least three respects. First, the subject of power—especially the problem of power inequality—is a central consideration. Sometimes the subject is addressed directly, as was the case at the conference, and sometimes it is merely assumed. Second, participants in conversations about power dynamics always seem to divide into two camps—the realists, like the Indian vice chancellor, for whom power is the primary determinant in any interaction between persons, organizations, or nations; and the idealists, like the American professor, who believe that skilled use of negotiation techniques, themselves tools of power, can reduce power differences between parties at the bargaining table. And third, conversations about power invariably employ metaphors—the lamb and the lion, David and Goliath, Jack and the Giant. Metaphors are themselves power tools. They seize the imagination and orient debate in a particular direction, but they can also distort reality.

A review of cases of negotiation between the weak and the strong in international relations does seem to reveal here and there instances when a lamb obtained better results from a lion than one might have anticipated at the start of their interaction. Examples include the U.S. negotiations with

Panama over the Panama Canal, the Algerian nationalist movement's (the F.L.N.) negotiations with France over Algeria's independence, Nepal's negotiations with India over water, and Canada's negotiation with the United States over the U.S.–Canada Free Trade Agreement, to name just a few.[2] Although these and similar cases offer many lessons, perhaps they teach one fundamental lesson above all others: An apparently less powerful party in an international negotiation is not always at the mercy of a seemingly more powerful party.

The cases also seem to teach that the weaker side is generally more powerful than it appears at first glance and that the more powerful side is often weaker than it first assumes. The reason for this initial erroneous assumption is that first judgments of relative power in a negotiation are made on the basis of each party's *aggregate* physical resources. Thus, at the beginning of negotiations, the United States seemed far more powerful than Panama, and France appeared much stronger than the F.L.N. But a negotiation is about specific issues and interests; consequently, power in a given negotiation consists of the particular resources and devices that will influence the other side with respect to the specific issues under discussion. Thus, one must distinguish between aggregate power and "issue power," the latter being a more accurate indicator of results in a particular negotiation.[3] The cases show that more important than a party's aggregate physical resources in influencing negotiation outcomes are: (1) the resources that a particular side brings to bear on the specific issues in a given negotiation; and (2) the skill and will with which a party applies its resources to the negotiating process. For the weaker party in an international negotiation, the resources and skills augmenting its power include the use of wise strategies and tactics. Strategies and tactics are a negotiator's power tools. Strategy refers to the grand plan by which a party hopes to carry out its goals. Tactics are the moves and actions taken to implement that strategy.

FOUR GRAND POWER STRATEGIES

A party in an international negotiation cannot determine a strategy until it has formulated a basic goal. And it is often at this point that weak parties show an initial lack of strength. Since they are unable to determine what they want, they cannot develop appropriate strategies. A country or company that, because of internal dissension and disorganization, fails to set clear goals for itself will be greatly weakened in its negotiations with international financial institutions such as the World Bank or multinational corporations such as General Motors. For any negotiator, setting clear goals is an act of empowerment, an initial step toward strengthening its position at the bargaining table.

Once goals are set, a party to an international negotiation needs to find a strategy that will enable it to attain its goals. What is the range of strategies available to a global negotiator?

In his book *Power: The Inner Experience*, the late Harvard University psychologist David C. McClelland examined the individual's drive for power and determined that people throughout the world seek power in one of four ways: (1) by obtaining support from others, often through a dependence relationship (I feel strong because another supports me); (2) by establishing one's autonomy and independence from others (I feel strong because I strengthen myself); (3) by assertively acting upon, influencing, and dominating others (I feel strong because I have an impact on others); and (4) by becoming part of an organization or group (I feel strong because of my group). He labels these four orientations support, autonomy, assertion, and togetherness.[4]

The four ways of experiencing power identified by McClelland can be translated into four grand strategies that countries, companies, and individuals use to seek power and achieve goals in negotiating with others. Let's examine each of them.

Support

One strategy often used by lambs in the international system is to seek support from larger companies by creating an agreed-upon dependence relationship. Small companies, such as an auto parts supplier, may consider that their best means of attaining economic benefits is to form a dependency or client relationship with a larger company, such as major auto manufacturer. Parties following a support strategy make it clear in all their interactions with the large company that they are prepared to do that larger company's bidding. At the same time, throughout their negotiations both before and after signing the deal, they indicate in direct and indirect ways that they and others expect the larger firm to behave toward them in particular ways, hoping that the strength of this expectation will lead the stronger party to feel that it has certain obligations toward the weaker party. The weaker party often proceeds on the assumption that expectations create obligations.

Dependence cannot, after all, be established unilaterally. The patron company must be convinced that it will gain advantages from the client's dependence or that it has an obligation to maintain it for other reasons; however, as the patron's situation changes, its view of the desirability of the support relationship may also change. Thus, when the U.S. auto manufacturer finds a less expensive Mexican auto parts supplier, it will terminate its relationship with its small American supplier.

Autonomy

Fearful of the costs of a support strategy, many countries and companies in their international relationships have chosen its opposite—autonomy—in many of their dealings with the world's lions. Some companies have a definite policy to undertake foreign investments only in the form of a wholly owned subsidiary, because this form gives them greater control over their activities than would a joint venture or a strategic alliance. In the 1960s and 1970s, policies of self-reliance and concerns about *dependencia* prompted many developing countries to restrict their economic interactions with powerful developed nations. They therefore strictly controlled the entry of foreign investment and they imposed high tariffs to limit imports. Ultimately, the failure of those policies to yield tangible benefits caused many countries to abandon autonomy strategies in the economic domain. Autonomy as a strategy does not necessarily mean an avoidance of interactions. In order to preserve autonomy successfully, a company ordinarily has to engage in constant negotiations toward that end. For example, a small, publicly held corporation threatened by a hostile takeover will engage in significant negotiations with banks and others in order to obtain the financing to take itself private and maintain its autonomy.

Assertion

Assertion of course is the traditional grand strategy of the powerful. Through coercion, threats, and unilateral action, powerful companies and countries compel others to give them what they want. But sometimes, seemingly weak parties can and do use it as well. Threatened by a hostile takeover, some small companies will mount aggressive public relations campaigns against the attacker and change election procedures of its board of directors in an effort to thwart the takeover.

Togetherness

A final strategy is to negotiate alliances, coalitions, and associations that enhance a party's power and ability to achieve its goals by sharing the resources of others. Thus, in the domain of global business, the drive by companies to create strategic alliances with other firms around the world is clearly a reflection of the togetherness strategy, since firms believe they will gain more economic benefits than they would alone by asserting themselves, by remaining aloof, or by becoming dependent on others.

Seemingly weak parties particularly try to follow this strategy. In particular, lambs in the international system often try to become part of an organization or association that includes a lion. The lamb thereby benefits from the lion's strength, and the organization's structures constrain the lion's ability to exercise its power abusively against the lamb. At the state level, for example, the lambs of Europe have clearly perceived that the best way to tame the German lion and at the same time benefit from its economic strength is to enclose it within the European Union. One may contrast Europe's current community strategy with the assertion strategies and balance of power politics that prevailed on that continent before the end of World War II. Similarly, after pursuing a strategy that vacillated between assertion and autonomy in its relations with the United States, Mexico appears to have shifted to a community strategy by negotiating the North American Free Trade Agreement. While negotiations based on a community strategy are often filled with assertive actions and statements by both weak and strong, they are merely tactics designed to maximize a party's interests within the organization or community to which both lion and lamb belong.

TACTICAL POWER TOOLS

Having chosen a strategy, a party in negotiation tries to augment its power through the skillful use of tactics. The following are several of the more common power tactics.

Build Relationships with Appropriate Third Parties

One of the most effective ways to increase your power in a negotiation is to build supportive relationships with a strong third party who may be willing to intervene on your side in the negotiation. In most cases, a strong third party means one who has influence over an adversary. A few years ago, Reebok, the international sports shoe manufacturer, wanted to renegotiate the terms of its contract with one of its major distributors. When the distributor refused, Reebok approached a noncompeting manufacturer whose products were also handled by the same distributor and asked it to help persuade the distributor to listen to reason. Fearful that a festering conflict between Reebok and the distributor would have negative consequences for the distribution of its own products, the noncompeting manufacturer decided to intervene and ultimately helped Reebok and the distributor arrive at a satisfactory solution to their problem. By involving the noncompeting manufacturer, Reebok was increasing its power with respect to the distributor, heightening its ability to influence the distributor's decisions in a way that Reebok desired.

In joint ventures and strategic alliances with more than two companies, this power tool usually takes the form of coalition building within the venture or alliance. In order to influence alliance policy in desired ways, two or more of the participants will implicitly or explicitly form coalitions. Thus, companies A and B in a three-party alliance might join together to cause the alliance to undertake an investment opposed by company C. In joint ventures of more than two parties, coalition building is a basic tool for deal management. On the other hand, while coalitions are easily formed, they break up just as easily. So while companies A and B in a venture with company C to manufacture air conditioners might form a coalition to control new investments, companies C and B might form a coalition to influence hiring policy.

A pervading lesson of international negotiations is that power is who your friends are; choosing your friends carefully is a key skill. No third party is an altruist. Third parties always pursue their own interests, even when they claim to work on behalf of other parties, and the pursuit of those interests may complicate and even obstruct the negotiation process. The noncompeting manufacturer was willing to intervene in Reebok's dispute with its distributor because it feared that a continuing conflict would have a negative effect on the distributor's ability to sell the noncompeting manufacturer's own goods. A *competing* manufacturer might have refused to undertake the task or have done it in such away as to disadvantage Reebok.

In choosing an appropriate third party with which to build a relationship, the weaker side has basically three options: a friend of the other side, an adversary of the other side, or a (preferably strong) neutral party. Probably the option with the greatest risk for the lamb is to select as an ally an adversary of the lion. That choice may indeed sometimes wring concessions from the stronger side, but it may also provoke the stronger party's hostility and increase its determination to dominate the weaker side because it now faces what it considers to be a genuine threat. On the other hand, raising the specter of a competitor, without actually involving it in the conflict, can be an effective form of influence as it was for many small countries during the cold war. A friend of the other side is usually the most appropriate third party, as long as that third party does not merely seek to hand over the weak party to the adversary. By virtue of their friendly relationship, the third party has the ability to influence the other side toward an acceptable solution. When Exxon Mobil wanted to undertake a petroleum development in Chad with a pipeline through Cameroon to export the oil, it knew it would face ferocious opposition from environmental and human rights groups. It therefore brought the World Bank, an organization with great influence in developing countries, into the project and gave it authority over important operational matters.[5] The presence of the Bank served to diminish opposition to the project.

Finally, it should be noted that in selecting a friend, lambs in the international system face an inherent constraint: The weak, by their very nature, usually have few potential friends to choose from.

Develop Alternatives Away from the Table

One of the most effective ways for a party to increase its power at the negotiating table is to develop alternative courses of action away from it. A party may ultimately decide to use that alternative instead of creating a relationship with a counterpart, or it may simply use it as leverage to persuade a counterpart to improve the terms of their agreement. Thus, the fact that the chairman of Daimler-Benz told the chairman of Chrysler that he had conducted exploratory discussions with Ford about a possible merger strengthened the German company in its successful negotiations to acquire Chrysler.[6] Throughout the cold war, small states in their negotiations with one of the superpowers often developed or threatened to develop alternative deals with the other. For example, Egypt's President Nasser, when faced with U.S. reluctance to finance the Aswan Dam in the 1950s, found an alternative sponsor in the Soviet Union. More recently, the development of the North

American Free Trade Agreement was an alternative trade arrangement that persuaded reluctant states in the Uruguay Round negotiations to come to terms with U.S. demands in 1994.

A related power tactic is to reduce an adversary's ability to develop its own alternatives away from the negotiating table. For example, in merger negotiations, one party may buy up another company in order to prevent its negotiating counterpart from acquiring that company itself, thereby gaining an alternative to a merger with the first company.

Get Attention

In order to influence the stronger side, the lamb must get the lion's attention at the highest level. The stronger side's lack of attention, often an indication that it does not consider the other side particularly powerful or significant, may take many forms, but it is almost always demonstrated by entrusting negotiations to relatively low-level officials with limited authority and access to their organization's leadership. The tactics of attention getting may include stalling or walking out of the negotiations. In the U.S.–Canada Free Trade Agreement talks, the Canadians walked out when they felt that the United States was not taking the negotiations seriously. That action provoked a diplomatic crisis between the two long-time allies and succeeded in getting the attention of the United States, which led to high-level American participation in the negotiations. Similarly, stalemated business negotiations can sometimes be unblocked by having the leader of one company go over the heads of the negotiators to deal directly with the president of the other company. The particular power tactics used by a weaker party in a negotiation depend on the whole network of relationships that exists between it and its stronger counterpart.

Take Initiatives

Often weak parties are paralyzed by their own sense of impotence. The evidence seems to show that organizations that take initiatives in their relations with others do better than those that do not. By making proposals to which the other side has to respond, the weaker side can influence the course of the negotiations. Thus, Canada took the initiative from the very beginning of the free trade talks, and this approach contributed significantly to Canada's success. On the other hand, developing serious initiatives often requires a commitment of resources, particularly human resources, that a weak state or company simply may not have.

Divide and Conquer

A strong company gains its power from the magnitude and diversity of its resources; however, its large size usually means that it has many interests, relationships, and constituencies to manage. The multiplicity of those interests, relationships, and constituencies can create opportunities for the other side to augment its power at the bargaining table. Conoco wanted to undertake drilling in an area of Ecuador's rain forest that was located in a national park. The Ecuadorian government needed the oil revenue and granted permission to drill, but an alliance of environmental and human rights groups within Ecuador and abroad mounted a ferocious campaign of public opposition. At one point, Conoco sought to break the opposition alliance by holding secret talks with some of the more moderate environmental organizations to get their approval of an environmentally sound management plan. Local groups, for their part, also sought to divide and conquer by pressuring the government to withdraw its participation in the project. In the end, Conoco decided to withdraw.

Global negotiators should remember that the other side in a negotiation is never a monolith. Consequently, they need to search constantly for divisions on the other side of the table and then seek to exploit them. For example, in a negotiation over a merger, the other side's marketing division may perceive fewer advantages from the proposed deal than its finance section. As a result, at the table it may be advantageous to address particularly the interests of the other side's finance department and seek to make it a covert ally in the negotiations.

Build Bridges

A gulf usually exists between the weak and the strong. The strong may hardly recognize the weaker party and see no reason to deal with it. One way that a weak party might increase its influence with the other side is to build a bridge across that gulf, to create a connection between the lamb and the lion. This tactic involves the search for a common element—a historical connection, a common language, or a similar culture—upon which to build that bridge. As noted in the earlier discussion of culture, Russian general Akhromeyev built a bridge to U.S. Secretary of State George Shultz by talking of his love for the novels of James Fenimore Cooper. By doing so, he gained credibility and therefore influence with Shultz. In short, he used literature as a power tool. Business negotiators engage in similar bridge building as they seek to learn of and relate to the special interests, backgrounds, and activities of their counterparts.

Exploit the International Context

Companies and states in a negotiation are not totally independent entities, and their negotiations with each other are not isolated from other relationships and events. They are, instead, integral parts of the international system, a system that is in constant flux. In the international domain, all negotiations between two parties either involve or have the potential to involve other parties. In this sense, there are few strictly bilateral negotiations. The international context in which states must operate can influence decisions in individual negotiations. Consequently, it is important for weaker states and organizations to understand that context and to seek to exploit it to their advantage. One can find numerous cases in which the weaker parties invoked this approach with varying degrees of success. In 2001 both Brazil and South Africa in their negotiations with multinational pharmaceutical firms exploited international public concern over the AIDS epidemic and built strong alliances with nongovernmental health organizations in order to lower prices of drugs needed to fight the disease.

Link Issues

Linkage involves the joining together of seemingly isolated issues into a single transaction to increase a party's influence with a counterpart. Often the linkage is unstated, but clearly implicit. Thus, in negotiating with the Chinese in April 2001 to gain the return of the crew of a spy plane that had landed in China, the United States exerted its influence with the Chinese on this issue by hinting at the detrimental effect that the dispute was having on China's trade relations with the United States.

In 2001, Enron was seeking to have India purchase its Dabhol power plant, which had been forced to close down after the Indian state of Maharashtra failed to pay nearly $50 million for electricity that it had received from the plant. Kenneth Lay, Enron's chairman and CEO and a strong campaign contributor and supporter of President George W. Bush, employed the power tool of bringing a third party, the United States government, into the negotiation. He threatened that the U.S. government would impose sanctions on India if it did not resolve the matter in a manner satisfactory to Enron's interests. In fact, the U.S. government did make some high-level contacts with the India government about the problem. After the terrorist attacks of September 11, however, the United States developed an overriding interest in making India a strong security partner in its war on terrorism. It understood that achieving that goal would be linked to ceasing to press India on settling Enron's Dabhol problem. Moreover, Enron's financial scandals that were revealed at about the same time gave President Bush a strong incentive to avoid a close public association with the troubled corporation and its chairman. Accordingly, the problem no longer appeared on the agenda of issues between India and the United States.

Frame Issues

Effective negotiators often rely on framing as a power tool to influence the other side. Framing is the use of analogies and metaphors to characterize a problem or issue in a way that is favorable to the negotiator. When the Indian university head characterized a negotiation between a weak and strong party as "a dialogue between the lamb and the lion," he was framing the issue in a way that was clearly to his advantage. Of course, most negotiations between the weak and the strong are not really negotiations between a lamb and a lion. But if, as in the case of the debate between the Indian and the American psychologist, you succeed in having the other side adopt that analogy, then you have effectively set the terms of the debate. The fact that the American psychologist did not challenge the appropriateness of the analogy, but instead began talking about how the lamb really did have tools to deal with the lion gave the Indian university head a clear advantage in their discussion.

HOW SHOULD THE LION
NEGOTIATE WITH THE LAMB?

Although discussions of the role of power in negotiations tend to focus on the tactics of the weak, one should be equally concerned about how the strong use their power. Rather than enabling the powerful to exploit the weak, appropriate advice to the strong might focus on making better agreements from which both the lamb and the lion benefit. A few lessons for the strong follow.

Carefully Study the Power Sources

Many international cases demonstrate that the stronger side should not take its power for granted but rather should analyze it carefully. In particular, it should ask what its sources of power are in this specific negotiation or dispute, rather than merely calculating its total resources. Had the United States objectively examined this question at the outset of the conflict in Vietnam, which Lyndon Johnson labeled a "piss-ant country," and had France asked the same question at the beginning of the war in Algeria, neither country might have squandered the men and resources that it did in the two wars. The failure of the strong to understand their power may also lead them to behave unwisely in a negotiation. Through words and actions, a party may communicate its power in provocative and arrogant ways, ways that antagonize the other side, make it defensive, and in the end impede negotiation.

Appearances May Deceive

The weaker party is often stronger than the stronger party first assumes. If the cases teach nothing else, they demonstrate that the weaker party has devices and tactics at its command to augment its power that the stronger party does not fully understand or appreciate at the outset of the negotiation. The multinational pharmaceutical companies at first did fully evaluate the power of South Africa and Brazil in negotiations over the AIDS drugs, and Conoco, which took pride in being "environmentally friendly," probably did not fully evaluate the potential power of the alliance of organizations opposing it in Ecuador. Blinded by the disparity in the two side's power, the stronger party often does not fully examine the other side's power potential and fails to grasp the degree of commitment and priority that the weaker side has placed on achieving a particular end.

Use Power Sparingly

The strong who seek to achieve stable advantageous agreements should avoid trying to overpower the weaker side through domineering words or actions.

Such an approach creates two types of risk for the stronger party. First, the lion's exploitative actions will often lead the lamb to become defensive and cautious, or indeed to avoid making any commitments until the last possible minute.

Second, while the coercive use of power may indeed result in an agreement, that agreement may prove unstable in the long run. Inevitably, weak organizations tied to agreements that they consider unfair will seek to escape them in the future. In the international system, the strong are in a constant process of negotiation with the weak; consequently, in any specific negotiation, they must weigh the short-term advantage to be gained through the overt application of power against the long-term benefits to be derived from a productive relationship brought about through wise restraint.

Part III

GLOBAL DEAL MENDING

15

DEAL STRESS

Parties to an international transaction always maintain and pursue their own separate interests. If marriage, according to a Chinese proverb is "one bed, two dreams," then a transaction, whether it is a one-shot sales contract or a multiyear joint venture, is one deal, two interests. So long as the parties' individual interests remain aligned and are not inconsistent with one another, their transaction will continue to function smoothly. But as soon as their interests begin to diverge, conflict will arise to place increasing stress on the deal. If the conflict is stressful enough, it will cause the deal to break.

As a result of the persistence of the parties' individual interests, the risk of conflict is inherent in any international business transaction. This conflict may take many forms. A host government may cancel an investment contract with a foreign company because of local political opposition. An emerging market company may not have the foreign currency to repay a loan from an international commercial bank. A foreign buyer may refuse to pay for a computer system that it claims does not meet contract specifications.

Although international and domestic transactions risk many similar conflicts, international deals face those of a kind and magnitude not commonly found in purely domestic deals. Global negotiators can divide the special elements of conflict in an international business transaction into two basic categories: (1) the special factors that increase the likelihood of dispute between the parties; and (2) the special factors that increase the likelihood that after a dispute breaks out, its resolution will not be fair, expeditious, or efficient. For example, in the long-term chemical supply transaction between Houston Glue and Budapest Adhesive mentioned earlier, the fact that the two parties speak different languages and come from different national and business cultures increases the risk that a conflict will break out between them. Once it does surface, the fact that both Hungary's and Texas's courts and laws may be applicable in the absence of special dispute planning measures increases the likelihood that the conflict will not be resolved fairly, expeditiously, and cheaply.

THE CAUSES OF DEAL STRESS

Although the causes of conflict in individual deals are numerous, they generally may be attributed to either the parties' imperfect contract with respect to their underlying transaction or the changed circumstances after they have signed their agreement.

The Parties' Imperfect Contract

The goal of any written contract is to express the full meaning of the parties' agreement concerning their proposed transaction. However, as shown earlier, in international transactions, the problem of accurately negotiating and articulating the parties' intent in a long-term arrangement is particularly difficult because of their differing cultures, business practices, ideologies, political systems, and laws—factors that often impede a true common understanding and inhibit the development of a working relationship. In connection with a contract between the government of the Sudan and an English company for the construction of housing for Nubians forced from their villages by the rising Nile waters from the construction of the Aswan Dam, an executive of the English company stated that it "expected" to complete the houses by the date specified in the government's public call for tenders. The Sudanese interpreted this as a firm commitment while the English executive later claimed that he was just stating an intent to make a good-faith effort. When the construction company failed to complete the houses on time, the Sudanese government demanded compensation. The resulting conflict caused by their imperfect contract was only settled years later in the company's favor through international arbitration.[1]

Changed Circumstances

A sudden fall in commodity prices, the outbreak of civil war, the development of a new technology, or the imposition of currency controls are exam-

ples of changes in circumstance that often force the parties back to the negotiating table. As chapter 12 argued, changes in circumstances can either
increase or decrease the costs and benefits of the agreement to the parties.
As the following diagram shows, when a change in circumstances means that
the cost of respecting a contract for one of the parties is greater than the
cost of abandoning it, the result is usually rejection of the deal or a demand
for its renegotiation.

Figure 15.1

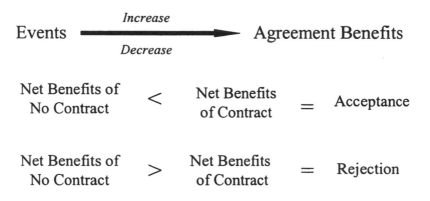

The notions of costs and benefits are not limited to purely economic calculations. Political and social costs and benefits must also be accounted for.
When the Islamic revolutionary government came to power in Iran, it realized that it would pay a significant economic cost for expropriating American
investment, but it also judged that the political benefits outweighed them.

DISPUTE RESOLUTION PROCESSES

In the face of a broken deal caused by severe conflict, the parties can resort to
one of four basic dispute settlement processes. These four processes, with
numerous variations, include: (1) negotiation, which in many cases results in
a renegotiation of the deal; (2) mediation, by which a third person assists the

disputants to resolve their conflict; (3) arbitration, by which the parties to the dispute agree to submit their dispute to a third person for a decision and to abide by that decision; and (4) adjudication by a court of law or some other governmental authority. As the diagram below indicates, these four dispute resolution processes form a continuum from negotiation on the one hand to adjudication on the other.

As the parties in conflict move along the continuum, they increasingly lose control of their dispute and are increasingly subject to the actions of a third party. In relying on negotiation alone, the parties retain complete control over their dispute. In mediation, they still maintain control over their dispute but the very presence of a third person changes the dynamics between them and can influence their actions. Arbitration requires an agreement by the parties to submit to the process. But once a dispute is referred to arbitration, the arbitral panel controls the dispute and has the power to impose a decision according to the applicable law. In adjudication, the jurisdiction and procedure of the courts is based on law, rather than on the parties' agreement as is the case in arbitration.

Lawyers and some executives tend to view arbitration and adjudication as the principal ways of resolving international business disputes. These two

Figure 15.2

Continuum of Dispute Resolution Processes

| Negotiation | Mediation | Arbitration | Adjudication |

Disputants increasingly lose control.
Third party increasingly intrudes.

dispute settlement processes, however, suffer from several disadvantages. They are costly, time-consuming, lack finality in some cases, and destroy the business relationship in nearly all cases. Indeed, if the goal of the parties in a dispute is to *mend* their deal, they should rely first and foremost on negotiation and mediation to solve their problem. Arbitration and adjudication, rather than mending the deal, are primarily means to liquidate it, to effect a legal divorce between the parties. The end result of both arbitration and adjudication is a decision as to whether or not one of the parties is entitled to a sum of money in satisfaction of its claim. Neither its aim nor its consequence is to repair a broken business relationship. Accordingly, given the ever-present potential for conflict in an international dealing, the parties to international transactions, particularly in long-term arrangements, should consider the role of renegotiation and mediation in resolving eventual disputes. Moreover, they might even build these dispute settlement processes into their transaction from the very beginning of their dealings together. The following two chapters will examine these basic techniques of deal mending.

16

RENEGOTIATING EXISTING TRANSACTIONS

The renegotiation of existing agreements is a constant in global business. The world witnessed the renegotiation of mineral and petroleum agreements in the 1960s and 1970s, often in the face of threatened host country nationalizations and expropriations; the loan reschedulings of the 1980s following the debt crisis in developing countries; and the restructuring of project and financial agreements as a result of the Asian financial crisis of the late 1990s.

THREE KINDS OF RENEGOTIATION

Discussions of "renegotiation" apply the term to three fundamentally different situations, and it is therefore important to distinguish them at the outset. The three situations are postdeal renegotiations, intradeal renegotiations, and extradeal renegotiations. Each raises different problems, and each demands different solutions.

Postdeal renegotiation takes place at the expiration of a contract when the two sides, though legally free to go their own ways, nonetheless try to renew their relationship. Consider the case of an international power company that built an electrical generating station in an emerging market country and entered into a twenty-year contract to supply electricity to a state public utility. At the end of twenty years, when local law considers their legal relationship at an end, the power company and the public utility begin discussions on a second long-term electricity supply contract, thereby renegotiating their original relationship. While this second negotiation process—a postdeal renegotiation—may seem at first glance to resemble the negotiation of their original contract, it also has some notable differences that influence renegotiation strategies, tactics, and outcomes.

Intradeal renegotiation occurs when the agreement itself provides that during specified times or after the happening of specified events during the term of the contract the parties may renegotiate or review certain of its provisions. Chapter 12 examined the various types of intradeal renegotiation provisions that parties might use in an agreement. Their purpose is to achieve a balance between contractual stability and the need to adapt to changing circumstances. For example, the just-mentioned electricity supply contract might include a provision calling for the renegotiation of the agreement's pricing terms in the event of dramatic changes in fuel costs that might occur over the twenty-year period. Here, renegotiation is anticipated as a legitimate activity in which both parties, while still bound to each other in a valid contract, are to engage in good faith. It is an intradeal renegotiation because it takes places within the legal framework established for the original transaction.

The most difficult, stressful, and emotional renegotiations are those undertaken in apparent violation of the contract or at least in the absence of a specific clause authorizing a renegotiation. These negotiations take place extradeal, for they occur outside the framework of the existing agreement. The negotiations to reschedule loans following the Third World debt crisis of the early 1980s and the renegotiation of investment agreements in the 1960s all fit within the category of extradeal renegotiations. In each case, one of the participants was seeking relief from a legally binding obligation without any basis for renegotiation in the agreement itself.

All three types of renegotiation are a constant and ever-present fact of contemporary life. Yet four important factors distinguish them from initial negotiations. They include: (1) increased mutual knowledge gained from working together; (2) increased transactional understanding as a result of experience with the deal; (3) increased mutual linkage because of the investments in the transaction; and (4) the option, by virtue of their contract, for one or both of the parties to invoke litigation to enforce its legal rights.

In each type of renegotiation, different relationships and process dynamics take place between the parties. These dynamics lead to possible strategies and tactics that skilled global negotiators should consider. Let's examine the processes at work in the three kinds of renegotiation.

Postdeal Renegotiations

Several factors distinguish a postdeal renegotiation from an initial negotiation. First, by virtue of law, custom, or contractual commitments expressed or implied, the parties may have a legal obligation to negotiate in good faith with one another despite the fact that their original contract has terminated. Consequently, their ability to refuse to engage in postdeal renegotiations may be limited. The existence and precise nature of such a duty will depend on the law governing the contract.

Anglo-American law has traditionally recognized a broad, unrestrained freedom of negotiation that permits a party to begin or end negotiations at any time for any reason.[1] The rationale for this rule is that a limitation on the freedom to negotiate might discourage persons from undertaking transactions in the first place. In contrast, the law in certain other countries is less liberal, holding that once the parties have commenced negotiations, they may have an obligation to negotiate in good faith.

But even in common-law countries, the parties may have an obligation to renegotiate an agreement in good faith at its end because of an express provision in the original contract, the prevailing practices and customs of the business concerned, or the conduct of the parties toward one another during the life of their agreement. In contrast, parties seeking to negotiate a transaction initially would have no such obligation and could abandon negotiations at any time.

The precise content of the obligation to participate in good faith negotiations varies from country to country. It may include a duty not to negotiate with a third person until postdeal negotiations with a party in the original transaction have failed. It may also require a party not to terminate renegotiations without reasonable cause and without having persevered for a reasonable length of time. Failure by either side to fulfill its obligations to renegotiate in good faith may result in liability to pay compensation.

Even if the applicable law imposes no legal obligation to renegotiate in good faith, the original contract, as well as economic factors, may constrain the postdeal renegotiation process in ways not present in the original negotiations. For example, the twenty-year electricity supply contract mentioned above might provide that if the power company and the public utility fail to negotiate a second twenty-year supply contract, the public utility company will be obligated to purchase the project company's electrical generating station according to a pricing formula specified in the original agreement.

Beyond legal and contractual constraints, the four factors mentioned above will significantly influence the course of negotiations. For example, in renegotiating the electricity supply agreement, the power company's approach will be more cautious and reluctant if the history of the first contract was plagued by late and contested payments than if the public utility had always paid on time and in full. Similarly, if over the first twenty years the price of power under the contract had proven to be much higher than that of competing forms of energy, the public utility would seek changes in the pricing formula during the renegotiation. And finally, the fact that the power company organized itself and trained its employees to provide electricity over the long term to a single specific purchaser will probably mean that, all other things being equal, the power company would prefer to enter into a new contract with the utility rather than to make an agreement with another purchaser, a course of action entailing significant new risks and costs. In addition, the public utility, having come to rely on the power company for a major portion of its electrical supply, may wish to avoid the costs of finding another supplier or of creating its own electrical generating capacity.

In any negotiation, a party's actions at the negotiating table are influenced by its evaluation of available alternatives to the deal it is trying to negotiate. Rational negotiators will not ordinarily agree to a transaction that is inferior to their best alternative to a negotiated agreement. In a postdeal renegotiation, each party's evaluation of its best alternative to a renegotiated deal be heavily influenced by its knowledge of the other side gained during the first agreement, its understanding of the transaction acquired during that time, and the extent of the investment it has made in the relationship.

In general, the success of postdeal renegotiations will depend on the nature of the relationship that developed between the parties during the original contract. If that relationship has been strong and productive, the atmosphere at the bargaining table will be that of two partners trying to solve a common problem. If the relationship has been weak and troubled, the prevailing mood will be that of two cautious adversaries who know each other only too well.

Rules to guide postdeal renegotiations. The factors discussed above give rise to the following principles that negotiators should consider as they structure and conduct the process of postdeal renegotiations.

1. *Provide for postdeal renegotiations in the original contract.* For transactions in which the desirability or likelihood of postdeal renegotiations is high, the parties should include in their original agreement the processes and rules that they will follow in conducting a postdeal renegotiation. For example, the contract should specify how soon before the end of the contract renegotiations are to begin; how long the renegotiations are to continue before either party may legally abandon them; where the renegotiations are to take place; and the nature of the information that each side is to provide the other. Recognizing that postdeal renegotiations may become problematic, the contract might also authorize the use of mediators or other third-party helpers in the process.

2. *Individually and jointly review the history of the relationship during the original contract.* As part of its preparation, each party to a postdeal renegotiation should review carefully and thoroughly the experience of working with the other side during the first contract. An understanding of the problems encountered during that period will enable each side to shape proposals to remedy them during a contemplated second agreement. To make that review an opportunity for creative problem solving rather than mutual acrimony over past mistakes, the parties should structure a joint review of past experience, perhaps with the help of a neutral facilitator, at the beginning of the postdeal renegotiation process. For example, the power company and the public utility might give a review team consisting of executives from each side the task of preparing a mutually acceptable history of their relationship. Inevitably, during the course of postdeal renegotiations, each side will refer to past events. The renegotiation process will proceed more smoothly and efficiently if at the beginning of the process the parties have a common understanding of their history together than if they engage in a continuing debate throughout the renegotiation about the existence and significance of past events.

3. *Understand thoroughly the alternatives to a renegotiated deal.* Negotiators should not only evaluate their own alternatives to the deal that they are trying to make, they should also try to estimate their counterparts' alternatives. In a postdeal renegotiation, these two tasks are often complicated by the fact that the parties may have conducted their activities in such a way during the first contract that few realistic alternatives to a second contract seem possible. For example, the power company that owns a generating facility may feel that it has few options other than making a second contract with the state

public utility. Or the public utility may see no realistic alternatives to making a second electricity purchase agreement with the power company. Rather than accept the inevitability of a second contract, each side, long before the termination of the first contract, should carefully examine all options and seek to develop possible new alternatives before entering into postdeal renegotiations with the other side.

Intradeal Renegotiations

Chapter 12 discussed the nature and purpose of intradeal renegotiations at length and is summarized here. The fundamental purpose of intradeal renegotiations is to balance the two imperatives in any transaction of contractual stability and adaptation to changed circumstances. Accordingly, renegotiation clauses in the original contract establish a framework in which such discussions about adapting to change are to take place. Their intent is to control the renegotiation process. They do not open all issues to reconsideration at any time. In general, a party that has agreed to an intradeal renegotiation has an obligation to participate in that process in good faith. The precise meaning of good faith will vary from country to country. The elements of good faith negotiation, outlined in the earlier discussion of postdeal renegotiations, would certainly apply in an intradeal renegotiation as well.

The existence of an intradeal renegotiation clause argues strongly for the parties to work hard at developing a strong working relationship during the life of their transaction. Intradeal renegotiations are likely to proceed more smoothly if such a relationship exists than if the parties consider themselves adversaries from the time they first sign the deal. It should be remembered, however, that although an intradeal renegotiation provision requires parties to negotiate, it does not compel them to agree.

Extradeal Renegotiations

In an extradeal renegotiation, one party is insisting on renegotiating terms of a valid contract that contains no express provision authorizing renegotiation. Unlike initial negotiations, which are generally fueled by both sides' hopes for future benefits, extradeal negotiations begin with both parties' shattered expectations. One side has failed to achieve the benefits expected from the transaction, and the other is being asked to give up something for which it bargained hard and which it hoped to enjoy for a long time. And whereas both parties to the negotiation of a proposed new venture participate willingly, if not eagerly, one party always participates reluctantly, if not downright unwillingly, in an extradeal renegotiation.

Beyond failed expectations, extra deal renegotiations by their very nature can create bad feelings and mistrust. One side believes it is being asked to give up something to which it has a legal and moral right. It views the other side as having gone back on its word, as having acted in bad faith by reneging on the deal. Indeed, the reluctant party may even feel that it's being coerced into participating in extradeal renegotiations since a refusal to do so would result in losing the investment it has already made in the transaction.

In most cases, it is very difficult for the parties to see extradeal renegotiations as anything more than a process in which one side wins and the other side loses. While initial negotiations are usually about the degree to which each side will share in expected benefits, an extradeal renegotiation is often about allocating a loss. At the same time, because the parties are bound together in a legal and economic relationship, it is usually much more difficult for one or both of them to walk away from a troubled transaction than it is for two unconnected parties from a proposed initial agreement.

In most countries, the law does not oblige a party to enter into renegotiations, no matter how much conditions have changed or how heavy the costs incurred by the other side since the contract was originally made.[2] Indeed, English common law at one time viewed renegotiated contracts under certain conditions as invalid since they lacked the legal requirement of consideration in those cases in which, as a result of renegotiation, a party was promising to do no more than it was already obligated to do under its original contract. In general, a party being asked to renegotiate an existing agreement has a legal right to refuse to renegotiate and to insist on performance in accordance with the letter of the contract. On the other hand, requests—or in some cases, demands—for renegotiation of an existing agreement are often accompanied by express or implied threats, including governmental intervention, expropriation, a slow down in performance, or the complete repudiation or cancellation of the contract itself.

Parties facing a demand for renegotiation usually have an available legal remedy to enforce their contract and will often threaten to go to court to assert it. However, a willingness to pursue a legal remedy to its conclusion, rather than renegotiate, will usually depend on the party's evaluation of that remedy in relation to the results it expects from renegotiation. To the extent that the net benefits (i.e., benefits minus costs) from renegotiation exceed the expected net benefits from litigation, a rational party will ordinarily engage in the requested renegotiation. But if either before or during the renegotiation, a party decides that the net benefits to be derived from litigation will exceed the net benefits to be gained in renegotiation, that party will normally pursue its legal remedies.

On its side, the party asking for renegotiation will be making its own cost-benefit analysis of the relative merits of contract repudiation and its probable fate in litigation. As long as this party thinks that the net benefits of repudiating the contract are less than the net benefits of respecting it, the contractual relationship will continue. But when (for whatever reason) it judges the respective net benefits to be the opposite, the result will be a demand for renegotiation with the threat of eventual repudiation in the background.

A party's reluctance to agree to an extradeal renegotiation may be due to the impact of renegotiation not only on the contract in question but on other contracts and relationships as well. Renegotiation of a transaction with one particular party may set an undesirable precedent for other renegotiations with other parties. For example, concessions by an international commercial bank to a debtor country in severe financial difficulties may lead another debtor country to seek equal treatment by demanding extradeal renegotiations of its own loan agreements.

A CASE OF EXTRADEAL RENEGOTIATION: ENRON'S DABHOL PROJECT IN INDIA

One may gain an understanding of the dynamics at work in extradeal renegotiations by examining a specific case, the renegotiations involved in Enron's Dabhol power project in India, an incident that received significant media attention in 1995–1996.

Background

India, the largest democracy in the world, had a population exceeding 920 million people in 1995. A poor country with per capita income of $370 a year, it also has a growing middle class of 250 million people located primarily in the cities. The former jewel in the crown of the British Empire, India gained its independence in 1947 and is a federation consisting of 26 states and 6 union territories with a strong central government whose 600-member Parliament is elected every five years. Following the British parliamentary model, the political party with the majority in Parliament forms the executive government and that party's leader becomes the Indian prime minister. Each of India's states has its own legislature and an executive consisting of a chief minister and a cabinet of state ministers chosen from the elected members of the state assembly. State elections are held every five years but not necessarily at the same time as central government elections.

From its independence in 1947 until the early 1990s, India had based its economic policies on self-sufficiency, import substitution, state control of basic industry and infrastructure, and restriction on foreign investment. These policies were probably no more apparent than in the electric power sector. The generation and distribution of electricity was the exclusive domain of the central and state governments, and political factors, rather than market forces, were primary considerations in its operation. The Indian Energy Supply Act of 1948 had initiated this monopoly, establishing state electricity boards to develop the power sector at the state level and the central government to set policy at the national level. Under this regime, total electricity generating capacity amounted to approximately 81,000 megawatts in 1995, of which state agencies accounted for 65 percent, the national government 31 percent, and private enterprise a mere 4 percent.

As India entered the 1990s, the country's demand for electrical power greatly exceeded its ability to supply it. As a result, it experienced serious power outages with a significant negative impact on industrial production. Furthermore, many rural areas received little electricity and some 95,000 Indian villages had none at all. Experts predicted that the situation would only grow worse in the years ahead. Neither the Indian central government nor the various state electricity boards had the necessary capital to develop the capacity to meet the nation's growing demand for electricity. Indeed, most state electricity boards were insolvent or nearly so due to the inefficiency of their operations. Power losses from their distribution grids were as much as 40 percent. Electricity was stolen from the system and in many cases pricing for certain privileged groups, such as farmers, resulted in it being sold for less than the cost of production. The entire system of electricity generation and distribution was beset by high costs, entrenched subsidies, and bloated employment rolls. As a result, the accumulated losses of the public power sector amounted to $6.4 billion in 1996.

One consequence of the system was the existence of entrenched constituencies opposed to reform of the power sector and especially to privatization. At the same time, growing public demand for electricity and the resolution of the energy shortage became an important political issue. In 1991, the Congress Party narrowly won an election victory with promises to address the problem. Prime Minister P. V. Rao, an advocate of market reforms, appointed as his finance minister Manmohan Singh, who began a series of reforms that sought to transform the economy from one based on state control to one based on market forces. A central focus of this package of reforms was the encouragement of private and foreign investment in India.

The new Indian government secured the adoption of the Electricity Laws Act of 1991, which represented a historic shift in policy. This legislation allowed private sector companies with 100 percent foreign ownership to build, own, and operate power plants, mandated a minimum rate of return of 16 percent on equity, allowed foreign investors to repatriate profits entirely, permitted new projects to have a debt-to-equity ratio of 4:1, outlined procedures by which private and foreign-owned projects could sell electricity to state electricity boards, and specified how electrical tariff rates should be set.

Despite these substantial reforms, foreign power companies did not immediately rush to India to develop new projects. The Indian government therefore took the initiative in May 1992 of sending its power secretary, S. Rajgopal, to the United States in an effort to attract American companies to invest in the Indian power sector. One company that responded positively to Mr. Rajgopal's overtures was Enron Corporation, based in Houston, Texas.

Negotiating the Project

Enron Corporation, then a diversified energy company that earned a net income of $453 million on revenues of approximately $9 billion in 1995, was facing the problem of slow growth in the U.S. energy market. It therefore made a strategic decision to focus its efforts abroad and so created Enron Development Corporation, a wholly owned subsidiary, to exploit the growing worldwide demand for energy, particularly in high-growth emerging market countries. The visit to Enron by the Indian power secretary in May 1992 persuaded the company's leadership that India offered the kind of opportunities that fit Enron's worldwide strategy. The following month, on June 15, 1992, a team of Enron executives arrived in Delhi, the capital of India, to continue discussions with central government officials and to explore concrete opportunities for power projects.

Under the guidance of these officials, the Enron team identified the state of Maharashtra as the most advantageous site from which to begin to serve the Indian electricity market. With a population of nearly 79 million people, Maharashtra was India's third largest state and the home of its commercial capital, Bombay (later to be Mumbai). Moreover, as the country's most important industrial state, Maharashtra had the highest gross national product per capita in India. At the time of the Enron visit, the Congress Party, which controlled the central government and had been the dominant force in Indian politics since before the country's independence, also controlled the Maharashtra state government.

In discussions with officials of the Maharashtra state government and the Maharashtra State Electricity Board (MSEB), Enron proposed the construction of a 2015-megawatt power plant at a cost of nearly $3 billion, which would make it the largest foreign investment project ever undertaken in India. A plant of that size would require a large reliable source of fuel, which Enron hoped to supply in the form of liquefied natural gas produced from its joint venture with the country of Qatar, 1,200 miles away across the Indian Ocean. In view of the substantial time and capital needed to develop facilities to liquefy, handle, and ship natural gas, Enron proposed to divide the electricity project into two phases: a first phase of 695 megawatts to use locally produced fuel and a second phase of 1,320 megawatts to use the imported liquefied natural gas. Dividing the project into two phases also permitted Enron to test India's credibility and for India to determine Enron's ability to deliver a reliable source of electricity. Enron decided that the best location for its power plant was the town of Dabhol, located on the Indian Ocean approximately 120 miles south of Bombay.

An essential requirement for the financial success of the proposed Dabhol project was the existence of a credible, long-term purchaser of its electricity to enable the project company to secure its needed long-term debt financing and to assure the equity investors an adequate return on their investment. For the Dabhol project to become a reality, it was therefore necessary for the Maharashtra State Electricity Board (MSEB), the only potential buyer in the state, to enter into a long-term power purchase agreement with the Dabhol Power Project Company, the entity to be created to build, own, and operate the power plant. On June 20, 1992, just three days after the Enron team's arrival in Bombay and only five days after entering the country for the first time, Enron and the MSEB signed a memorandum of understanding outlining the project as described above and proposing a power purchase agreement stipulating that the price to be charged by the Dabhol Power Company would be no more than 2.40 rupees (7.3 cents) per kilowatt-hour.

During the next year, Enron, the MSEB, and various concerned Indian central and state government departments negotiated the precise arrangements under which the proposed Dabhol power project would come into existence and sell electricity in Maharashtra. The negotiation encountered three major problems. First, the World Bank, which served as a consultant to the central government, wrote a report claiming that the Dabhol project was too large and would create excess capacity for years to come. It also asserted that the electricity produced by the proposed project would be too expensive when compared to electricity generated by more traditional fuels such as coal. In response, Enron, stressing the environmental benefits of the Dabhol project and the long-term power needs of India, undertook a lobbying campaign in key departments of the Indian government and succeeded in countering the negative effects of the Bank's report.

The second and more difficult problem concerned the project's expected rate of return. Enron projected a rate of return to equity holders of 26.52 percent, which the government of Maharashtra as well as the central government's Foreign Investment Promotion Board considered too high. The Indian side felt that 20 percent was much more reasonable. Enron insisted that given the risks involved and the prevailing market expectations for similar projects, the projected rate of return on the Dabhol project was reasonable and that even 30 percent would be appropriate. Although the negotiations nearly collapsed over the issue, the two sides finally agreed on a rate of return of 25.22 percent, which various government officials still considered too high. Other difficult issues concerned the project's capital costs, government guarantees, the pricing escalation factor in the power purchase agreement, and the provisions on monetary exchange rate fluctuations.

The third problem that surfaced during the negotiations was a growing negative view of the project among certain segments of the Indian public. Opponents of the project strongly criticized its high rate of return, the high electricity tariff that Indians would ultimately have to bear, and the government's failure to engage in competitive bidding as had been standard practice with other Indian power plants. Accusations were made that Indian officials had been bribed to approve the project. Public demonstrations against the project took place and at one point a bomb exploded in the hotel in which the Enron team was staying. Despite public opposition, negotiations continued.

To undertake the project, Enron with two American minority partners, General Electric and Bechtel, each of which held 10 percent of the equity, formed the Dabhol Power Company in April 1993. On December 8, 1993, some 20 months after the Indian power secretary's first contact with Enron, the Dabhol Power Company and the MSEB signed the power purchase agreement, formally launching the Dabhol project, the biggest foreign investment project ever undertaken in India. The basic provisions of the power purchase agreement were as follows:

- The Dabhol Power Company agreed to design, finance and build within 33 months an electrical generating plant with a base load capacity of 625 megawatts and additional peak load capacity of 70 megawatts. Failure to provide commercial service within 33 months of the deadline or to reach base load capacity of 625 megawatts within one year after the beginning of commercial service would result in penalty payments by the company to the MSEB.
- The MSEB and the government of the State of Maharashtra agreed to provide the land and the necessary infrastructure, including roads to the site, communications, and transmission lines from the power plant to the MSEB grid.
- The MSEB agreed to purchase what amounted to at least 90 percent of the Dabhol plant's output. It was obligated to pay for electricity from the Dabhol Power Company under a complex payment formula for an initial period of 20 years. The result of the formula was that the estimated cost of power to the MSEB would be 7.05 cents per kilowatt-hour at the commencement of commercial operations. The tariff was indexed to Indian inflation rates and was expected to rise to 11.34 cents per kilowatt-hour by 2015.
- Although the MSEB's payments were to be made in rupees, it also had the responsibility of bearing any changes in the dollar-rupee exchange rate over time.

- The Maharashtra state government guaranteed the MSEB payment obligations to the Dabhol Power Company, and the central government issued a counter guarantee.
- Although the power purchase agreement was governed by Indian law, the parties agreed to settle any disputes arising under the agreement by binding arbitration in London.
- At the end of 20 years, MSEB had the option to extend the power purchase agreement for an additional 5 or 10 years at its option. If it chose not to renew the Agreement, the MSEB would be required to purchase the plant at 50 percent of its then-depreciated replacement value.

Enron then moved rapidly to finance and implement the project. In addition to the equity contribution of $279 million from the project partners, it ultimately secured loan commitments of $643 million from banks and lending agencies for Phase I of the project.[3]

The Forces for Change

Public opposition to the Dabhol power project grew as construction activity proceeded. Indian activists and organizations filed lawsuits in the Bombay High Court, challenging the legality of the project and the processes by which it was negotiated. Although the court dismissed the complaints, political opposition continued to mount. Specifically, the political opposition alliance of the Bharatiya Janata Party (BJP) and the Shiva Sena took up the issue on the floor of the Maharashtra State Assembly. As they prepared for state elections scheduled for March 1995, they made opposition to the Dabhol project a centerpiece in their campaign. Emphasizing Hindu nationalism and warning against the dangers of American economic and cultural imperialism, BJP–Shiv Shena politicians encouraged public opposition to the project in their campaign rhetoric. They charged that Enron was offering India nothing that India could not do for itself, that the power tariff was exorbitant and would hurt the poor, that Enron's rate of return was exploitative, and that the whole negotiation process had been tainted by corruption. According to one observer, the Dabhol project became "a national icon . . . rallying economic nationalists suspicious of the post-liberalization arrival of foreign investment."[4]

In the state assembly elections of March 1995, the BJP–Shiv Sena alliance won a majority of seats and thereby ousted from government the incumbent Congress Party. In May, the new government appointed a cabinet subcommittee, chaired by Deputy Chief Minister Shri Gopinath Munde, to investigate the Dabhol project. The committee submitted a report in July recommending that the state repudiate Phase I of the project and cancel Phase II. The committee based its recommendation on several grounds, including the absence of transparency in the negotiation process, the lack of competitive bidding procedure, the relaxation by the previous government of certain regulations relating to the project, the great expense of the project, the high electricity tariff rate and its continuing escalation, the obligation of the MSEB to pay for electricity whether or not it was actually used, the World Bank report's objections to the project, and the failure of the project negotiations to address environmental concerns.

On the basis of this report, the state government, under its new chief minister, Manohar Joshi, and the MSEB formally canceled the power purchase agreement with the Dabhol Power Company. At this point in its development, the Dabhol project had incurred sunk costs of approximately $300 million, and each day of delay on construction was estimated to cost an additional $250,000.

In response, the Dabhol Power Company and the project sponsors invoked their legal rights under the power purchase agreement by instituting arbitration in London against the MSEB and the Maharashtra state government, claiming damages in excess of $300 million. The State of Maharashtra reacted by bringing suit in the Bombay High Court to invalidate the arbitration clause and the guarantee of MSEB payments on the grounds that both had been secured through illegal means. The United States government issued a statement critical of the contract repudiation, asserting that it would have negative consequences for foreign investment in India. Foreign investors considering India became demonstrably more cautious and expressed their concern over the incident. The Indian press appeared to be divided over the wisdom of Maharashtra's action. In the face of this growing controversy, Deputy Chief Minister Munde, who had chaired the Dabhol project review committee stated: "Our decision is firm. We do not wish to renegotiate."

Renegotiating the Deal

While pursuing arbitration, Enron made it clear to the Maharashtra authorities that it would be willing to renegotiate the Dabhol project. In the fall of

1995, discussions to revive the project took place between Enron executives and Maharashtra officials and political leaders, which culminated in a meeting with Chief Minister Joshi. Shortly thereafter, Joshi announced that Maharashtra state would undertake a review of the project and promised to reopen negotiations in November. To carry out the review and renegotiation, he appointed a panel consisting of the president of the MSEB, the power secretary of Maharashtra State, and four other academic and industry experts, in contrast to the first review panel that had consisted solely of government ministers.

For two weeks, the review panel not only met with Enron to discuss proposals for restructuring the Dabhol project, but it also listened to principal critics of the project. The key issues in the discussions with Enron concerned the electricity tariff, capital costs, payment terms, and the environment. Finally, on November 19, 1995, the panel submitted a proposal to the Maharashtra state government outlining the renegotiated terms of the Dabhol project to which the panel and Enron had agreed. Enron agreed to suspend its arbitration proceedings in London until December 10. On January 8, 1996, after some delay, the Maharashtra government agreed to accept the panel proposal for renegotiated terms, which eventually became the basis for amending the power purchase agreement between the Dabhol Power Company, the state of Maharashtra, and the MSEB, an event that took place on February 23, 1996. Ultimately, in July after much debate, the Indian central government approved the amended power purchase agreement and extended the central government's counterguarantee of Maharashtra's obligations, thereby removing the final barrier to the revived project. In August 1996, Enron agreed to abandon its arbitration proceeding in London, and Maharashtra state agreed to drop its case in the Mumbai (Bombay) high court.

Despite the renegotiation and government approvals, Enron was not able to resume construction immediately. While the conflict and renegotiation between Enron and the government were evolving, various labor unions, public interest groups, and activists brought 24 suits in the Indian courts to stop the project. Even though the Maharashtra government had approved the terms of the renegotiated agreement, the courts ruled that until these suits were resolved, construction on the project would have to remain suspended. Eventually, the Indian courts held against the plaintiffs in all of these cases, but it was not until December 1996 that the last suit was dismissed and construction was resumed on the Dabhol Project.

The Renegotiated Terms

The renegotiation resulted in a modification of all of the principal terms of the power purchase agreement. Below is a summary of the changes.

Equity Participation.   Although the project company originally had only three U.S. shareholders (Enron 80 percent, Bechtel 10 percent, and General Electric 10 percent), the renegotiated deal provided for the introduction of the MSEB as a 30 percent shareholder with a proportionate reduction in Enron's interest to 50 percent.

Output Capacity.   Although the World Bank's report had criticized the original proposed power plant as being too large, the renegotiated terms provided for a plant of even greater output capacity. The capacity of Phase I was increased from 695 megawatts to 826 megawatts, and total capacity after the completion of Phase II under the renegotiated agreement was increased to 2,450 megawatts, as compared to 2015 in the original proposal.

Capital Costs.   To respond to the criticism that the project was too expensive, the renegotiation reduced the capital costs from $2.85 billion to $2.5 billion. The panel achieved this result by removing the regassification plant from the Dabhol project and treating it as a separate project, for which the power plant would pay a fixed charge, thus transforming a portion of capital costs to an ongoing variable cost that would be included in the new power tariff. A portion of the reduction in capital costs can also be attributed to the worldwide fall in the price of generation equipment.

Power Tariff.   The politics of Maharashtra demanded a reduction in the power tariff to be paid by the MSEB. Accordingly, the panel with the agreement of Enron recommended a reduction in the power tariff from approximately 7.03 cents per kilowatt-hour subject to a 4 percent annual escalation on fixed charges, to 6.03 cents per kilowatt-hour subject to fuel price and exchange rate fluctuations, until Phase II became operational, at which time the tariff would become 5.08 cents per kilowatt-hour subject to fuel price and exchange rate fluctuations for 20 years, but with no escalation.

Fuel.   The original proposal had called for distillate oil to be used in Phase I and liquefied natural gas in Phase II. The renegotiated terms provided in

Phase I for the use of naphtha, a locally produced fuel, thus sparing India foreign exchange costs of importing oil for the project.

Environment. The original power purchase agreement contained no provisions with respect to environmental protection. The renegotiated terms stated that Enron and the Dabhol Power Company would pay for monthly air and water surveys, would plant trees, manage effluent discharged into the sea to protect marine life, and would employ one person from any family displaced due to the construction of the plant.

Other Terms. Various other terms were introduced into the renegotiated agreement. For example, Enron and the Dabhol Power Company agreed to use local suppliers and supplies to the extent possible and to employ a bidding procedure in purchasing power equipment. Moreover, Enron agreed to bear costs of approximately $175 million caused by the state's cancellation of the contract provided that the construction was renewed by February 1, 1996. Although Maharashtra state failed to meet this deadline, Enron later also agreed to waive the daily interest charges of $250,000 that had been accruing as a result of work stoppage, thereby saving Maharashtra state approximately $10 million.

The Aftermath

Both Enron and the State of Maharashtra claimed the renegotiation as a victory. The Maharashtra government pointed to the reduction in the power tariff and the reduced capital costs as major concessions favoring the state. On the other hand, the enlarged project capacity was clearly a renegotiated term favorable to Enron, and a significant portion of the capital cost reduction resulted from favorable market developments with respect to generating equipment, not a transfer of value from Enron to the State of Maharashtra.

Despite government statements of satisfaction with the renegotiation, significant public opposition to the project continued. Although the Indian courts eventually dismissed all the numerous lawsuits against the project, public protests and demonstrations at the project site persisted. The measures taken by the Maharashtra state government and the police to deal with these protests prompted human rights complaints. Nonetheless, in May 1999 Phase I of the Dabhol power project was completed and began commercial operation. In that same month, Enron secured financing of $1.87 billion for Phase II of the Project, which was scheduled for completion at the end of 2001.

Ultimately, the MSEB found itself unable to pay for the electricity it was obligated to take under the power purchase agreement. In 2001, with unpaid electricity bills of approximately $45 million, the Dabhol Power Company closed down operations and began a series of legal actions against the Maharashtra State Electricity Board, the State of Maharashtra, and the Indian Central Government to secure payment and to sell its interest in the plant. In that same year, Enron itself went into bankruptcy because of losses sustained in its other businesses. At the end of 2002, the Dabhol power plant remained closed and none of the competing claims surrounding its operations had been resolved. Eventually, those claims and the Dabhol project itself will become the subject of yet another extradeal renegotiation.

GUIDING PRINCIPLES FOR EXTRADEAL RENEGOTIATIONS

Since the risk of extradeal renegotiations is always present in any international transaction, global negotiators, as stated earlier, need to ask two basic questions:

- How can the likelihood of extradeal renegotiations be reduced?
- When renegotiations actually occur, how should the parties conduct them to make the process as productive and fair as possible?

In answering these questions, negotiators need to distinguish actions they should take before and after the transaction has broken down. Thus in the case of the Dabhol project, one needs to consider the actions that Enron might have taken to avoid the conflict and renegotiation that actually took place, as well as the actions that it did take when faced with the cancellation of the power purchase agreement.

Before the Breakdown

Some principles that should guide negotiators before the deal breaks down were discussed earlier and are restated briefly below within the context of the Dabhol project case.

1. *Work to create a business relationship between the parties and recognize that a signed contract does not necessarily create an international business relationship.* Earlier chapters of this book have stressed the importance of developing effective working relationships for the success of any deal. The principles discussed in those chapters not only assist the parties in maximizing the potential of their transaction, but they also help to reduce the likelihood of extradeal renegotiations. The existence of a valuable relationship between the parties is more likely to facilitate a negotiated resolution of their dispute than if no such relationship exists. The reason for this phenomenon is that the aggrieved party views the relationship with the offending party as more valuable than the individual claim arising out of the failure to honor the contractual provision. Thus, a bank is often more willing to renegotiate loans with delinquent debtor countries or companies when the bank considers the prospect of future business with the debtor likely.

In reviewing the Dabhol project case, one concludes that although the parties had negotiated a detailed contract to govern their deal, no real business relationship appears to have existed at all between Enron, the MSEB, and the various concerned Indian government departments. Specifically, at the time the power purchase agreement was signed, there was no real connection between Enron and India itself. No Indian party was to participate in any meaningful way in the development and management of the Dabhol Power Company. The Indian public had little knowledge of Enron or of the proposed Dabhol project, which was negotiated largely in secrecy. The only role for any Indian entity was to buy electricity according to the power purchase agreement. The negotiation of the contract had been contentious, and Enron appeared to have little appreciation of Indian concerns about foreign investment in general and the Dabhol power project in particular. Finally, given the size and importance of the Dabhol project, Enron and India seemed to know relatively little about one another. After nearly eighteen months of negotiation, Enron emerged with a contract but no real business relationship. It had established no basis for cooperation and trust with the Maharashtra State Electricity Board, with the Maharashtra state government, or with the Indian public.

Had Enron thought in terms of relationship building and acted accordingly, it might have avoided the cancellation of the contract. Involving the Maharashtra State Electricity Board as a partner in the project from the very start of the project might have been a crucial step in building an effective business relationship between Enron and India. Moreover, given India's historical ambivalence toward foreign investment, it was essential that a deal of the magnitude of the Dabhol project *appear* to be and be balanced and fair to both sides. The project's high rate of return and high power tariff raised important questions in the minds of the Indian public, something that Enron should have sought to address.

2. *Building a relationship takes time, so don't rush negotiations.* Global negotiators concerned to lay the foundation for a business relationship as well as to conclude a contract know that sufficient time is required to achieve this goal. In the case of the Dabhol project, the speed with which Enron and the Maharashtra State Electricity Board achieved a contract not only prevented the parties from developing a relationship, but the project's opponents viewed that speed as a defect in the negotiation process itself. Opponents and the Indian press criticized the original Enron transaction as having been executed in "unseemly haste," and the Maharashtra state government cited "fast track procedures" as a reason for canceling the power purchase agreement. In particular, the Cabinet subcommittee pointed to the fact that the memorandum of understanding had been signed less than three days after the Enron team's arrival in Bombay.

While speed of negotiation may have appealed to Enron negotiators as efficient and a recognition of the fact that time is money, in India a quick negotiation implied overreaching by one of the parties, insufficient consideration of the public interest, or even corruption. Negotiations done in haste may be subject to challenge later on. While Enron seems to have taken pride in the speed with which it concluded the memorandum of understanding and the power purchase agreement, one may ask whether a greater investment of time in the early stages of the negotiation process would have proved cost-effective in the end by avoiding the expense and the delays of renegotiation later on.

3. *Provide for renegotiation in appropriate transactions.* As suggested in previous chapters, rather than to view a long-term transaction as frozen in the detailed provisions of a lengthy contract, it may be more realistic and wiser to think of an international deal as a *continuing negotiation* between the parties to the transaction as they seek to adjust their relationship to the rapidly changing international environment in which they must work. Accordingly, another approach to the problem of contractual instability is to provide in the contract that at specified times or on the occurrence of specified events, the

parties may renegotiate or at least review certain of the contract's provisions. In this approach, the parties deal with the problem of renegotiation before, rather than after, they sign their contract. Rather than dismiss the possibility of renegotiation and then be forced to review the entire contract at a later time in an atmosphere of hostility between the partners, it may be better to recognize the possibility of renegotiation at the outset and set down a clear framework within which to conduct the process.

4. *Consider a role for mediation or conciliation in the deal.* A third party can often help the two sides with their negotiations and renegotiations. Third parties, whether called mediators, conciliators, advisers, or something else, can assist in building and preserving business relations and in resolving disputes without resorting to arbitration or adjudication. Consequently, persons planning and negotiating international business and financial transactions should consider the possibility of building into their deals a role for some form of mediation. For example, the contract might require the parties to use the services of a mediator or conciliator to try to negotiate a settlement of their conflict before either side can invoke arbitration.

After the Breakdown

When one side has demanded renegotiation of the basic contract governing their relationship, how should one or both of the parties proceed? The following are some principles to guide negotiators after a deal has broken down.

1. *Resist the temptation to make belligerent or moralistic responses to demands for renegotiation but seek to understand the basis of the demand.* A party facing a demand for extradeal renegotiations often counters it with hostile, belligerent, or moralistic objections. Such responses are never effective in persuading the other side to end its insistence on renegotiation since that party has already determined that its own vital interests require a repudiation or a renegotiation. Normally, it is only by dealing with those interests that the two sides in a renegotiation can resolve the conflict. Moreover, as the state of Maharashtra did, the party asking for renegotiation almost always asserts equally moralistic arguments to justify its own demands: the contract is exploitative; the negotiators were corrupt; one side used duress; the other side was ignorant of all the underlying factors; the basic circumstances of the deal have changed in a fundamental way.

While respect for agreements is indeed a norm in virtually all societies, most cultures also provide some kind of relief from the binding force of a contract in various circumstances. "A deal is a deal" (*pacta sunt servanda*) is certainly an expression of a fundamental rule of human relations, but so is the statement "things have changed" (*rebus sic stantibus*). While a request for extradeal renegotiations may provoke bad feelings in one party, an outright refusal to renegotiate may also create ill will on the other side since it will be seen as an attempt to force adherence to an unjust bargain. Throughout the crisis provoked by the Maharashtra state government's cancellation of the power purchase agreement, Enron consistently expressed its willingness to renegotiate the agreement, a posture that ultimately led to a satisfactory resolution of the conflict. While it did begin to pursue its legal remedy in arbitration as soon as the power purchase agreement was canceled, it did not become belligerent or hostile toward the Maharashtra government.

In some cases, extradeal renegotiation can also be justified on the grounds that it is implicit in the parties' relationship. One may argue that in many transactions there are in effect two agreements, the legal contract that sets out enforceable rights and duties and the foundation agreement that reflects the parties' fundamental understanding in all its dimensions, legal and nonlegal. An important, implied aspect of this agreement is an understanding, given the impossibility of predicting all future contingencies, that if problems develop in the future the two sides will engage in negotiations to adjust their relationship in a mutually beneficial way.

2. *Evaluate the benefits of a legal proceeding against the value of a continuing relationship with the other side.* The extent of a party's willingness to renegotiate an existing agreement will usually be in direct proportion to the value it attaches to its potential future relationship with the other side. If a party judges that relationship to be worth more than the claim for breach of contract, it will ordinarily be willing to engage in extradeal renegotiations. For example, one of the factors that encouraged Enron to renegotiate with the Maharashtra government after the cancellation of the power purchase agreement was the prospect of undertaking numerous energy projects throughout India in the years ahead. Enron clearly evaluated that relationship to be worth much more than winning an arbitration award in a case that would certainly be a long protracted struggle. Even if it won an award for $300 million, that victory would drastically reduce its business prospects not only in

the economically important state of Maharashtra but probably in all of India as well.

A willingness to renegotiate does not mean that a party should not at the same time invoke legal remedies granted by the contract, such as litigation or arbitration, for failure to perform specified legal obligations. The aggrieved party will only pursue them fully and to the end, however, if it judges the benefits of a legal remedy to be greater than its costs, one of which is the loss of any relationship with the other side. But a party usually cannot accurately make that calculation unless it has engaged in some form of renegotiation first. Nor can it make the other side aware of the costs that side will face as a result of litigation without bringing legal action. Consequently, in appropriate cases it may be advisable to initiate legal action while at the same time conducting extradeal renegotiations.

One can argue that one of the purposes of the delays inherent in pursuing legal remedies such as a lawsuit or arbitration is to give the parties an opportunity to negotiate an efficient solution to their conflict. Although Enron began arbitration in London immediately after the Maharashtra government's cancellation of the power purchase agreement, it also immediately communicated to the government its willingness to renegotiate. The slow pace of the arbitration process allowed a successful renegotiation to take place, and Enron eventually abandoned arbitration.

3. *Look for ways to create value in the renegotiation.* A party facing a demand for renegotiation has a tendency to see the process as one in which anything gained by the other side is an automatic loss to itself. As a result, an unwilling participant in an extradeal renegotiation tends to be intransigent, to quibble over the smallest issues, and to voice recriminations. By pursuing this approach, the parties may fail to capture the maximum gains possible from their encounter.

Joint problem-solving negotiation and integrative bargaining are as applicable to an extradeal renegotiation as to an initial negotiation. The challenge for both sides in a renegotiation is to create an atmosphere in which problem solving can take place. Even if a party feels forced into an extradeal renegotiation, it should approach the process as an opportunity to secure gains. In the renegotiations between Enron and the Maharashtra state government over the Dabhol project, even though Maharashtra state gained a reduced power tariff and a project that was no longer exclusively foreign, Enron secured certain additional benefits including an enlarged power plant, increased capital from a new joint venture partner, and more influence in India through a local partner.

4. *The parties should fully understand the alternatives to success in the renegotiation—especially their costs.* The alternative to a successful extradeal renegotiation in most cases is litigation. Litigation has risks and costs for both sides, and it is important that both sides understand them thoroughly as they approach the renegotiation process so that they can accurately evaluate the worth of any proposal put forward.

Often the party demanding renegotiation has a tendency to undervalue the risks and costs of litigation while the party facing that demand tends to overvalue its benefits. It is therefore important for each side as part of its negotiating strategy to be sure that the other has a realistic evaluation of its litigation alternative. Sometimes an aggrieved party may try to focus the other's attention on those costs by commencing a lawsuit while the renegotiation discussions are in progress.

In the Dabhol case, at the time the Maharashtra government canceled the electricity supply agreement, it probably assumed that its action would entail relatively little cost. It also may have assumed that other investors would be willing to step into the shoes vacated by Enron or that it would be able to find indigenous solutions to the state's power shortage. Once those assumptions proved false and once Enron had begun an arbitration case in London with a claim of $300 million, the State of Maharashtra became considerably more open to renegotiation than it had been at the time it canceled the contract.

5. *Involve either directly or indirectly all necessary parties in the renegotiation.* A successful renegotiation may require the participation not only of the parties who signed the original agreement but also of those who gained an interest in the transaction after the signing. Such secondary parties may include labor unions, creditors, suppliers, government departments, and, in the case of diplomatic negotiations, other states. As an example, in the renegotiation of a loan between a bank and a troubled real estate developer with a partially completed office building, it may be impossible to reach a new agreement without the participation, directly or indirectly, of the unpaid construction contractor whose lien on the property can block refinancing of the project. In the Dabhol case, the Indian central government was such a secondary party since it had counterguaranteed the Maharashtra government's payments under the power purchase agreement and needed to ap-

prove the terms of any renegotiated contract. It is therefore important in organizing any renegotiation to involve all the parties, both primary and secondary, and to decide whether secondary parties should be involved in the face-to-face renegotiations between the primary parties or be dealt with in separate discussions.

6. *Design the right forum and process for the renegotiation.* Both sides should think hard about the appropriate process for launching and conducting extradeal renegotiations. Renegotiations often emerge out of severe conflict, threats, and high emotion. An appropriate process for the renegotiation may help to mollify the parties and reduce the negative consequences of the conflict on their discussions. An inappropriate process, on the other hand, may serve to heighten those negative consequences and impede the renegotiations. The government of the State of Maharashtra canceled the power purchase agreement and declared publicly that it would not renegotiate. In that context, if renegotiations were ever to take place, the parties would need to create a process that would preserve the government's dignity and prestige. The use of a review panel to conduct what amounted to a renegotiation, rather than face-to-face discussions between the government and Enron, served this purpose. Moreover, the panel's independent status gave its recommendations the legitimacy needed to persuade the public that the renegotiated agreement protected Indian interests.

In some cases, the way that the parties frame the renegotiation may influence its success. For example, rather than using "renegotiation," a term that conjures up negative implications, the parties may refer to the process as a review, restructuring, rescheduling or an effort to clarify ambiguities in the existing agreement rather than to change basic principles. Waiver, by which one side grants the other temporary relief from an obligation, is yet another way of framing a request for renegotiation, an approach that respects the agreement yet enables the burdened party to obtain relief for a time from certain contractual burdens. This approach may avoid some of the friction and hostility engendered by demanding outright extradeal renegotiations.

7. *Involve the right mediator in the renegotiation process.* In the stress and hostility of extradeal renegotiations, a mediator or other neutral third person may be able to help the parties overcome the obstacles between them. A mediator may help design and manage the renegotiation process so that the parties can maximize value creation. By facilitating communications between the

two sides and by suggesting substantive solutions to problems that the parties have not considered, a mediator can contribute to a successful extradeal renegotiation. To be effective, the mediator must have the skills, experience, and confidence of the parties appropriate to the renegotiation in question.

17

DEAL-MENDING MEDIATION

If one defines mediation as a voluntary process by which a third person assists parties in their negotiations, then mediation has a role throughout the life of an international business transaction. Third persons, like Michael Ovitz and Robert Strauss in Matsushita's acquisition of MCA, can help parties make deals. And like consulting engineers in major international construction projects, they also can help manage them. In addition, a third person can help parties mend their deal when it becomes broken due to severe conflict.

Efforts at deal-mending mediation take place in the shadow of a pending lawsuit or arbitration proceeding. But a mediator, unlike a judge or an arbitrator, has no power to impose a decision on the parties. Indeed, each party always retains the right to withdraw from mediation at any time. Mediators participate in settling a dispute only because the parties have specifically sought them out and invited them into the negotiation process. Unlike international political disputes such as the Arab-Israeli conflict, in which third countries often advance themselves as mediators, it is extremely rare for persons to volunteer their services as mediators in an international business dispute. The parties to the dispute must take the initiative in seeking a mediator when it might be helpful. In all cases, mediators in international business disputes are private individuals, not organizations, institutions, or governmental officials. Institutions such as the International Chamber of Commerce or the International Centre for Settlement of Investment Disputes only facilitate the search for an appropriate mediator or conciliator. They do not themselves conduct the mediation. Once on the job, the mediator works independently of these organizations, is not their representative, and does not operate under their direction.

MEDIATION AND ITS ALTERNATIVES

Mediation does not exist in a vacuum. It stands among other dispute settlement processes, especially international commercial arbitration and litigation, that one or both of the parties might invoke in seeking to settle their dispute. In the background of all international business disputes is the prospect of binding arbitration or litigation if the parties, alone or with the help of a third person, are unable to resolve the conflict. This prospect influences the ways that the parties deal with their dispute, and it also affects the strategy of any mediator who may be invited to help them settle their conflict. In this regard, international business disputes are unlike international political disputes between states where no such arbitral or adjudicative process is waiting in the wings to impose a binding decision.

When parties to an international business transaction find themselves embroiled in a dispute that they judge to be irreconcilable, they will invariably commence arbitration or litigation to settle the matter. In no country is arbitration or litigation a painless, inexpensive, quick solution. Like litigation in the courts, arbitration is costly, may take years to conclude, and invariably results in a final rupture of the parties' business relationship. Even when an arbitration tribunal makes an award in favor of one of the parties, the losing side may then proceed to challenge it in the courts, thus delaying or even preventing a final settlement.

The prospect of such a costly, lengthy, and potentially destructive process does encourage parties in a business dispute to negotiate a settlement. For this reason, approximately two-thirds of all arbitration cases filed with the International Chamber of Commerce Court of Arbitration are settled by negotiation before an arbitral award is made.[1] In order to build on this dynamic, third persons, whether called mediators, conciliators, or something else, could in theory help parties embroiled international business disputes settle their conflicts without the intervention of an arbitrator's decision.

Initially, one may ask whether arbitrators themselves can and should seek to facilitate a negotiated settlement of the dispute. On this question, practice seems to vary considerably among countries. Generally, Americans and some Europeans consider it improper for an arbitrator to facilitate a settlement of the dispute. In their view, arbitrators should do no more than to suggest the possibility of settlement but should not actively engage in mediating efforts. The reason for this reluctance is their fear that if their mediation efforts fail, they will have compromised their ability to act as arbitrators because of the information gained from and contacts made with the individual disputants, often in private meetings. In other cultures—for example China and Germany—arbitrators often take a more active role by proposing at the parties' request possible formulas for settlement, by participating in settlement negotiations, and even meeting separately with the parties with their consent. In Asian cultures, which have a particular aversion to confrontation, arbitrators are even more energetic than their European and American counterparts in seeking to facilitate agreement among the disputants rather than merely imposing a decision.[2]

Generally speaking, an arbitrator's efforts, however minimal, to facilitate settlement tend to have the effect of persuading the parties that if they allow the dispute to be arbitrated, they will not achieve all that they hope. Such efforts by arbitrators have a predictive effect. When arbitrators strongly encourage settlement, they are actually saying to the claimant company that it probably will not receive all that it desires, and they are also telling the respondent that if the case goes to an award, it will have to pay something. The strategy of arbitrators who seek to play a mediating role is to give the parties a realistic evaluation of what they will receive or be required to pay in any final arbitration award.

MEDIATION OF INTERNATIONAL BUSINESS DISPUTES

Traditionally, companies engaged in an international business dispute have not actively sought the help of mediators. They first try to resolve the matter themselves through negotiation, but when they judge that to have failed, they immediately proceed to arbitration or litigation. As the preceding chapter indicated, in many cases a party will commence litigation or arbitration of a dispute and undertake negotiations at the same time. Various factors explain the failure of companies to use mediation: their lack of knowledge about mediation and the availability of mediation services, the fact that companies tend to give control of their disputes to lawyers whose professional inclination is to litigate, and the belief that mediation is merely a stalling tactic that only delays the inevitability of an arbitration proceeding or a lawsuit.

With increasing recognition of the disadvantages of arbitration and litigation, some companies are beginning to turn to more explicit forms of mediation to resolve business disputes. But what does a mediator bring to the process that the parties themselves, with their own lawyers and experts, do not already possess? First, an appropriate mediator brings expertise regarding both the processes of dispute settlement as well as the substance of the dispute. Second, the mediator brings neutrality and objectivity. And third, the mediator brings legitimacy because the parties themselves have chosen the mediator. During the course of the mediation, the mediator will deploy these resources in different ways and at different times in an effort to help the parties reach a solution to their conflict.

The way mediators go about their task will vary from dispute to dispute. Basically, the mediator assists with three important functions in the settlement of a dispute: procedures, communications, and substance. With respect to the procedures, the mediator may help to arrange meetings between the parties and to shape the rules for their interactions. With respect to communication, a mediator may interpret one party's statements to the other, reduce the emotional content of communications, and facilitate the flow of information between the two sides. And finally, the mediator may assist with the substantive aspects of the dispute, by offering an opinion on the parties' stated positions, evaluating the competing claims of the parties, and suggesting solutions that the parties should consider.

In some cases, the parties will only grant a mediator a very limited role in the dispute. Increasingly, when a dispute can be quantified—for example the extent of damage to an asset by a partner's action or the amount of a royalty fee owed to a licensor—the parties will engage an independent third party such as an international accounting or consulting firm to examine the matter and give an opinion. The opinion is not binding on the parties, but it has the effect of allowing them to make a more realistic prediction of what may happen in an arbitration proceeding or a lawsuit. Although neither the parties nor the outside expert may consider this kind of intervention to be "mediation," it does fit the term because a third person is helping the two sides reach agreement.

Some companies accept a more extensive role for mediators in solving their international business disputes. General Electric has developed a program known as the Early Dispute Resolution Initiative that seeks to save money and time through the effective use of dispute resolution techniques outside of formal litigation and arbitration, often with external mediators. One of GE's subsidiaries, Nuovo Pignone, an Italian manufacturer of heavy equipment, was sued by an insurance company for money that it had paid to a Nuovo Pignone customer who had lost business when some heavy equipment manufactured by Nuovo Pignone and other companies failed. At Nuovo Pignone's suggestion, the two sides brought in a retired Italian judge to mediate their dispute. The mediator began a process of shuttle talks between the insurer and the various defendants in the case. Although the mediator did not himself suggest a solution, his presence and the process he launched focused the parties' attention on settlement, rather than on litigation. This led them to evaluate realistically the strengths and weaknesses of each other's case. It also led Nuovo Pignone to persuade the equipment purchaser, which was still a Nuovo Pignone customer, to put pressure on its insurance company, who still had a business relationship with the customer, to settle the matter for a reasonable amount. Ultimately, the parties did reach a settlement, something that probably would not have occurred without the participation of a mediator.[3]

A mediator can also help shape a solution that the parties, left to their own devices, would probably not have been able to reach. In one case, a California product manufacturer had authorized an Argentinean company to act as its distributor for all of Latin America. After a period of time, although the manufacturer was achieving significant sales in Argentina and increasing volume in Chile, it was disappointed in the low level of sales elsewhere in Latin America. It therefore canceled the distribution agreement. Claiming unjustified and unlawful cancellation of their contract, the Argentinean distributor sued the California manufacturer for $10 million in damages. Instead of proceeding to trial, the two sides decided to mediate their dispute. During private meetings with each party, the mediator learned that the Argentinean company' was making progress in creating a distribution network in Argentina and Chile and that the California manufacturer still wanted to sell into the Latin American market. The mediator therefore helped the parties fashion a new agreement whereby the California manufacturer and the Argentinean company would enter into a new distribution contract limited to Argentina and Chile, with compensation to the Argentinean company for the lost territory.[4] In effect, the mediator helped to mend the deal, preserving in a new form a productive business relationship for both companies. Neither litigation in court nor arbitration under the auspices of an international institution could have brought about this result.

CONCILIATION: A MEDIATION VARIATION

Conciliation is a formal type of deal-mending mediation used occasionally in international business. Many arbitration institutions, such as the International Chamber of Commerce and the International Centre for Settlement of Investment Disputes, offer this service. The United Nations Commission on International Trade Law has also prepared a set of conciliation rules that parties may use without reference to an institution.

Generally in institutional conciliation, a party to a dispute may address a request for conciliation to an institution offering this service. If the institution concerned secures the agreement of the other disputant, it will appoint a conciliator. While the conciliator has broad discretion to conduct the process, in practice this person will invite both sides to state their views of the dispute and will then make a report proposing an appropriate settlement. The parties may reject the report and proceed to arbitration or a lawsuit, or they may accept it. In many cases, they will use it as a basis for a negotiated settlement. Conciliation is thus a kind of nonbinding arbitration. Its function is predictive. It tends to be rights-based in its approach, affording the parties a third person's evaluation of their respective rights and obligations. Conciliators do not usually adopt a problem-solving or relationship-building approach to resolving the dispute between the parties. The process is confidential and completely voluntary. Either party may withdraw from conciliation at any time.

Deal-Mending Mediation in Trinidad and Tobago

Since conciliation is confidential, public information on the process itself is scant. One of the few published accounts concerns the first conciliation conducted under the auspices of the International Centre for Settlement of Investment Disputes (ICSID).[5] An affiliate of the World Bank, ICSID provides arbitration and conciliation services to facilitate the settlement of investment disputes between host countries and foreign investors. One such dispute, between Tesoro Petroleum Corporation and the government of Trinidad and Tobago, arose out of a joint venture that the two sides established in 1968, each with a 50 percent interest, to develop and manage oil fields in Trinidad. By their joint-venture contact and subsequent agreements, the two partners developed a complex arrangement regarding profits and reinvestment. Their agreement also provided that in the event of a dispute the parties would first attempt conciliation under ICSID auspices.

By 1983, following the rise of oil prices and the continued turbulence in the world petroleum industry, Tesoro and the government of Trinidad and Tobago disagreed over whether and to what extent accumulated profits should be used for reinvestment to develop new oil properties. Tesoro sought a distribution of its share of the profits so that it might develop oil-producing properties elsewhere in the world. The government of Trinidad and Tobago wanted the joint venture to reinvest its profits in Trinidad. Unable to reach agreement, Tesoro decided to sell its shares and, pursuant to their agreement, offered them first to the Trinidad and Tobago government. The two parties then began to negotiate a possible sale but made little progress. In August 1983, Tesoro filed a request for conciliation with the ICSID secretary-general, claiming that it was entitled to 50 percent of the profits as dividends and that the government had breached the joint-venture agreement on dividend payments.

Recognizing the importance of a conciliator in whom the parties have confidence, the ICSID conciliation rules give the parties wide scope in the conciliator's appointment. The rules allowed them to choose anyone, provided that person was "of high moral character and recognized competence in the fields of law, commerce, industry, or finance, and [might] be relied upon to exercise independent judgment." Tesoro and the Trinidad and Tobago government agreed to a single conciliator (instead of a commission of three or more conciliators as the rules allow) and through direct negotiations chose Lord Wilberforce, a distinguished retired English judge, to serve as their conciliator.

Lord Wilberforce held a first meeting of the parties in London, where they agreed upon basic procedural matters, including a schedule for the filing of briefs and other documents by the parties in support of their positions. The parties proceeded to file their documents and then met once again with Lord Wilberforce in July 1984 in Washington, D.C. In this meeting, at the conciliator's suggestion, they agreed that no oral hearing or argument by the parties would be necessary, that the parties could confidentially submit to Lord Wilberforce their views on an acceptable settlement, and that he would then give them his recommendation.

In February 1985, Lord Wilberforce delivered a lengthy written report to the parties in which he stated that his task as a conciliator had three dimensions: (1) to examine the contentions raised by the parties; (2) to clarify the issues in dispute; and (3) to evaluate the respective merits of the parties' positions and the likelihood of their prevailing in arbitration. Thus, he saw his task as giving the parties a prediction of their fate in arbitration, with the hope that such prediction would assist them in negotiating a settlement. He concluded his report with a suggested settlement, which included a percentage of the amount sought by Tesoro, based on his estimate of the parties' chances of success in arbitration on the issues in dispute.

Following receipt of the report, Tesoro and the Trinidad and Tobago government began negotiations, and by October 1985 they had reached a settlement by which the joint-venture company would pay dividends to the two partners in cash and petroleum products totaling $143 million. The conciliation thus helped the parties reach an amicable settle of their dispute with minimum cost, delay, and acrimony. The whole conciliation process from start to finish took less than two years, and total fees and administrative costs amounted to less than $11,000. Equally important, conciliation preserved the business relationship between the parties. After the conciliation, the Trinidad and Tobago government purchased a small portion of Tesoro's shares in the joint venture to gain a majority interest, but Tesoro continued as a partner in the enterprise. Had the matter proceeded to arbitration, without conciliation, the case would have lasted several years, cost at least a million dollars and perhaps more, and would have resulted in a complete rupture of business relationships between Tesoro and the government.

Few companies avail themselves of conciliation to settle international business disputes. For example, out of a total of ten cases on the docket of ICSID in 1996, only one was for conciliation.[6] Five years later, the situation had not improved. Out of 44 cases on the ICSID docket as of June 30, 2001, none involved conciliation.[7] Similarly, from 1988 to 1993, a period in which over 2,000 arbitration cases were filed at the International Chamber of Commerce, the ICC received only 54 requests for conciliation. Of that number, the other party in the dispute agreed to conciliation in only 16 cases; however, the ICC appointed only ten conciliators, since the parties settled the dispute or withdrew the request in six cases. Of the ten conciliations, nine had been completed by 1994, five resulting in complete settlement.[8]

THE FUTURE OF INTERNATIONAL BUSINESS MEDIATION

The use of mediators in international business is fragmented and uneven. If one defines a mediator broadly as a third person who helps the parties nego-

tiate an agreement, then their use in dealmaking is fairly extensive. Their use
in deal managing seems to be growing, particularly in the international construction industry. But in deal mending, where the parties to a transaction are
embroiled in a genuine conflict, the use of mediators is relatively rare.

Effective international business mediation requires three things: disputant
motivation, mediator opportunity, and mediator resources, including skills. No
mediation can take place unless the parties to the business conflict want or at
least acquiesce to the presence of a mediator. Variations in the degree of disputant motivation in deal making, deal managing, and deal mending may explain the difference in the frequency of use of mediators in these three types of
negotiation. Motivated to achieve a deal because of expectations of profit, parties have a strong incentive to use third persons to achieve their deal-making
goals and may view the alternatives as the loss of the deal with no compensation. Similarly, agreement to use mediators in deal managing may be a condition for achieving agreement or for securing financing from institutions such as
the World Bank; consequently, disputant motivation may also be high in these
cases. However, in the case of a broken deal, at least one of the parties will lack
motivation so long as it believes that it can obtain compensation or secure enforcement of its version of the deal in the courts or in international commercial
arbitration. In short, that party does not see the failure to mend a deal through
mediation as an absolute loss. As long as it considers litigation or arbitration an
acceptable alternative to a mediated agreement, it will have little motivation to
accept the presence of a mediator. Unfortunately, most of the time, one of the
parties to a business dispute does, in fact, believe that it will gain more in litigation or arbitration than it could through the services of a mediator.

Mediators have an opportunity to mediate international business disputes only if both parties invite them into the process. Parties to international business transactions can enhance mediator opportunity by agreeing at
the time they make their contract to use third persons, such as dispute review
boards, to help them with future disputes. However, outside of the international construction industry, such provisions are relatively rare. To a certain
extent, the low degree of disputant motivation to use mediators in international business disputes is also caused by the general lack of knowledge by
businesses executives and their lawyers of the potential value of mediation
and their belief that mediation will be used by one of the parties merely to
delay the inevitability of a law suit or arbitration case.

To be effective, mediators in international business, like mediators in
other domains, must possess certain resources, including skills. The essence

of their resources resides in their ability to influence the parties to arrive at an agreement. Mediators in international business transactions derive their power to influence the parties from various factors. Unlike some mediators in the political arena, business negotiators generally have no coercive power. The basis of their power first and foremost resides in their expertise. The power of Ovitz, Wilberforce, and consulting engineers to influence the parties clearly resided in their knowledge about the respective industries and the issues they were dealing with. In the kind of rights-based mediation engaged in by Wilberforce, where the source of his influence was his ability to give the parties an accurate prediction of how they might fare in arbitration, expertise in the law and the functioning of the arbitral process was an important source of mediator power.

Mediators may also have power because of their relationships with the disputants. This relational power is particularly present in deal-making mediation in international business. Thus, the relationships of Ovitz and Strauss with both sides in the MCA-Matsushita negotiation gave weight to their advice and recommendations. And finally, international business negotiators may also rely on legitimacy in influencing the parties to a dispute. Wilberforce had legitimacy because the parties specifically selected him to make a recommendation; a dispute review board for a major construction project has legitimacy because the parties created it to resolve future disputes at the time they signed the construction contract; and Strauss had great legitimacy because MCA and Matsushita had designated him in a formal document as "counselor to the transaction."

The magnitude, complexity, and duration of international business transactions create a substantial and continuing risk of conflict. International commercial arbitration, the primary dispute settlement mechanism designed for international business, has proven itself to be expensive, destructive, time consuming, and in some cases lacking in finality. Mediation of various types offers international business executives a possible attractive alternative, an alternative that they should explore at the time they negotiate their transactions. As Tesoro Petroleum and Trinidad and Tobago did in their joint venture, parties to international transactions might include in their contracts from the outset mechanisms such as dispute advisers to help in the problem of deal management. And, they might also commit themselves to try mediation or conciliation before they take the usually irrevocable step of submitting their disputes to arbitration.

18

THE ART OF DEAL DIPLOMACY

As you apply this book's principles and techniques for making, managing, and mending international business transactions, it is important to remember above all that you are engaged in deal diplomacy. The dynamics of twenty-first century global business compel international negotiators to understand and manage forces that diplomats have had to cope with since the practice of diplomacy began. Today's global negotiators need to be deal diplomats. They can therefore usefully find guidance not only in the techniques of modern business but also in the principles of traditional diplomatic practice.

Nearly three hundred years ago, François de Callières, a distinguished French diplomat, gave that guidance in one of the first practical manuals of modern diplomacy, *On the Manner of Negotiating with Princes.*[1] Originally published in 1716, the book is still considered a model introduction to the subject. While de Callières's language may sound quaint to us today, its pages contain much useful advice for global negotiators in the twenty-first century. Based on de Callières's thoughts, the following ten simple rules of the art of deal diplomacy are offered to guide you as you go about the tasks of making, managing, and mending international business transactions. They are precisely the principles developed in this book.

1. Recognize the Necessity of Continual Negotiation

De Callières stressed "the necessity of continual negotiation"[2] between states though their permanent representatives as the basis of modern diplomacy, a novel idea in its time but one that modern diplomats take for granted today. Twenty-first century global negotiators must also recognize, as this book has argued, that a modern business deal of any significant duration requires a constant process of negotiation. Just as negotiations do not stop when two countries seal a treaty, negotiations do not end when two companies sign a contract. You need to develop your business strategies and deploy your resources with that principle constantly in mind.

2. Study and Saturate Your Mind

Prepare thoroughly for every negotiation. You should not only understand the substance of the transaction, you should exhaustively research the countries, organizations, cultures, and persons involved in the deal. De Callières's constant and repeated message to negotiators is "to study" before undertaking negotiations. His list of matters to study includes virtually every dimension of the country and the people with whom the negotiator will come into contact. Recognizing that all negotiators are agents, he also advises a negotiator to "saturate his mind with the thoughts of his master."[3] Global negotiators in the twenty-first century need to prepare no less, as chapter 3 and other sections of this book have emphasized.

3. Be an Apt Listener

People often think that negotiation is mostly about talking and that the best negotiators are the best talkers. That view misconceives the nature of the negotiation process. In the words of de Callières, "one of the most necessary qualities in a good negotiator is to be an apt listener," and, "in order to succeed in this kind of work one must rather listen than speak."[4]

More generally, successful negotiation requires keen perception of yourself as well as the other side. As we have seen, the ability to understand interests and to overcome the seven barriers to an international deal depends first and foremost on your perceptive powers. As you sit at the negotiating table, you are like a director in a television studio watching three TV monitors showing the images taken by three different cameras from three different angles of the same set. The negotiator's three cameras are focused on (1) the words and actions of the other side; (2) his or her own words and actions; and (3) the effect of his or her words and actions on the other side. Like the television director, a global negotiator must constantly process information from each of the monitors and then make a decision about the next steps.

4. Know and Stay Faithful to Your Goal

An important step in preparation is to carefully determine what you want from a deal before you start negotiations. As we saw, you need to identify in advance precisely at what point an agreement is not in your interest compared to other options and to beware of changing objectives in the heat of negotiations. On this issue, global negotiators should heed de Callières's advice: "The lack of firmness of which I speak here is a common fault of those who have a lively imagination for every kind of accident which may befall, and hinders them from determining with vigor and dispatch the means by which action should be taken. They will look at a matter on so many sides that they forget in which direction they are traveling."[5]

5. Have a Mind Fertile in Expedients

While you should know your bottom line, you should also realize that there are many ways to arrive at it. Earlier chapters have stressed the need for creativity and flexibility in shaping global deals. Remain open to new approaches and search for novel solutions to allow both sides to advance their interests. In the words of de Callières, "[A negotiator] must also have a mind so fertile in expedients as easily to smooth away the difficulties which he meets in the course of his duty . . ."[6]

6. Have the Patience of a Clockmaker

As we have seen, negotiating an international transaction and then managing it through unexpected difficulties is a time-consuming process, one that invariably takes longer than you originally planned. If you are not prepared to commit the time, don't get into the negotiation. Shortcuts usually fail. Establish deadlines with care and avoid ultimatums. De Callières's advice of three hundred years ago is valid today for global negotiators encountering difficulties in the process of making, managing, and mending deals: "Indeed, he must behave as a good clockmaker would when his clock has gone out of order; he must labor to remove the difficulty, or at all events to circumvent its results."[7] A global negotiator needs "a patience which no trial can break down."[8]

7. Be Master of Yourself and Avoid the Choleric Word

Never become emotional at the negotiating table. Emotions cloud judgment and interfere with perception. Equally important, different cultures interpret displays of emotion differently. An angry statement that might be tolerated in negotiations in the United States may be taken as evidence of insanity in Thailand. In such a setting, your outburst may entirely destroy your credibility with the other side, as de Callières recognized three hundred years ago when he stressed the need for a negotiator to be "master of himself," for " . . . a choleric word may poison the minds of those with whom negotiations are in process."[9] In short, keep your cool.

8. Show Respect

International negotiations, as we have seen, bring you into contact with many different cultures, governments, ideologies, customs, values, and personalities. Approach each one with a respect and willingness to learn. Negotiation is fundamentally a learning process. One of the marks of inexperienced negotiators is the attitude that they have little to learn from the other side. That attitude is not only perceived as arrogance by the other side, but it also prevents executives from getting the information they need to make a good deal. De Callières counseled negotiators in the eighteenth century to "reveal an innate respect for the person whom they are addressing," and "to show genuine and sincere interest in the welfare of his new associates and in all the customs of the court and the habits of the people." A negotiator quickly discovers that "it is easy to single out the good points, and that there is not profit to be had in denouncing the bad ones, for the very good reason that nothing the diplomatist can say or do will alter the domestic habits or laws of the country . . ."[10] That remains good advice today.

9. Search Constantly for the Needs and Interests of Others

This book has stressed the importance of understanding interests, both yours and the other side's, in making, managing, and mending global deals. Throughout his manual, de Callières also emphasized the key role that interests, both the public interests of governments and the private interests of negotiators, play in diplomacy. "The secret of negotiation is to harmonize the interests of the parties concerned."[11] To understand interests, negotiators must put themselves in the position of others. "The more often he thus puts himself in the position of others, the more subtle and effective will his arguments be."[12] "He should therefore at the outset think rather of what is in their minds than of immediately expressing what is in his own."[13]

10. Accentuate the Positive

Throughout your discussions with the other side, emphasize the positive aspects of the deal and the relationship. Stress the points of agreement with your counterparts and the progress you are making in the talks. Try to make negative points in a positive way. For de Callières, "the great secret of negotiation is to bring out prominently the common advantage to both parties of any proposal and so to link those advantages that they may appear equally balanced to both parties."[14]

Keep in mind these ten rules of the art of deal diplomacy as you go about the task of making, managing, and mending deals in the twenty-first century. They have successfully guided relationships among nations over the last three hundred years. They will also allow you to take advantage of vast new business opportunities in the decades ahead.

APPENDIX A

THE GLOBAL NEGOTIATOR'S CHECKLIST

Use this checklist as a guide to preparing for and conducting your negotiations.

I. Prenegotiation and Preparation
   A. Goals
      1. What are our goals and interests in this negotiation?
         Our maximum objectives?
         Our minimum objectives?
      2. What is our best alternative (BATNA) to this deal? At what point is it preferable not to make a deal? What is our walk-away point?
      3. What are the goals and interests of the other side? At what point do we think they will walk away?
      4. What is our relationship and history with the other side?
         How will that relationship affect the discussions?
      5. Who are our competitors for this deal?
      6. What advantages do we have over our competitors?
      7. What advantages do our competitors have over us?
      8. How will the existence of competition affect our goals, interests, strategies, and tactics in this negotiation?
   B. Environment
      1. Where should the negotiation take place?
      2. When will the negotiation take place? Have we checked the local calendar for conflicts, holidays, and other events that may affect the negotiation?
      3. How long should we plan for the negotiation to last?
      4. When should our team plan to arrive at the negotiation site? Will we arrive far enough in advance of the negotiation to adjust to the surroundings and prepare for the talks?
      5. When will we leave the negotiation site? Have we informed the other side of our arrival and departure plans?
      6. Have we and the other side agreed on where the various negotiating rounds or sessions will take place?
      7. Have we designated a home office person to back-stop the negotiations? Have we agreed on a fixed time to communicate with the home office?
      8. What language will be used in the negotiation?
      9. Will an interpreter be used? Who will provide the interpretation?

10. What will the language of the contract be?
11. Have we made arrangements to brief the interpreter on the nature of the deal, the technical language, etc.?

C. Our Negotiating Team
1. Who will be the members of our negotiating team? Who will be our spokesperson?
2. Does our team have the right balance of functional skills, language ability, knowledge of the country, and negotiating experiencing?
3. Have specific responsibilities been allocated to individual team members for matters such as logistics, communications, note taking, etc.?
4. Has our team met to prepare our strategy, to formulate necessary draft documents, conduct simulations, etc.?
5. What specific authority does our team have to make commitments in the negotiation?
6. What third persons can help us negotiate this deal?

D. The Other Side
1. Are we certain we are dealing with the organization that can deliver what we want?
2. Are we dealing with the right persons or departments in that organization?
3. Are there other parties (especially the government) who should be at the negotiating table?
4. Are we fully informed of the other side's standing within the country and with its government?

E. Information and Documentation
1. What information do we need about the other country, company, transactions, etc., before we begin negotiations? How will we obtain it?
2. What information do we need about the members of the other team? How will we get that information? By what date do we need that information?
3. What draft documents, slides, reports, and publications need to be prepared for the negotiations?
4. What books, journals, reports, and equipment need to accompany our team to the negotiation site?
5. What local consultants and experts will we need to hire? Should they be present at the negotiations?
6. What documents and other information should we send to the other side before negotiations take place?

F. Agenda
1. Have we agreed on an agenda with the other side?
2. What items are on the agenda?
3. Does the agenda allow for surprises and topics we would rather not discuss?
4. What items do we want to discuss first?

II. Opening Moves
1. Have we fully introduced all the members of our team?
2. Has the other side fully introduced all the members of its team?
3. Do we know the identity of the leader of the other team and the roles played by its other members?
4. What will the physical arrangements for the negotiations be?
5. Have we spent sufficient time on getting to know the members of the other team?

6. Will we make a comprehensive opening statement? What will it include? What information should we provide about our organization? Should we brief the other side on our mission statement, code of ethics, statement of corporate responsibility, etc.?

7. Have we reviewed the agenda with the other team?

8. Do we have an accurate idea of the other team's negotiating authority? Does the other team have an accurate idea of our negotiating authority?

III. Negotiating Dynamics

1. Have we obtained sufficient information from the other side? Are we listening to them carefully? Do they know that we are listening carefully? What questions do we need to ask them?

2. Do we have knowledge of the other side's culture? How will that culture affect the way we communicate with each other?

3. What are the principal issues in this negotiation? What order of importance does each have on a scale of 1 to 10?

4. What will be our strategy with respect to each issue? In what sequence will we address the issues?

5. At what point do we put forward our draft agreement as a basis for negotiation?

6. If the other side submits its draft agreement to us, how will we respond?

7. Are we watching for nonverbal as well as verbal forms of communication by the other side?

8. What social occasions with the other side will arise during the course of this negotiation? Are we sure we know how to respond and act appropriately according to local culture?

9. To what ideological factors must we be sensitive during the negotiations?

10. Who will bear the foreign exchange risk in this deal? If we are to bear it, how should we protect ourselves?

11. Have we examined the relevant exchange controls? How will they affect our deal? Will countertrade be a part of this transaction?

12. Has our team agreed to meet at the end of each day to review progress and plan for the next day's activities?

13. Have we prepared an adequate written record of the negotiations? What communication do we need to make with the other side after each negotiating session?

14. What other follow-up will be necessary? Who will be assigned to do it?

15. What options does the other side have to attain its goals and interests?

16. What options do we have to attain our goals and interests?

17. Are we sure that we really understand the other side's goals and interests?

18. Are we sure that the other side really understands our goals and interests?

19. Have we fully explained the nature of the transactions we are proposing? Do they fully understand the deal and its implications?

20. What kind of dispute resolution processes should we build into this deal? Mediation? Conciliation? A dispute adviser?

IV. End Game

1. If we do make a deal, are we sure it will last?

2. What future events and trends might affect the agreement? How do we protect ourselves against these events?

3. How do we structure the agreement to minimize future uncertainties?
4. Is the deal balanced? Is it good for both sides?
5. Have we developed a plan for effective implementation of the deal?
6. What is our strategy for managing this deal once the contract is signed?
7. What do we need to do to build a good working relationship with the other company?

APPENDIX B

A PRIMER ON INTERNATIONAL BUSINESS TRANSACTIONS

The goal of any negotiation is to create a transaction that the parties perceive is in their interests. That transaction, regardless of where it is negotiated and when it is to take place, is founded upon one or more contracts. Indeed, in virtually all business negotiations, the parties while seeking to create a business relationship also envision embodying their agreement in a written, legally enforceable contract. The fact that the contract is legally enforceable gives a party some assurance that the other side will perform its part of the bargain according to plan. The existence of a contract allows a party injured by the other side's failed performance to seek compensation in a court of law or arbitration proceeding.

For a contract to come into existence as a legally enforceable set of rights and duties, the laws of some country must recognize it as a contract. In nearly all cases, contracts for international transactions are governed by the laws of a particular country. National contract laws, while similar in many respects, also exhibit important differences. In planning and negotiating any transaction, negotiators need to decide whose laws will govern their contract. For example, in a joint venture to undertake a mining venture in the Congo between a Japanese company located in Tokyo and a U.S. company incorporated in Delaware with headquarters in New York, what laws will apply to their joint venture contract? Japan's laws? Delaware's laws? New York's laws? The Congo's laws? In any future litigation, a court or arbitrator would have to answer that question first before proceeding to determine the substantive rights and duties of the two companies. In making that determination, the court would refer to its own choice of law rules. A problem in deciding on the applicable body of law is that different countries have different rules for choosing the laws to be applied to a contract, a fact that creates uncertainty as to how the courts will interpret and apply a contract's provisions if the parties fall into conflict in the future. In order to give increased certainty to their legal relationship, parties to nearly all international commercial agreements specify in the agreement itself the country whose laws will govern their contract. Courts in virtually all countries will enforce a choice of law made by the parties, unless that law includes provisions that violate the public policy of the country in which the court is sitting. So the Japanese and U.S. companies might agree in their joint-venture contract that it will be governed by the laws of New York, in which case a court or arbitrator in England or France or Japan would be bound to apply New York's laws in interpreting and applying the contract in any future dispute. In some cases when the parties are unwilling or unable to agree on the laws of a particular country to govern their transaction, they may opt instead for the application of international law or even general principles of law appropriate to the industry or trade in question. Accompanying a choice of applicable law in most international agreements is the selection of the courts of a particular country or a specific form of arbitration as the exclusive means for settling disputes that may arise under their contract.

A contract is an agreement that creates, modifies, or ends a legal relationship between two or more persons. A valid contract is binding on the parties and can be modified or terminated only in accordance with its terms, by agreement of the parties themselves, or otherwise by law. In short, a party to a valid contract cannot unilaterally change its provisions. In most systems of law, a contract comes into existence if one side has made an offer that the other side has accepted. Unless the law provides otherwise, a contract may be oral or written. Moreover, a written contract need not exist in a single document. Two documents, for example, one a written offer and the other a written acceptance, together may form a legally valid contract.

The words of a contract, written or oral, may be subject to various interpretations. One significant source of conflict arises out of differing interpretations of a contract by each of the parties after it is made. The risks of conflict over interpretation are particularly significant in international contracts since the parties usually come from different cultures, employ different business practices, and speak different languages. When faced with such a conflict over interpretation, a court or arbitrator ordinarily will first seek to interpret a contract according to the common intention of the parties. The evidence that courts consider in determining that intent may vary from country to country. If they are unable to determine that common intention, the courts or arbitrators will give the contract the meaning that reasonable persons of the same kind as the parties would give to it in the circumstances. That meaning, for example, might be determined by reference to the particular trade or business in which the two sides are engaged.

For example, suppose that Akbar Petroleum Company in the United Arab Emirates makes a contract to sell 100,000 barrels of oil at a price of $20.50 a barrel to Basic Industries, Ltd., a United Kingdom company located in London. When the oil is delivered, Basic claims that Akbar did not fulfill the contract because it delivered 100,000 barrels consisting of 42 standard gallons each (i.e., 231 cubic inches per gallon), instead of 100,000 barrels of 36 imperial gallons (i.e., 277.42 cubic inches per barrel), as Basic had expected. If there is no evidence of the common intention of the parties on the question of the intended size of the barrel, a court or arbitrator would refer to the practices in the international oil business, in which case it would find that it is standard practice in international petroleum transactions to measure barrels of oil in 42 standard gallons, not 36 imperial gallons.[1]

The contract law of any country is complex, so the global negotiator would be wise to secure the services of a competent lawyer in helping to negotiate, structure, and draft an appropriate contract for a desired transaction. Nonetheless, effective negotiators should be aware of some of the basic elements in the contracts underlying the deals they are trying to make. With that in mind, the aim of this primer is to provide a basic introduction to seven of the fundamental contracts and transactions involved in global business.

International Sales of Goods

One of the most common transactions in international business, indeed the bulk of international trade, is the sale of goods—that is, movable, tangible objects—from one country to another. International sales of goods are negotiated in one of two ways. Most contracts for the sale of substantial, costly goods, such as electrical generators or airplanes, are arrived at through face-to-face negotiations between the buyer and the seller and are embodied in a single lengthy document that may be subject to long negotiations and painstaking drafting. On the other hand, the sale of items of lesser value—for example a shipment of ten binoculars or twenty videodisk players—whose total cost does not warrant the expense of travel and lengthy negotiations are often concluded by e-mail, fax, or correspondence. In this case, the buyer or the seller sends an offer to buy or to sell and the other side responds with an acceptance. The two documents together constitute the contract for the transaction.

A problem known as "the battle of the forms" sometimes arises in the sale of goods. Companies often use preprinted, standard forms to purchase and sell goods. The form used by the buyer often does not correspond exactly to the terms of the form used by the seller. Under the laws of many countries, if the terms of the intended acceptance differ from the terms of the offer, the intended acceptance is instead considered a counteroffer, so no contract comes into existence. For example, if a Belgian seller faxes on its standard form an offer to sell 100 binoculars to a Brazilian buyer at 100 euros each, plus the cost of transportation, and the buyer's form accepts the offer but also contains a provision that Brazilian law governs the contract and all disputes are to be decided in Brazilian courts, a court might find that the Brazilian form is legally a counteroffer and does not create a contract with the Belgian seller. If the seller ignores this difference in terms and ships the binoculars anyway, the act of shipment could be considered an acceptance of the terms in the counteroffer. Persons engaged in making deals at a distance through the use of printed forms should carefully compare the terms of the offer and acceptance to be sure they are consistent and that they reflect the buyer's and the seller's intentions.

One of the principal functions of the international sales contract is to determine the extent that the parties to the transaction will bear the various risks involved. For example, in the case of a sale of Belgian binoculars to a Brazilian buyer, who will bear the risk of loss of the goods if the ship transporting them sinks or if the truck transporting them to the ship crashes? Who will bear the risk of loss or delay if the goods are seized by the government in the country of shipment, a transit country, or the importing country for a violation of customs or other regulations? Who will bear the risks of fluctuation in monetary exchange rates between the date of contract and the contractual date of payment?

Some of the most important elements covered in any international sales contract are the identification of the goods to be sold, their price, the terms for delivery (including time, mode, and place), and the payment for the goods (including time, mode, place, and currency). The importance of these terms lies in the fact that they allocate some of the principal risks in the transaction to one side or the other. An exporter with sufficient bargaining power could shift all of the risks inherent in these terms to the importer by requiring that payment be made in the exporter's own currency in advance of delivery of the goods and that delivery take place at the exporter's warehouse or factory. The importer, on the other hand, would ideally wish to pay for the goods in its currency, after the goods have been delivered to its premises, and after an opportunity to determine that the goods received met the specifications stated in the contract.

For example, suppose an importer in Paris, France, wants to purchase a high-speed printing machine from a manufacturer in Chicago, Illinois, for $250,000. The Chicago manufacturer, naturally, wishes to minimize its risks and maximize its profits. It would therefore ideally like to structure this transaction so that it would be paid in dollars in advance of shipment, that delivery of the goods would take place at its factory or warehouse in Chicago, and that the $250,000 purchase price would oblige it to do nothing more than allow the purchaser or its agent to take delivery of the machine in Chicago.

The Parisian importer, on the other hand, who is also seeking to minimize its risks and maximize its profits, would want to organize this transaction so that delivery would take place at its Paris factory, that payment would be made after delivery in Paris and an opportunity to inspect and test the machine, that the price be specified and payable in euros rather than dollars, and that the price include not only the cost of the machine but also all of the other costs, such as insurance, shipping, and freight-forwarding fees involved in transporting the machine from Chicago to Paris.

Between the ideal position of the Chicago manufacturer and the ideal position of the French importer are a host of variations that allocate the risks of the transaction in different proportions between the two parties. The precise allocation of risk will be determined by negotiations between the buyer and the seller. For example, they might agree that delivery will take place in New York City when the goods are loaded on a ship bound for France and that payment is due when the American manufacturer presents the bill of lading covering the shipment to the Parisian importer or its bank.

In face-to-face negotiations, terms for payment, delivery, and other matters in the sales contract may be the subject of detailed and complex contractual provisions. In other situations, particularly in which the parties are contracting at a distance by fax or e-mail, they may use shorthand trade terms commonly understood in international commerce. Over the years, international commerce has evolved a series of simplified, more-or-less standard contractual terms that are commonly used in international sales transactions to specify some of the rights and obligations of the parties. These terms, which generally take the form of abbreviations, include "free along side ship" (F.A.S.), "free on board" (F.O.B.), and "cost, insurance, and freight" (C.I.F.). Even these terms have different meanings in different countries. In order to bring some uniformity to their use, the International Chamber of Commerce has prepared a publication known as INCOTERMS that gives standard and detailed definitions of all the principal trade terms in use. Many contracts and forms specifically provide that they are to be interpreted by reference to INCOTERMS.[2]

Trade terms have implications both for the price of the goods and the way delivery is to take place. For example, through an exchange of forms, a German optical goods manufacturer and an American department store might agree on a shipment of 1,000 binoculars at a total price of "100,000 euros F.O.B. named vessel Hamburg," or "100,000 euros C.I.F. Akron, Ohio." In the first case, the price would include the cost of transporting the goods to the ship at Hamburg, where delivery is to take place. In the second case, the price quoted includes not only the cost of the binoculars, but of shipping and insuring them from the manufacturer's factory to the purchaser's warehouse in Akron, Ohio.

An international sales contract may cover a single sales transaction or it may provide for a series of sales over a period of time, thereby creating a continuing relationship between the buyer and the seller. For example, the American department store, in order to gain a price advantage, might agree with the German optical manufacturer to purchase a fixed number of binoculars each quarter for the next three years at a specified price.

The normal international sales transaction, in addition to the basic contract of sale between the buyer and the seller, consists of at least three other contracts that are usually required by the basic sales agreement. The first of these is the transportation contract by which the seller ships the goods to the buyer. This contract usually takes the form of a bill of lading issued by the carrier. In most cases, the bill of lading is "negotiable," which means that the shipping company may turn over the goods only "to the order of" the person named in the bill of lading or to a person to whom the bill is endorsed and who physically has possession of the bill of lading. The second is the contract of insurance to cover any loss or injury to the goods during shipment. Normally, the beneficiary of the insurance policy is the person, buyer or seller, to whom title to the goods has passed at the time of shipment. And finally, the third additional contract is the letter of credit issued by the buyer's bank promising to pay the seller the purchase price upon presentation by the seller of certain specified documents, such as the bill of lading covering the shipment of the goods. In view of the importance of letters of credit in a wide variety of international business transactions, let's examine these documents in detail.

Letters of Credit

Sales of goods between businesses within the United States are usually made on "open account," which means that the buyer first receives the goods and then pays for them within a specified time period, for example thirty, sixty, or ninety days after delivery. If, on the other hand, the seller is concerned about the buyer's credit-worthiness, the seller may demand payment on delivery or in advance of shipping the goods. In the case of payment on account, the seller bears the risk of payment. In the case of payment in advance, the buyer bears the risk of nonperformance.

In international sales of goods between unaffiliated parties, neither payment in advance nor payment on account is commonly used, primarily because of the heightened risks created by the international environment. For example, the fact that the buyer and the seller are located in two different countries usually means that the seller, because of lack of information, is less able to make a reliable evaluation of the buyer's credit than if the two were located in the same country. Moreover, the seller who sells on open account to a buyer in another country faces a greater risk of not being able to enforce its payment rights under the contract than if the buyer and the seller were located in the same country. On the other hand, the buyer who pays in advance faces an increased risk that the goods may not be delivered. Finding a remedy in the courts of the seller's home country may prove to be difficult.

In order to surmount payment risks in international business, banks and businesses have developed the letter of credit. Fundamentally, the purpose of the letter of credit is to shift payment risks inherent in an international sale of goods from the buyer and the seller to a bank.

Contracts for the international sale of a product often provide that the buyer will make payment by securing an "irrevocable, confirmed letter of credit payable at a bank acceptable to the seller" upon presentation by the seller of certain specified documents. Suppose, for example, that American Stores, a regional chain of home appliance stores with headquarters in Boston, Massachusetts, agrees to buy 1,000 food processors for 100,000 euros from La Cucina Italiana, an Italian manufacturer located in Milan, Italy. The sales contract provides that the payment of the purchase price is to be made under an irrevocable letter of credit confirmed by an Italian bank in Milan, calling for payment of 100,000 euros upon presentation by La Cucina Italiana of specified documents including a bill of lading, a transportation insurance policy, an invoice, and a draft. When the Italian bank confirms the letter of credit, it accepts an independent obligation to pay La Cucina Italiana. The execution of this transaction will take place in several steps:

1. Once the contract is made, American Stores will ask its bank, Fleet Bank Boston, to arrange for the required letter of credit. For a fee, Fleet, which is called the issuing bank, will contact Banca Nazionale del Lavoro in Milan, with which it has a correspondent banking relationship, and ask it to inform La Cucina Italiana that Banca Nazionale del Lavoro will pay La Cucina the required amount when La Cucina presents the specified documents to it. Fleet also promises Banca Nazionale del Lavoro, known as the confirming bank, that Fleet will pay it the specified amount plus commission when Banca Nazionale del Lavoro transfers to Fleet the documents it receives from La Cucina Italiana.

2. Banca Nazionale del Lavoro then sends a letter of credit to La Cucina Italiana, promising to pay La Cucina 100,000 euros when La Cucina presents to Banca Nazionale del Lavoro the specified documents. When La Cucina receives the letter of credit, it knows that the payment risk in the transaction has been considerably reduced since it now can rely for payment on Banca Nazionale del Lavoro, a strong financial institution in Italy, rather than American Stores, an organization of uncertain credit standing (at least from La Cucina's point of view) located in a foreign country.

3. With the letter of credit, La Cucina knows that if it ships the goods and presents the documents to the bank it will be paid the sales price promised in the contract. It therefore prepares the goods for shipment and gives them to an ocean carrier for transportation to American Stores in Boston. In return, it receives a negotiable bill of lading, made out "to the order of the shipper," as well as an insurance certificate covering the shipment.

4. La Cucina then presents these documents to Banca Nazionale del Lavoro, with a draft and the letter of credit, in return for which Banca Nazionale del Lavoro will pay 100,000 euros to La Cucina.

5. Banca Nazionale del Lavoro transfers these documents to Fleet Bank Boston and debits Fleet's account with it for the required amount.

6. Fleet then notifies American Stores of the arrival of the documents and transfers them to American Stores in return for payment of the dollar equivalent of 100,000 euros plus fees associated with the transaction.

7. Upon arrival of the goods in Boston, American Stores will present the bill of lading to the carrier or its agent in order to take possession of the 1,000 food processors that it had agreed to buy.

Negotiators contemplating the use of a letter of credit in a sales transaction should always bear two things in mind. First, banks pay under letters of credit upon presentation of the specified documents, regardless of factors affecting the underlying transaction. So, if a buyer changes its mind or if it discovers that the food processors do not meet its expectations, it cannot order the bank to stop payment. If the seller presents the specified documents, the bank must pay the seller, despite any protests by the buyer. Second, the documents that the seller presents must strictly comply with the documents specified in the letter of credit. If they do not strictly and precisely comply, the bank is justified in refusing to pay under the letter of credit. So, for example, if the letter of credit calls for an invoice specifying goods consisting a "three electrical motors with spare parts," but the actual invoice presented states that the shipment consists of "three electrical motors with miscellaneous equipment," the bank would be justified in refusing payment.

A letter of credit may also be used as a means to finance an international transaction. For instance, suppose that in contemplation of a large sale, a manufacturer needs cash in order to buy raw materials to fill the order. It might negotiate an agreement by which the buyer would secure a letter of credit in favor of the seller that would specify payment in installments, the first payment to be made by the seller's simple written demand for payment in the form of a draft presented to the bank as soon as the letter of credit is issued. The first payment is, in effect, an advance to the seller to enable it to finance the purchase of the necessary raw materials.

In most cases, the seller insists on a letter of credit in order to avoid or reduce the credit risk in the transaction. In some instances, a buyer may require a letter of credit to gain protection from the risk of nonperformance by the seller. This type is known as a "performance letter of credit" or "standby letter of credit." Suppose that the Indian Ministry of Transport contracts with an American company to install new air traffic control systems at several of its airports for a total of $200 million. The contract calls for installation of the systems over a period of four years with 25 percent of the purchase price payable at the end of each year. The American company would ordinarily require a letter of credit to secure the payments. India, however, faces the risk the system will not work or will not be installed on time in accordance with the contract. It might therefore require the American company to secure a performance letter of credit from a recognized international bank, providing that upon the presentation of specified documents—for example, a statement, certified by the Minister of Transportation and a particular consulting engineer—that the control system failed to meet contract specifications, a specified sum would be paid to the Indian government. Here, too, the bank will pay under the letter of credit upon presentation of the appropriate documents. It will not itself evaluate whether the installed systems actually meet the terms of the contract.

International Agency and Distributorship

Instead of selling into a foreign market on an ad hoc basis, a manufacturer or exporter might wish to set up a more or less permanent arrangement to conduct such sales on a regular, expanded basis. In fashioning such an arrangement, a company has a broad array of options from which to choose. Two of the most common means are to appoint a foreign agent (sometimes called a sales representative) or a distributor in the country concerned.

In the former arrangement, the agent or representative in the foreign country seeks to secure orders that the exporter will accept if it so chooses. Normally, the representative or agent works on a commission basis, assumes no risk or responsibility for the sale itself, and does not take ownership or possession of the goods. While it is possible for the agent or representative to have the authority to make contracts on behalf of the exporter, most sales representation agreements specifically deny the agent or representative that power because of the risks that it entails for the exporter.

Under a distributorship, a person or company in the foreign market buys the goods for its own account from the exporter and then resells them at a markup, using the exporter's trademarks and logos. Under this arrangement, the distributor takes ownership of the goods, is responsible for making retail sales to customers for which it bears the entire credit risk, and also must usually provide after-sales service to retail customers.

Both foreign sales representation and distributorship arrangements are normally concluded after careful negotiation and preparation of a lengthy contract. The most difficult and at the same time most important single task in establishing a sale representation or distributorship abroad happens before negotiations actually take place: the identification and selection of an appropriate person or company to act as representative or distributor. The selection of an inappropriate agent or distributor may not only thwart any hope for increases in sales in that country but may also result in significant costs to the exporter, including failure to pay for goods delivered, misappropriation of product advertising, damage to the exporter's reputation and the standing of its products, and loss of existing customers. In addition, an exporter may find that getting rid of an inappropriate representative or distributor will require the payment of damages, indemnifications, and other costs.

Although the relationship between a manufacturer and its agent or distributor will fundamentally be subject to the contract negotiated between the parties, the laws of the country in which the agent or distributor is to operate will also influence that relationship in several important respects. First, many countries have enacted legislation to protect local agents and distributors from unfair or arbitrary termination of the relationship. Because the agent or distributor may have devoted considerable efforts and resources to developing the market for the manufacturer's products in the country, many countries have enacted legislation to prohibit cancellation of an agency or distributorship agreement without appropriate notice or compensation. Second, provisions in the contract that seek to prevent a foreign agent or distributor from engaging in certain activities, such as handling competing goods, may be judged to violate local anticompetition laws. And finally, negotiators of agency and distributorships need to assure themselves that local labor and taxation laws will not have adverse effects on the deal.

International Licensing Agreements

Much global business is concerned with the transfer of intangible rights rather than physical objects. Persons and companies that own valuable intellectual property rights, such as patents, trademarks, copyrights, or unpatented trade secrets, earn billions of dollars each year by giving permission to persons and companies in other countries to use those rights. Suppose that a U.S. company, KIDSTIME, Inc., has developed a digital children's watch whose face changes every day. It has successfully marketed the watch in the United States with the advertising slogan "The KIDS-TIME Watch—A New Face Every Day." It has patented the watch, has registered the trademark "KIDSTIME," has a copyright on advertising materials and instruction booklets, and has various trade secrets about manufacturing and marketing the watch. Rather than selling the watches directly to foreign markets through its own subsidiary, or through a foreign agent or distributor, KIDSTIME, Inc. might license its intellectual property to a company abroad to permit it to manufacture and sell KIDS-TIME watches. It would therefore negotiate one or more contracts whereby it would grant the foreign company the right to use its patent rights, its trademarks, its copyrighted materials, and any trade secrets under specified conditions in return for which it would receive a royalty, which in most cases is a percentage of gross sales of products made and marketed using the licensed intellectual property. KIDSTIME, Inc., the licensor, remains the owner of the intellectual property. It merely permits the foreign company, the licensee, to use its intellectual property rights under specified conditions.

Licensing, like any other transaction, has both rewards and risks. A company like KIDSTIME may decide to license rather than sell directly or establish a sales or manufacturing subsidiary in order to gain additional revenue without significant investment or expenditure. Moreover, licensing may be a way to penetrate a foreign market that is protected by high tariffs or stiff import regulations. On the other hand, poor manufacturing or marketing practices by the licensee may damage the reputation of the goods produced and thereby diminish the value of the intellectual property that is licensed. In addition, the licensee may divert the intellectual property to other purposes or become a competitor of the licensor once the license ends. In addition, a third party in the country may gain access to the technology and manufacture competing goods.

In order to deal with these risks, the license contract normally contains detailed conditions on how the licensed intellectual property may be used. It also provides a means for the licensor to police the use of the intellectual property and to audit the proceeds earned from its use. As a result, a license agreement creates a continuing relationship between the licensor and the licensee. The governments of both the licensor and the licensee may seek to regulate licensing transactions. For example, the licensor's government may be concerned that licensing intellectual property and technology not have an adverse effect on its national security. Thus, the United States government, under the Export Administration Act, has the power to restrict the flow of certain kinds of technology to countries that it feels threaten U.S. security. Governments in licensees' countries, on the other hand, are often concerned about the cost of the licensed intellectual property and the anticompetitive effects of the conditions imposed on the licensee. As a result, a license in those countries may require government approval before it goes into effect.

Negotiators of intellectual property licenses must deal with a wide range of issues. These include an accurate description of the intellectual property to be transferred or licensed, the royalty and payment terms, quality controls that the licensee must respect, geographical and other controls on the use of the licensed rights and the resulting products by the licensee, the duration of the license and the means by which it may be terminated, auditing and reporting requirements, confidentiality and secrecy provisions to protect the intellectual property from being leaked to third parties, and mechanisms to settle disputes that may arise between the licensor and the licensee.

International Management and Technical Services Agreements

A significant portion of global business consists in selling services to companies and governments in other countries, either alone or in connection with a patent, technology, trademark, or know-how licensing agreements. For example, when KIDSTIME,

Inc. licenses its patent and trademarks to manufacture and sell KIDSTIME Watches to a company in France, it might also make a technical services agreement with the French licensee to assist it, for a fee, in organizing itself and training its workers to manufacture the KIDSTIME watch. The specific nature of the service to be provided will depend on the recipient's needs.

Service contracts are of many different types. They may provide for training, design and engineering, technological assistance (such as the improvement of production methods at a factory), marketing and commercial services, planning, research and development, and general or specialized management. In effect, service agreements in international business are mechanisms for transferring technology from one country to another. Like any other technology transactions, service transactions are normally subject to lengthy and detailed contracts that are the product of careful negotiations between the parties. The issues to be covered in the negotiation and the resulting contract include the specification of the precise services to be provided, the method by which the provider will be compensated, the nature of the ongoing relationship between the personnel of the transferor and the transferee, and the conditions that the transferee must create in order to allow the service to be rendered as promised. For example, if the transferor of the service is to manage a factory or hotel, the management services agreement will ordinarily specify the transferee's obligations to provide adequate support staff, maintenance of facilities, and general security to allow effective management to take place.

International Franchising Agreements

Franchising is an increasingly important means of global business. Franchised businesses, such as McDonald's, Pizza Hut, and Bennetton, cover the globe. A franchise is an agreement by which the franchiser authorizes the franchisee to engage in the business of selling goods or services using trademarks owned by the franchiser in accordance with a business plan or system prescribed by the franchiser and based on its intellectual property. For example, suppose that Louisiana Foods Corp. has developed a spicy pizza that it calls "Cajun Pizza," which it sells at small restaurants having a distinctive architectural design and bearing the name "Cajun Pizza" with a logo consisting of an alligator wearing a straw hat. Within a few years, Cajun Pizza restaurants become extremely popular and some 1,500 of them are located throughout the United States. Seeking to capitalize on the popularity and reputation of Cajun Pizza, which has now extended beyond the U.S. borders, Louisiana Foods considers options to sell its product in foreign markets. One option would be to establish its own subsidiaries to produce and market Cajun Pizza in individual countries. That approach would require Louisiana Foods to invest substantial amounts of capital and to incur significant risk. Another would be to produce Cajun Pizzas in the United States and sell them through appointed distributors in various foreign markets. This option is hardly practical since the pizza would be at least a week old before it got to the buyer.

A third option is franchising. Louisiana Foods might authorize carefully selected individuals or companies located in markets around the world to establish Cajun Pizza restaurants, identical to those in the United States, to produce and sell Cajun Pizzas in a such a way that the foreign restaurants are acting as part of a common business system. These individuals and businesses would provide the capital necessary to build the restaurants, thus sparing Louisiana Foods the burden and risk of investing its own funds to build a global network of pizza restaurants. With an obligation to pay Louisiana Foods a percentage of gross sales and to purchase various inputs from it, the local franchisees would also assume the responsibility for managing the restaurants efficiently and profitably.

At the heart of a franchise system is the franchise contract, a standard form agreement that franchisees must accept with little opportunity for amendment. A franchise agreement is more than an intellectual property license. In return for an initial investment or franchise fee paid by the franchisee as well as the payment of an ongoing royalty or service fee normally calculated as a percentage of the franchisee's gross sales, the franchisor grants the franchisee a package of rights in the form of various intellectual property rights, including the use of a common name and uniform presentation of the premises, the communication of substantial know-how to carry on the franchised business effectively, and the continuous provision of commercial and technical assistance during the life of the agreement. For a franchise to succeed, a high level of uniformity needs to exist among the franchised businesses, whether in Bangor or Bangkok, even though they are each legally separate enterprises. In order to achieve that uniformity, the franchisor must be able to exert a significant degree of control over the franchisees and their operations. The instrument that allows this control is the franchise agreement. If the franchisee does not follow the franchisor's rules concerning franchise operations, the franchisor usually has the right to cancel the contract. This is a serious sanction because the franchisee's business, deprived of the right to use the franchisor's trademarks and to benefit from its advertising and image, will be much less valuable than it was as part of the franchise system.

International Direct Investment and Joint Ventures

One of the most significant forms of global business entails the transfer of capital from one country to another for purposes of investment. Foreign investment has traditionally been divided into two categories: direct and portfolio investment. A direct investment establishes or purchases an interest in a permanent enterprise or facility, such as a hotel, factory, or plantation, in whose management the investor will have some role. A portfolio investment, because of its size, gives the investor no right to participate in management. For statistical purposes, an investment of less than 10 percent of the equity in an enterprise is considered a portfolio investment.

A direct foreign investment may take the form of a branch of the investor's enterprise, a separately incorporated subsidiary, or a joint venture with other investors. A direct investor may build its own foreign operations (known as "green field development") or acquire it by buying existing facilities through merger, acquisition, or privatization. A joint venture may be a separately incorporated enterprise, in which case it is called an "equity joint venture," or simply a type of unincorporated partnership between two companies known as a contractual joint venture. In either case, the parties to the joint venture will negotiate a detailed contract to govern their relationship.

For a wholly owned subsidiary or joint venture to become a reality as a functioning business, it must secure various resources and services, many of which will be provided by the investors themselves. Normally individual contracts between a specific direct investor and the enterprise entity will govern the provision of these resources and services. Many of these contracts will take the form of the agreements discussed earlier in this chapter. For example, if a wholly owned subsidiary will use the trademarks of the parent corporation, it will ordinarily enter into a trademark license with the parent and pay a stipulated royalty for the privilege.

In the case of joint ventures, in order to give legal certainty to its eventual formation and the joint-venture investors' commitments to provide the necessary resources and services, the joint-venture partners will ordinarily prepare these contracts at the time the joint-venture agreement is negotiated and stipulate that the partners, as shareholders in the joint-venture company, will take all appropriate action to cause the joint-venture company once it is formed to enter into these contracts, which are usually annexed to the joint venture agreement. The agreement between the joint-venture partners has various names: joint-venture agreement, pre-incorporation contract, or founder's agreement.

For example, suppose that American Air Conditioners, Inc., a New York corporation, decides to form a joint venture with Agraria Refrigerator Corporation, a family-owned company, to manufacture air conditioners in Agraria, a developing country. American Air Conditioners will contribute 40 percent of the capital and Agraria Refrigerator will contribute 60 percent to form the joint-venture company, Agraria Air Conditioners, Ltd. The business plan negotiated by the two partners provides that Agraria Air Conditioners, Ltd., will build a manufacturing facility on land to be purchased from Agraria Refrigerator and employ used manufacturing equipment and machinery to be bought from American Air Conditioners, Inc. The manufacturing process will rely on American Air Conditioners' patented technology, and the air conditioners will bear the trademark "MultiCool," also owned by American. In the initial stages of production, Agraria Air Conditioners will use components purchased from American Air Conditioners. American will also provide the joint venture with management and marketing expertise. In order to protect American as a minority partner, it is also agreed that American will appoint the general manager of Agraria Air Conditioners and that the joint venture company will make no major policy decision over American's opposition.

To give legal certainty to these various understandings, the parties to the joint venture would agree to and prepare the following contracts:

1. Company Statutes, stating the rules by which the joint venture company would be run, including special provisions to protect American Air Conditioners, Inc. as a minority shareholder

2. Management Structure Description, outlining the internal management organization of the joint venture company

3. Land Purchase Agreement, by which the joint-venture company is to obtain the land for its factory from Agraria Refrigerator Corporation

4. General Assistance Agreement, by which American Air Conditioners for a fee will provide technical assistance and advice to the joint-venture company

5. Components Supply Agreement, by which the joint-venture company agrees to purchase components from American Air Conditioners for a specified period of time

6. Machinery and Equipment Purchase Agreement, by which the joint-venture company agrees to buy from American Air Conditioners the necessary used equipment and machinery to manufacture air conditioners

7. Technical License, by which American agrees to license its patented technology to the joint-venture company for use in manufacturing air conditioners

8. Trademark License Agreement, by which American Air Conditioners agrees to license its trademark "MultiCool" to the joint venture for use in marketing the air conditioners

9. Shareholder Agreement, by which the two partners agree to vote the shares in the joint venture company to carry out specific policies and agreements
10. Marketing Policy, by which the two partners agree that the joint-venture company will carry out a predetermined marketing policy

At the time the two partners sign their joint-venture agreement, the joint-venture company is not yet in existence. The process of forming the company can take considerable time, depending on the legal and bureaucratic environment of the country concerned. Therefore, to be certain that, once formed, the joint-venture company will enter into contracts containing the terms agreed upon, the parties in their joint venture-agreement commit themselves to vote their shares and to take all necessary actions to cause the board of directors of Agraria Air Conditioners, Ltd. to enter into all of the specified contracts that are annexed to and made an integral part of the joint venture agreement. In effect, these various contracts form a hub-and-spoke structure, with the pre-incorporation or joint-venture agreement as a hub that holds the annexed contracts as spokes to form a single agreement, as illustrated in the following diagram.

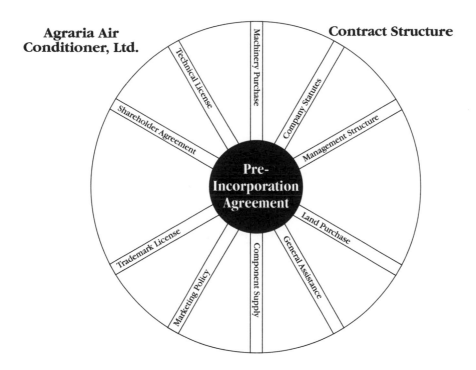

In addition to the contracts among themselves, the investors will also need to negotiate various agreements with the host country government to cover such matters as customs duties exemptions on capital equipment, guarantees on repatriation of profits and capital, and protection against expropriation.

Other Contracts

The number and variety of international business contracts is infinite. International loans, concession agreements, build-operate-and-transfer transactions, mineral exploration and development contracts, and international equipment leasing arrangements are just a few of the many other types of contracts that are used in the world of global business. Indeed, their number and type are limited only by the ingenuity of negotiators during the deal-making process.

APPENDIX C

SUGGESTIONS FOR FURTHER READING

The following books and articles provide additional helpful information and advice for global negotiators generally and in specific areas.

GENERAL SOURCES

Acuff, Frank L. *How to Negotiate Anything with Anyone Anywhere Around the World.* New York: American Management Association, 1993.

Brake, Terrence, Danielle Medina Walker, and Thomas Walker. *Doing Business Internationally: The Guide to Cross-cultural Success.* Burr Ridge, IL: Irwin Publishing, 1995.

Brett, Jeanne. *Negotiating Globally: How to Negotiate Deals, Resolve Disputes, and Make Decisions Across Cultures.* San Francisco: Jossey-Bass, 2001.

Foster, Dean Allen. *Bargaining Across Borders: How to Negotiate Business Successfully Anywhere in the World.* New York: McGraw-Hill, 1992.

Gesteland, R.R. *Cross-cultural Business Behavior.* Copenhagen: Copenhagen Business School Press, 1996.

Ghauri, Pervez. and J.C. Usunier, *International Business Negotiations.* Oxford: Pergamon, 1996.

Hendon, D.W., R.A. Hendon, and P. Herbig. *Cross-cultural Business Negotiations.* Westport, Conn: Quorum Books, 1996.

Hodge, Sheida. *Global Smarts: The Art of Communicating and Deal Making Anywhere in the World.* New York: John Wiley, 2000.

Moran, Robert T., and William G. Stripp. *Dynamics of Successful International Business Negotiations.* Houston: Gulf Publishing, 1991.

Morrison, Terri, Wayne A. Conaway, and George A. Borden. *Kiss, Bow, or Shake Hands: How to do Business in Sixty Countries.* Holbrook, MA: B. Adams, 1994.

Silkenat, James R. and Jeffrey M. Aresty, editors. *The ABA guide to International Business Negotiations: A Comparison of Cross-Cultural Issues and Successful Approaches.* Chicago: Section of Law Practice Management, Section of International Law and Practice, American Bar Association, 1994.

SPECIFIC AREAS

Africa

Bigsten, Arne, et al. "Contract Flexibility and Dispute Resolution in African Manufacturing" in *Journal of Development Studies* 36, no. 4 (April 2000): 1–37.

Algeria

Zartman, I. William, and Antonella Bassani. *Algerian Gas Negotiations.* PEW Case Studies, 103.0-C-86-J. Washington., D.C.: School of Advanced International Studies, Johns Hopkins University Press, 1986.

Argentina

Stiles, K.W. "Argentina's Bargaining with the IMF" in *Journal of Inter-American Studies and World Affairs* 29, no. 3 (Autumn 1987): 55–86.

Asia

Chu, Chin-Ning. *The Asian Mind Game: Unlocking the Hidden Agenda of the Asian Business Culture: A Westerner's Survival Manual.* New York: Rawson Associates; Toronto: Collier Macmillan Canada, 1991.

Engholm, C. *When Business East Meets Business West: The Guide to Practice and Protocol in the Pacific Rim.* New York: John Wiley, 1991.

Paik, Yongsun. "Negotiating with East Asians: How to Attain "Win-Win" Outcomes" in *Management International Review*, Wiesbaden 39, no. 2 (1999): 103–23.

Tung, R.L. "Managing in Asia" in *Managing Across Cultures: Issues and Perspectives*, edited by P. Joynt and M. Warner. London: Routledge, 1996.

Australia

Fletcher, Richard. "Network Theory and Countertrade Transactions" in *International Business Review* 5, no. 2 (April 1996): 167–89.

Brazil

Graham, John L. "Brazilian, Japanese, and American Business Negotiations" in *Journal of International Business Studies* 14, no. 1 (Spring-Summer 1983): 44–66.

———. "The Influence of Culture on the Process of Business Negotiations: An Exploratory Study" in *Journal of International Business Studies* 16, no. 1 (Spring 1985): 81–96. (Study of the United States, Japan, and Brazil.)

Hurrell, Andrew, and Ellen Felder. *U.S.-Brazilian Information Dispute.* PEW Case Studies, 122.0-E-88-J. Washington, D.C.: School of Advanced International Studies, Johns Hopkins University Press, 1988.

Pinto dos Santos, V.B.M. "Genre Analysis of Business Letters of Negotiation" in *English for Specific Purposes* 21, no. 2 (2002): 167–99.

Volkema, Roger J. "Ethicality in Negotiations: An Analysis of Perceptual Similarities and Differences between Brazil and the United States" in *Journal of Business Research* 45, no.1 (May 1999): 59–67.

Canada

Alder, Nancy J., and John L. Graham. "Cross-cultural Interaction: The International Comparison Fallacy?" in *Journal of International Business Studies* 20, no. 3 (Fall 1989): 515–37. (Study of Japanese, American, and Canadian Francophones and Canadian Anglophones.)

Bemmels, Brian, E.G. Fisher, and Barbara Nyland. "Canadian-American Jurisprudence on 'Good Faith' Bargaining" in *Industrial Relations* 41, no. 3 (Canada, 1986): 596–620.

Grey, Rodney de C. "Negotiating about Trade and Investment in Services" in *Trade and Investment in Services/U.S. Perspectives*, edited by R.M. Stern, 1985, 181–202. Toronto: Ontario Economic Council.

China

Adler, N. J., R. Brahm, and J. Graham. "Strategy implementation: a comparison of face-to-face negotiations in the People's Republic of China and the United States" in *Strategic Management Journal* 13 (1992): 449–46.

Blackman, C. *Negotiating China: Case Studies and Strategies.* St. Leonards, NSW, Australia: Allen & Unwin, 1997.

Chen, M. "Understanding Chinese and Japanese Negotiating Styles" in *International Executive* 35, no. 2 (1993): 147–59.

Child, J., and S. Stewart. "Regional Differences in China and Their Implications for Sino-Foreign Joint Ventures" in *Journal of General Management* 23, no. 2 (1997): 65–86.

Fang, Tony. *Chinese Business Negotiating Style.* Thousand Oaks, CA: Sage Publications, 1999.

Ghauri, Pervez, and Tony Fang. "Negotiating with the Chinese: A Socio-Cultural Analysis" in *Journal of World Business* 36, no. 3 (Autumn 2001): 303–25.

Lam, Maria Lai-Ling. *Working with Chinese Expatriates in Business Negotiations : Portraits, Issues, and Applications.* Westport, CT: Quorum, 2000.

Li Ji, "Negotiating with China: Exploratory Study of Relationship-Building" in *Journal of Managerial Issues* 13, no. 3 (Fall 2001): 345–60.

Pye, Lucian W. *Chinese Negotiating Style: Commercial Approaches and Cultural Principles.* New York: Quorum Books, 1992.

Roehrig, Michael Franz. *Foreign Joint Ventures in Contemporary China.* New York: St. Martin's Press, 1994.

Shi Xinping, and R.I. Westwood. "International Business Negotiations in the Chinese Context" in *Management and Organizations in China*, edited by J.T. Li, A. Tsui, and E. Weldon. London: Macmillan, 2000.

Wagner, C. L. "Influence on Western-Chinese Joint Venture Negotiations" in *Asia-Pacific Journal of Management* 7, no. 2 (1994): 79–100.

Worm, Verner. *Vikings and Mandarins: Sino-Scandinavian Business Cooperation in Cross-Cultural Settings.* Copenhagen: Handelshojskolens Forlag: distributed by Monksgaard International Publishers, 1997.

Zhao, Jensen J. "The Chinese Approach to International Business Negotiation" in *Journal of Business Communication* 37, no. 3 (July 2000): 209–38.

Colombia

Kline, Harvey F. *The Coal of El Cerrejon: Dependent Bargaining and Colombian Policy Making.* University Park: Pennsylvania State University Press, 1987.

Costa Rica

Sebenius, James K., and Hannah Riley. "Case Brief: Stone Container in Honduras and Costa Rica." Harvard Business School case 800137, October 1999.

Denmark

Kjaerbeck, Susanne. "The Organization of Discourse Units in Mexican and Danish Business Negotiations" in *Journal of Pragmatics* 30, no. 3 (September 1998): 347–62.

Egypt

Quandt, William B. "Egypt: A Strong Sense of National Identity" in *National Negotiating Styles* edited by Hans Binnendijk, ed. Washington, D.C.: Foreign Service Institute, U.S. Department of State, 1987.

Europe

Altanny, David. "Europe 1992: Culture Crash" in *Industry Week* 238, no. 19 (October 2, 1989): 13–20.

Angwin, Duncan. "Mergers and acquisitions across European borders: National perspectives on preacquisition due diligence and the use of professional advisers" in *Journal of World Business* 36, no. 1 (Spring 2001): 32–57.

Bruce Leigh. "North vs. South" in *International Management* 44, no. 5 (United Kingdom, May 1989): 20–26. (Cultural differences between the nations of northern and southern Europe)

Campbell, Nigel C. G., John L. Graham, Alain Jolibert, and Hans Gunther Meissner. "Marketing Negotiations in France, Germany, the United Kingdom and the United States" in *Journal of Marketing* 52, no. 2 (April 1988): 49–62.

Le Poole, Smafrits. "Negotiating with Clint Eastwood in Brussels" in *Management Review* 78, no. 10 (October 1989): 58–60.

Millington, A. I. and B. T. Bayliss. "Instability of Market Penetration Joint Ventures: A Study of U.K. Joint Ventures in the European Union" in *International Business Review* 6, no. 1 (February 1997): 1–17.

Sebenius, James K. "Dr. Sergio Ceccuzzi and SMI: Negotiating Cross-Border Acquisitions in Europe." Harvard Business School case 897085, January 1997.

Finland

Beamish, Paul W., and R. Azimah Ainuddin. "Nora-Sakari: a proposed joint venture in Malaysia." Harvard Business School case 95G002, February 2000.

France

Kenna, Peggy. *Business France: A Practical Guide to Understanding French Business Culture.* Lincolnwood, IL: Passport Books, 1994.

Germany

Kenna, Peggy. *Business Germany: A Practical Guide to Understanding German Business Culture.* Lincolnwood, IL: Passport Books, 1994.

Streeck, Jürgen, and Werner Kallmeyer. "Interaction by Inscription" in *Journal of Pragmatics* 33, no. 4 (April 2001): 465–90.

Wever, Kirsten S. *Negotiating Competitiveness: Employment Relations and Organizational Innovation in Germany and the United States.* Cambridge, MA: Harvard Business School Press, 1995.

Ghana

Tsikata, Fui S. *Essays from the Ghana Valco Renegotiations*, 1982–1985. Accra: Ghana Publishing, 1986.

Guatemala

Krznaric, Roman. "Civil and Uncivil Actors in the Guatemalan Peace Process" in *Bulletin of Latin American Research* 18, no. 1 (January 1999): 1–16.

Moreno, Josephine and Mary Ann Littrell. "Negotiating Tradition: Tourism Retailers in Guatemala" in *Annals of Tourism Research* 28, no. 3 (2001): 658–85.

Honduras

Sebenius, James K. and Hannah Riley. "Case Brief: Stone Container in Honduras and Costa Rica," Harvard Business School case number 800137, October 1999.

India

Bullis, Douglas. *Doing Business in Today's India*. Westport, CT: Quorum, 1998.

Ghuari, Pervez N. "Negotiating with Firms in Developing Countries: Two Case Studies" in *Industrial Marketing Management* 17, no. 1 (February 1988): 49–53. (Study of India and Nigeria).

Japan

Adair, Wendi L., Tetsushi Okumura, and Jeanne M. Brett. "Negotiation Behavior When Cultures Collide: the United States and Japan" in *Journal of Applied Psychology* 86, no. 3 (June 2001): 371.

Chen, M. "Understanding Chinese and Japanese Negotiating Styles" in *International Executive* 35, no. 2 (1993): 147–59.

Conway, Mara Eleina. *Negotiating for Success: How U.S.-Japan Negotiations Are Affected by Different Legal Systems and Cross-Cultural Miscommunications*. J.D. Thesis, Syracuse University, 1996.

Deutsch, M. F. *Doing Business with the Japanese*. New York: NAL Books, 1993.

Graham, John. "The Japanese Negotiation Style: Characteristics of a Distinct Approach" in *Negotiation Journal* (April 1993): 123–40.

Hodgson, James D. *Doing Business with the New Japan*. Lanham, MD:Rowan & Littlefield, 2000.

Nishiyama, Kazuo. *Doing Business with Japan: Successful Strategies for Intercultural Communication*. Honolulu: University of Hawaii Press, 2000.

Kazakhstan

Neumann, Michael J. "A Company Perspective on Doing Business in the Former Soviet Union: A Mining Venture in Kazakstan" in *Resources Policy* 23, no. 3 (September 1997): 137–46.

Kenya

Jamison, David. "Tourism and Ethnicity: The Brotherhood of Coconuts" in *Annals of Tourism Research* 26, no. 4 (October 1999): 944–67.

Kimuyu, Peter. *Enterprise Attributes and Corporate Disputes in Kenya.* Nairobi, Kenya: Institute of Policy Analysis and Research, 1997.

Korea

De Mente, B. L. *Korean Etiquette & Ethics in Business.* Lincolnwood, IL: NTC Business Books, 1994.

Griffin, T. J. "Doing Business in Korea" in *Washington State Business News* 43 (March 1989): 19–22.

Odell, John, David Land, and Tracy Tierney. *Bilateral Trade Negotiations Between South Korea and the United States.* PEW Case Studies, 129.0-G-88-S. Los Angeles: School of International Relations, University of Southern California, 1988.

Latin America

Mendoa, Eugene L. "How to Do Business in Latin America" in *Purchasing World* 32, no. 7 (July 1988): 58–59.

Malaysia

Beamish, Paul W., and R. Azimah Ainuddin. "Nora-Sakari: A Proposed Joint Venture in Malaysia." Harvard Business School case 95G002, February 2000.

LeCraw, Donald J., and Boon Lim. "Kanzen Berhad: A Proposed Joint Venture with Pacific Dunlop Ltd." Harvard Business School case 97G004, February 2000.

Mexico

Grayson, George W. "Mexico: A Love-Hate Relationship with North America" in *National Negotiating Styles,* edited by Hans Binnendijk. Washington D.C.: Foreign Service Institute, U.S. Department of State, 1987.

Heydenfeldt, Jo Ann G. "The Influence of Individualism/Collectivism on Mexican and US business Negotiation" in *International Journal of Intercultural Relations* 24, no. 3 (May 2000): 383–407.

Kenna, Peggy. *Business Mexico: A Practical Guide To Understanding Mexican Business Culture.* Lincolnwood, IL: Passport Books, 1994.

Kjaerbeck, Susanne. "The Organization of Discourse Units in Mexican and Danish Business Negotiations" in *Journal of Pragmatics* 30, no. 3 (September 1998): 347–62.

Middle East

Al-Khatib, J. A., C. J. Robertson, A. D'Auria Stanton, and S. J. Vitell. "Business Ethics in the Arab Gulf States: A Three-Country Study" in *International Business Review* 11, no. 1 (February 2002): 97–111.

Nigeria

Bierstecker, Thomas J. *Reaching Agreement with the IMF: The Nigerian Negotiations, 1983–1986.* PEW Case Studies, 205.0-C-88-S. Los Angeles: School of International Relations, University of Southern California, 1988.

Ghuari, Pervez N. "Negotiating with Firms in Developing Countries: Two Case Studies" in *Industrial Marketing Management* 17, no. 1 (February 1988): 49–53. (Study of India and Nigeria)

Norway

Nye, D. A. "Formation of Contracts: The Law in Norway" in *North Carolina Journal of International Law and Commercial Regulation* 12 (Spring 1987): 187–248.

Philippines

Calantone, Roger J., John L. Graham, and Alma Mintu-Wimsatt. "Problem-solving Approach in an International Context: Antecedents and Outcomes" in *International Journal of Research in Marketing* 15, no. 1 (February 1998): 19–35.

Mintu-Wimsatt, Alma. "Exploring Personality Traits of Filipino Industrial Exporters and Their Implications on the Negotiation Activity" in *Journal of Asia-Pacific Business* 2, no. 4 (2000): 3–19.

Russia

Schecter, Jerrold L. *Russian Negotiating Behavior: Continuity and Transition.* Washington, D.C.: United States Institute of Peace Press, 1998.

Sebenius, James K. "Doing Business in Russia: Note on Negotiating in the 'Wild East." Harvard Business School case 899048, August 1999.

Saudi Arabia

Mackey, Sandra. *The Saudis: Inside the Desert Kingdom.* Boston: Houghton Mifflin, 1987.

Scandinavia

Worm, Verner. *Vikings and Mandarins: Sino-Scandinavian Business Cooperation in Cross-Cultural Settings.* Copenhagen: Handelshojskolens Forlag: distributed by Monksgaard International Publishers, 1997.

Singapore

Ang, Swee Hoon and Georgina Teo. "Effects of Time Processing Orientation, Agreement Preferences and Attitude towards Foreign Businessmen on Negotiation Adaptation" in *International Business Review* 6, no. 6 (December 1997): 625–40.

Spain

Bruton, Kevin. *The Business Culture in Spain.* Boston: Butterworth-Heinemann, 1994.

United Kingdom

Millington, A. I., and B. T. Bayliss. "Instability of Market Penetration Joint Ventures: A Study of UK Joint Ventures in the European Union" in *International Business Review* 6, no. 1 (February 1997): 1–17.

United States

Campbell, Nigel C. G., John L. Graham, Alain Jolibert, and Hans Gunther Meissner. "Marketing Negotiations in France, Germany, the United Kingdom and the United States" in *Journal of Marketing* 52, no. 2 (April 1988): 49–62.

Volkema, Roger J. "Ethicality in Negotiations: An Analysis of Perceptual Similarities and Differences Between Brazil and the United States" in *Journal of Business Research* 45, no.1 (May 1999): 59–67.

Wever, Kirsten S. *Negotiating Competitiveness: Employment Relations and Organizational Innovation in Germany and the United States.* Cambridge, MA: Harvard Business School Press, 1995.

Notes

CHAPTER 2

1. Author's interview with "Janet," January 25, 1998, New York City.
2. Terrence P. Hoppmann, "Two Paradigms of Negotiation: Bargaining and Problem Solving," *ANNALS, AAPSS* 542 (1995): 24–47.
3. See Abba Kolo and Thomas W. Walde, "Renegotiation and Contract Adaptation in International Investment Projects," *Journal of World Investment* 1 (2000): 5, for an excellent summary of major renegotiation cases in the petroleum and minerals industry.
4. Jeswald W. Salacuse, "Ten Ways that Culture Affects Negotiating Style: Some Survey Results," *Negotiation Journal* 14 (1998): 221.
5. Akilagpa Sawyer, "Redoing An Old Deal: Case Study of the Renegotiation of the Valco Agreement," (unpublished paper, 1991). See also Fui S. Tsikata, ed., *Essays from the Ghana-Valco Renegotiations: 1982–85* (Accra: Ghana Publishing, 1986).
6. For a discussion of this tripartite analysis within the context of diplomatic negotiations, see I. William Zartman and Maureen R. Berman, *The Practical Negotiator* (New Haven, CT: Yale University Press, 1982).
7. D. M. Kolb and G. G. Coolidge, "Her Place at the Table: A Consideration of Gender Issues in Negotiation," in *Negotiation Theory and Practice*, ed. J. W. Breslin and J. Z Rubin (Cambridge, MA: PON Books, 1991).
8. "Enron's Rebecca Mark: 'You Have To Be Pushy and Aggressive,'" *Business Week*, February 24, 1997, at http://businessweek.com/1997/08/b351586.htm.
9. Jeswald W. Salacuse, "Renegotiating International Project Agreements," *Fordham International Law Journal* 24 (2001): 1319.
10. C. Buhring-Uhle, *Arbitration and Mediation in International Business* (New York: Kluwer, 1996), 318–319.
11. Nael G. Bunni, "Major Project Dispute Review Board," *In-House Counsel International* 1 (June-July 1997):13.

CHAPTER 3

1. Author's interview with Frank, December 24, 2000, Concord, MA.
2. Robert H. Mnookin and Lawrence E. Susskind, eds., *Negotiating on Behalf of Others: Advice to Lawyers, Business Executives, Sports Agents, Diplomats, Politicians and Everybody Else* (Thousand Oaks, CA: Sage Publications, 1999).

3. For a discussion of the process of giving advice, see Jeswald W. Salacuse, *The Wise Advisor: What Every Professional Should Know About Consulting and Counseling* (Westport, CT: Praeger, 2000).
4. Roger W. Fisher, William Ury, and Bruce Patton, *Getting to YES: Negotiating Agreement Without Giving In* (New York: Penguin, 2nd ed., 1991).
5. See Bill Vlasic and Bradley A. Stertz, *Taken for a Ride: How Daimler-Benz Drove Off with Chrysler* (New York: W. Morrow, 2000).
6. Edmund L. Andrews, "AOL-Time Warner Merger is Cleared by the Europeans," *New York Times*, October 12, 2000, p. C4.
7. Kenneth J. Vandevelde, "The Bilateral Investment Treaty Program of the United States," *Cornell International Law Journal* 21 (1988): 201, 203–6, Jeswald W. Salacuse, "BIT by BIT: The Growth of Bilateral Investment Treaties and Their Impact on Foreign Investment in Developing Countries," *The International Lawyer* 24 (1990): 655.
8. W. Pengilley, "International Franchising Arrangements and Problems in Their Negotiation," *Northwestern Journal of International Law and Business* 7 (1985): 185.

CHAPTER 4

1. See Robert Mnookin et al., *Beyond Winning: Negotiating to Create Value in Deals and Disputes* (Cambridge, MA: Harvard University Press, 2000) 11–43. See also David A. Lax and James K. Sebenius, *The Manager as Negotiator: Bargaining for Cooperation and Competitive Gain* (New York: The Free Press, 1986) 29–45.
2. See Kathleen Valley and Michael Wheeler, "Luna Pen," Harvard Business School Case no. 9–396–156 (rev. May 8, 2000).
3. Jeswald W. Salacuse, "Implications for Practitioners," in *Culture and Negotiation*, ed. G. O. Faure and J. Z. Rubin (Newbury Park, CA: Sage Publications, 1993) 206.
4. For a detailed description of a joint venture that adopted similar techniques in order to assure both parties sufficient control over the enterprise, see David Goldsweig and Mark Sandstrom (eds.), *International Joint Ventures* (Chicago: American Bar Association, 1990) 3–106.
5. Jeswald W. Salacuse, "Renegotiating International Project Agreements," *Fordham International Law Journal* 24 (2001): 1319.
6. Author's interview with Abdullah al-Omran, Legal Advisor, Counsel of Ministers, Saudi Arabia, November 6, 1983.
7. C. Buci, "The World of Business—Leap of Faith," *New Yorker*, September 9, 1991, 38–74.
8. C. Buhring-Uhle, *Arbitration and Mediation in International Business* (New York: Kluwer, 1996) 318–319.
9. Author's interview with a Reebok executive, November 25, 2000, Canton, Massachusetts.
10. Lance N. Antrim and James K. Sebenius, "Formal Individual Mediation and the Negotiator's Dilemma: Tommy Koh at the Law of the Sea Conference," in *Mediation in International Relations*, eds. J. Bercovitch and J. Rubin (New York: St. Martin's Press, 1992), 97.
11. Nael C. Bunni, " Major Project Dispute Review Boards," *In-House Counsel International*, (June-July 1997): 13.

CHAPTER 6

1. See Adrian Furham and Stephen Bochner, *Culture Shock: Psychological Reactions to Unfamiliar Environments* (New York: Methuen, 1986).
2. Ibid.
3. Ann Williams, "Mobil Oil Corporation and Petro Zaire: Post Nationalization Negotiations in Zaire" (unpublished manuscript, 1988).
4. See Diana B. Henriques, "New Take on Perpetual Calendar: If This is Taipei in 2002, Are Businesses Open on Friday?" *New York Times*, August 24, 1999, p. C1.

CHAPTER 7

1. Edward T. Hall, *The Silent Language* (Garden City, NY: Doubleday, 1959).
2. William C. Frederick, *Values, Nature and Culture in the American Corporation* (New York: Oxford University Press, 1995) 88.
3. Charles Hampden-Turner and Alfons Trompenaars, *The Seven Cultures of Capitalism: Value Systems for Creating Wealth in the United States, Japan, Germany, France, Britain, Sweden and the Netherlands* (New York: Doubleday, 1993).
4. S. E. Weiss, "Negotiating With the Romans," *Sloan Management Review* 35 (1994): 51, 85.
5. See, for example, Hans Binnendijk (ed.), *National Negotiating Styles* (Washington, D.C.: U.S. Department of State, 1987); N. C. G. Campbell et al., "Marketing Negotiations in France, Germany, the United Kingdom and the United States," *Journal of Marketing* 52 (1993): 49–62; and J. L. Graham et al., "Buyer-Seller Negotiations Around the Pacific Rim: Differences in Fundamental Exchange Processes," *Journal of Consumer Research* 15 (1988): 48–54.
6. Author's interview with Cordell Hull, Executive Vice President, Bechtel Group Inc., March 3, 1990, San Francisco, California.
7. Edward T. Hall and M. Reed Hall, *Understanding Cultural Differences* (Yarmouth, ME: Intercultural Press, 1990) 48.
8. "Enron's Rebecca Mark: 'You Have to be Pushy and Aggressive'" *Business Week*, February 24, 1997, at http://www.businessweek.com/1997/08/b351586.htm.
9. The students in the survey were graduate students, primarily in law and business, with considerably less work experience than the other professional groups surveyed. The student responses may be treated as representing persons without significant occupational experience.
10. Hall and Hall, *Understanding Cultural Differences*, 152.
11. Geert Hofstede, *Culture's Consequences: International Differences in Work-related Values* (Newbury Park, CA: Sage Publications, 1980), 152.
12. George Shultz, *Turmoil and Triumph: My Years as Secretary of State* (New York: Charles Scribner's Sons, 1993), 763.

CHAPTER 8

1. Philippe Hasplespleigh, Tomo Nada, and Fares Boulos, "Managing For Value: It's Not Just About Numbers," *Harvard Business Review* (July-August 2001), 65, 67–68.

2. Author's Interview with Ara Oztemel, chairman, the Satra Group, August 1, 1990, Medford, Massachusetts.

CHAPTER 10

1. Author's interview with Charles Francis Adams, former chairman of Raytheon, April 6, 1993, Lexington, Massachusetts.
2. Jack Welch and John A. Byrne, *Jack: Straight From the Gut*, (New York: Warner Books, 2001) 366.
3. David Lax and James K. Sebenius, *The Manager as Negotiator: Bargaining for Cooperation and Competitive Gain* (New York: Free Press, 1986) 354–55.
4. See E. Alan Farnsworth, "Precontractual Liability and Preliminary Agreements: Fair Dealing and Failed Negotiations," *Columbia Law Review* 87(1987): 217, 221–22.
5. "When Political Masters Fall Out, Whom Does Business Obey?" *The Economist* (July 10, 1982): 63.

CHAPTER 11

1. *Consolidated Power Purchase Agreement between the Dabhol Power Company and the Maharashtra State Electricity Board, as amended as of 9 December 1998* (unpublished documents).
2. Laurent Jacque, *Management and Control of Foreign Exchange Risk* (Boston: Kluwer Academic, 1996) 237–52.
3. Laurent Jacque and Gabriel Hawamini, "Myths and Realities of the Global Capital Market: Lessons for Financial Managers," *Journal of Applied Corporate Finance* (Fall 1993) 81, 89–90.
4. United States International Trade Commission, *Assessment of the Effects of Barter and Countertrade Transactions on U.S. Industries* (Washington, D.C.: USITC, 1985) 137.

CHAPTER 12

1. Raymond Vernon, *Sovereignty at Bay: The International Spread of U.S. Enterprises*, (New York: Basic Books, 1971) 46.
2. Award in the Arbitration of S.P.P. (Middle East), Limited, Southern Pacific Properties Limited, and the Arab Republic of Egypt, *International Legal Materials* 22 (1983): 752.
3. J. W. Carter, "The Renegotiation of Contracts," *Journal of Contract Law* 13 (1999) 185, 189.
4. The noted American legal scholar Karl Llewellyn underscored this point more than seventy years ago: " . . . the major importance of a legal contract is to provide a frame-work for well-nigh every type of group organization and for well-nigh every type of passing or permanent relation between individuals and groups, up to and including states—a frame-work highly adjustable, a frame-work which almost never accurately indicates real working relations, but which affords a rough indication around which such relations vary, an occasional guide in cases of doubt, and a norm of final appeal when the relations cease in fact to work." Karl Llewellyn, "What

Price Contract? An Essay in Perspective," *Yale Law Journal* 40: (1931) 704, 736–37.

5. Wintershall, A. G., et al. v. Government of Qatar, *International Legal Materials* 28 (1989): 795, 814.

CHAPTER 13

1. Benjamin Gomes-Casseres, "Joint Venture Instability: Is It a Problem?" *Columbia Journal of World Business* 22 (Summer 1987) 97.
2. Another explanation is that joint ventures and alliances are inherently unstable because they are fundamentally temporary and evolving arrangements undertaken to achieve specific goals. When they achieve their goals, they often terminate. Thus, in many cases the instability of an alliance may be an indication of success rather than failure. See Benjamin Gomes-Casseres, *The Alliance Revolution: The New Shape of Industry Rivalry* (Cambridge, MA: Harvard University Press, 1996) 213–214.
3. Rosabeth Moss Kanter, "Collaborative Advantage: The Art of Alliances," *Harvard Business Review* (July-August 1994) 96, 99.

CHAPTER 14

1. Raymond Vernon, *Sovereignty at Bay: The International Spread of U.S. Enterprises* (New York: Basic Books, 1971) 46.
2. See I. William Zartman and Jeffrey Z. Rubin, Zartman, *Power and Negotiation* (Ann Arbor: University of Michigan Press, 2001).
3. William Mark Habeeb, *Power and Tactics in International Negotiation: How Weak Nations Negotiate with Strong Nations* (Baltimore, MD: Johns Hopkins Press, 1988) 19–23.
4. David C. McClelland, *Power: the Inner Experience* (New York: Irvington Publishers, 1975).
5. Benjamin C. Esty, *The Chad-Cameroon Petroleum Development and Pipeline Project* (Harvard Business School case N9–202–010, January 17, 2002).
6. Bill Vlasic and Bradley A. Stertz, *Taken for a Ride: How Daimler-Benz Drove Off with Chrysler* (New York: W. Morrow, 2000) 206.

CHAPTER 15

1. Turriff Construction Co. v. Government of the Sudan, unpublished file no. 862, Attorney General's Chambers, Khartuom, Sudan.

CHAPTER 16

1. E. A. Farnsworth, "Precontractual Liability and Preliminary Agreements: Fair Dealing and Failed Negotiation," *Columbia Law Review* 87 (1987): 217–94.
2. J. W. Carter, "The Renegotiation of Contracts," *Journal of Contract Law* 13 (1999): 185.
3. For background, see Richard P. Teisch and William A. Stoever, "Enron in India: Lessons From a Renegotiation," *Mid-Atlantic Journal of Business* 35 (1999): 51- 62; Harvard Business School, "Enron: Development Corporation:

The Dabhol Power Project in Maharashtra, India (A)" (HBS Case 9–596–099, March 25, 1997); Harvard Business School, "Enron Development Corporation: The Dabhol Power Project in Maharashtra, India (B)" (HBS Case 9–596–100, Dec. 16, 1996); Harvard Business School, "Enron Development Corporation: The Dabhol Power Project in Maharashtra, India (C)" (HBS Case 9–596–101, Dec. 16, 1996).

4. John F. Burns, "Indian Politics Derail a Big Power Project," *New York Times,* July 5, 1995, D1.

CHAPTER 17

1. E. Schwartz, "International Conciliation and the ICC," *ICSID Review* 10 (1995): 98.
2. See C. Buhring-Uhle, *Arbitration and Mediation in International Business* (London: Kluwer, 1996).
3. Harvard Business School, *"GE's Early Dispute Resolution Initiative"* (HBS Case N9–801–395, 2001).
4. Jeanne Brett, *Negotiating Globally: How To Negotiate Deals, Resolve Disputes and Make Decisions Across Cultures,* (San Francisco: Jossey-Bass, 2001) 87–89, 128–29.
5. L. Nurick and S. J. Schnably, "The First ICSID Conciliation: Tesoro Petroleum v. Trinidad and Tobago," *ICSID Review* 1 (1986): 340–53.
6. ICSID, *1996 Annual Report* (Washington, D.C.: International Centre for Settlement of Investment Disputes, 1996).
7. ICSID, *2001 Annual Report* (Washington, D.C.: International Centre for Settlement of Investment Disputes, 2001).
8. Schwartz, 107–17.

CHAPTER 18

1. François de Callières, *De La Manière de négocier avec les souverains. De l'utilité des négociations, du choix des ambassadeurs et des envoyés et des qualitiés nécessaires pour réussir dans ces emplois* (Amsterdam: Pour la Compagnie, 1716.) The book has been published in many languages since it was written. The most recent English language version is Francois de Callières, *On the Manner of Negotiating With Princes,* trans. A. F. Whyte, with introduction by Charles Handy, (New York: Houghton Mifflin, 2000.) The quotations in this chapter are from this edition. A recent French version with a useful bibliography is Francois de Callières, *De La Manière de négocier avec les souverains,* ed. Alain Pekar Lempereur (Paris-Cergy: Essec Irene, 2001).
2. *On the Manner of Negotiating with Princes* (New York: Houghton Mifflin, 2001): 6.
3. Ibid., p. 6.
4. Ibid., p. 91.
5. Ibid., p. 20.
6. Ibid., p. 12.
7. Ibid., p. 80.
8. Ibid., p. 25.
9. Ibid., p. 24.

10. Ibid., p.95.
11. Ibid., p. 82.
12. Ibid., p. 77.
13. Ibid., p. 46.
14. Ibid., p. 82.

APPENDIX B

1. UNIDROIT, *Principles of International Commercial Contracts* (Rome: International Institute for the Unification of Private Law, 1994), 94.
2. International Chamber of Commerce, INCOTERMS (Paris: ICC, 2000).

Index